BRYOATT.

Attributes of British and Irish Mosses, Liverworts and Hornworts

With Information on Native Status, Size, Life Form,
Life History, Geography and Habitat

M O Hill, C D Preston,
S D S Bosanquet & D B Roy

NERC Centre for Ecology and Hydrology
and Countryside Council for Wales

2007

© NERC Copyright 2007

Designed by Paul Westley, Norwich

Printed by The Saxon Print Group, Norwich

ISBN 978-1-85531-236-4

The Centre of Ecology and Hydrology (CEH) is one of the Centres and Surveys of the Natural Environment Research Council (NERC). Established in 1994, CEH is a multi-disciplinary environmental research organisation.

The Biological Records Centre (BRC) is operated by CEH, and currently based at CEH Monks Wood. BRC is jointly funded by CEH and the Joint Nature Conservation Committee (www.jncc/gov.uk), the latter acting on behalf of the statutory conservation agencies in England, Scotland, Wales and Northern Ireland. CEH and JNCC support BRC as an important component of the National Biodiversity Network. BRC seeks to help naturalists and research biologists to co-ordinate their efforts in studying the occurrence of plants and animals in Britain and Ireland, and to make the results of these studies available to others.

For further information, visit www.ceh.ac.uk

Cover photograph: Bryophyte-dominated vegetation by a late-lying snow patch at Garbh Uisge Beag, Ben Macdui, July 2007 (courtesy of Gordon Rothero).

Published by Centre for Ecology and Hydrology, Monks Wood, Abbots Ripton, Huntingdon, Cambridgeshire, PE28 2LS.

Copies can be ordered by writing to the above address until Spring 2008; thereafter consult www.ceh.ac.uk

Contents

Introduction

In recent years the availability in electronic form of 'attribute data' for all British vascular plant species has greatly enhanced our ability to interpret distribution patterns, and in particular to interpret changes in those patterns in response to environmental pressures. Whereas in the past plants tended to be grouped simply by broad habitat, such as woodland or calcareous grassland, they can now usefully be grouped by attributes that indicate additional features such as the life-form of species, their pH preferences and their shade-tolerance. Attributes thus allow many of the individual factors which together comprise the autecology of a species to be identified, and then allow species sharing particular traits to be grouped together even though they may grow in very different broad habitats. Thus a number of recent studies have shown a marked tendency for species characteristic of nutrient-rich places to have been more successful than those that grow in nutrient-poor habitats, and this is true over a range of broad habitats, time periods and spatial scales (e.g. Braithwaite *et al.*, 2006; Haines-Young *et al.*, 2000; Walker & Preston, 2006).

This compilation is a sequel to *PLANTATT* (Hill, Preston & Roy, 2004), presenting for bryophytes similar attribute information to that which we presented for vascular plants. Just as for *PLANTATT*, we have assembled the information over a period of years, either for our own use or for particular projects. However, previously compiled information for bryophytes is much less plentiful than for vascular plants. Dierssen (2001) and Düll (1991) present data on the habitats and indicator values of European bryophytes. Neither of these is ideal for British users. Dierssen's comprehensive compilation is not available in database form and uses a rather complex typology of vegetation types and units of geographical range. Düll's indicator values do not agree well with experience in Britain and lack values for nitrogen. There was therefore a need for a similar compilation to *PLANTATT*.

The dataset presented here as *BRYOATT* is mainly new (Table 1). We have incorporated taxonomic information and data on geographical elements from existing sources. Ellenberg values were drawn from an existing set of values calculated for an unpublished report (Hill, Roy & Preston, 2005). Other data have been compiled from research papers, books and personal communications, or calculated from existing datasets. In a few cases they have simply been added from personal experience.

The BRYOATT dataset is published as a book, which may be downloaded as a pdf file from the Biological Records Centre website (http://www.brc.ac.uk). The spreadsheet of data (which includes some columns which are not published in the printed document) may also be downloaded from the BRC website, and we will update this spreadsheet from time to time with additions and corrections to the data published here.

Table 1
Attributes, codes and names listed as columns in BRYOATT.

Column name	Abbreviation	Source or other comment
(a) Taxonomic & status		
Taxon name		Name, mostly as in Blockeel & Long (1998)
Moss, liverwort or hornwort	ML	M moss, L liverwort, H hornwort
Order	Ord	Order; mosses from Goffinet & Buck (2004), liverworts from Forrest et al. (2006)
Native status	Stat	Our own opinion, using criteria from Crundwell (1985)
(b) Size and life history		
Length	Len	Length of shoot or thallus (or diameter of rosette)
Perennation	Per	Perennation (annual or perennial)
Life form	LF1, LF2	Life form; categories modified for BRYOATT
Tubers	Tub	Frequency of tubers, either on rhizoids (mosses) or thallus (liverworts)
Gemmae	Gem	Gemma frequency on leafy plant or thallus, not on protonema
Bulbils	Bul	Bulbil frequency
Deciduous branchlets	Bra	Deciduous branchlet frequency
Deciduous leaves	Lvs	Deciduous leaf frequency
Sex organs	Sex	Sexuality, whether monoecious or dioecious
Fruit	Fr	Occurrence and frequency of sporophytes
Spore size	Sp1, Sp2	Spore size minimum and maximum
(c) Geography		
Presence in parts of British Isles	E, W, Sc, IR, NI, CI	From Blockeel & Long (1998) and additional vice-county records up to 2006
Element	Elem	Element, from Hill & Preston (1998)
GB hectad number	GBno	Number of 10-km squares in GB + Man 1950 onwards
Irish hectad number	IRno	Number of 10-km squares in Ireland 1950 onwards
CI hectad number	CIno	Number of 10-km squares in Channel Islands 1950 onwards
January mean temperature	TJan	Mean January temperature of hectads where found
July mean temperature	TJul	Mean July temperature of hectads where found
Annual precipitation	Prec	Mean precipitation (mm) of hectads where found
Maximum altitude	Alt	Max altitude (m) in Britain and Ireland
(d) Habitat		
Ellenberg indicator value	L, F, R, N, S, HM	Compiled for an unpublished report (Hill et al., 2005)
Substrate	14 categories	Compiled for BRYOATT; see Table 18
EUNIS habitat	32 categories	Compiled for BRYOATT; see Table 19

Taxonomy and native status

Species and orders

In the main tabulation, codes H, L and M are used to denote hornworts, liverworts and mosses respectively. The list of 1057 species comprises 4 hornworts, 297 liverworts and 756 mosses (Table 2). In addition, we include data on 36 species aggregates (mostly species *sensu lato*), 13 subspecies and 85 varieties. The orders are those recognized by Forrest *et al.* (2006) for liverworts and Goffinet & Buck (2004) for mosses. The largest orders are Hypnales and Jungermanniales each with about 200 members. At the other extreme, three liverwort orders, namely Blasiales, Haplomitriales and Pleuroziales and three moss orders, Archidiales, Diphysciales and Oedipodiales, have each only a single member in the British and indeed in the European flora.

Taxonomy and nomenclature

Our taxonomy and nomenclature follow the British Bryological Society's *Census Catalogue*, published as a book by Blockeel & Long (1998) and recently updated on the internet (Blackstock, Rothero & Hill, 2005). We depart from this nomenclature by retaining *Grimmia sessitana* for the plant listed as *G. ungeri* in the updated *Census Catalogue* and adopting the name *Bryum moravicum* for the plant referred to there as *B. laevifilum*. We have added eight taxa recently identified in Britain, *Anastrophyllum alpinum*, *Bryum valparaisense*, *Conocephalum salebrosum*, *Ephemerum hibernicum*, *Hypnum cupressiforme* var. *heseleri*, *Lophocolea brookwoodiana*, *Thamnobryum maderense* and *Tortella bambergeri*, and have deleted *Brachythecium appleyardiae*, *Didymodon mamillosus*, *Fissidens exiguus* and *Pictus scoticus*, which are no longer thought to be good taxa. We have treated the segregates of *Barbula convoluta* as var. *convoluta* and var. *sardoa*. Within *Seligeria trifaria* s.l. we have provided data (albeit very incomplete data) for just one of the two segregates, *S. patula*; data for *S. trifaria* s.str. are lacking. We have not included a separate treatment for the varieties of *Amblystegium serpens*, *Bryum capillare*, *Campylopus pyriformis*, *Ditrichum zonatum*, *Hygrohypnum luridum*, *Hypnum lacunosum*, *Orthotrichum cupulatum*, *Pterigynandrum filiforme*, *Tortella flavovirens*, *Tortula muralis* and *Trichostomum tenuirostre*, all of which are recognized by the updated *Census Catalogue*, and we have also excluded *Campylopus atrovirens* var. *gracilis*, *Ctenidium molluscum* var. *fastigiatum*, *Ephemerum serratum* var. *praecox*, *Fontinalis antipyretica* var. *cymbifolia* and var. *gigantea*, *Palustriella commutata* var. *sulcata*, *Polytrichum commune* var. *humile* and *Tortula subulata* var. *subinermis*.

Thirty-six species aggregates are included (Table 3) because data such as counts of grid squares may be unavailable or very incomplete for the segregates, so that sometimes aggregates have to be included in numerical analyses.

Table 2
Bryophyte orders and main groups. Counts are of the number of taxa in each group.

Code	Groups and orders	Species	Infraspecific	Aggregates
H	Hornworts	4	0	1
Anth	Anthocerotales	4		1
L	Liverworts	297	12	8
Blas	Blasiales	1		
Foss	Fossombroniales	14		1
Hapl	Haplomitriales	1		
Jung	Jungermanniales	202	7	5
Lepi	Lepicoleales	4		
Marc	Marchantiales	9	3	1
Metz	Metzgeriales	16		1
Pleu	Pleuroziales	1		
Pore	Porellales	27	2	
Radu	Radulales	6		
Ricc	Ricciales	14		
Sphae	Sphaerocarpales	2		
M	Mosses	756	86	27
Andr	Andreaeales	10	4	
Arch	Archidiales	1		
Brya	Bryales	118	11	2
Buxb	Buxbaumiales	2		
Dicr	Dicranales	109	4	6
Diph	Diphysciales	1		
Enca	Encalyptales	6		
Funa	Funariales	11		
Grim	Grimmiales	74	4	5
Hedw	Hedwigiales	3	2	1
Hook	Hookeriales	5		
Hypn	Hypnales	189	26	4
Oedi	Oedipodiales	1		
Orth	Orthotrichales	31	4	1
Poly	Polytrichales	16	4	
Pott	Pottiales	123	21	4
Rhiz	Rhizogoniales	2		
Sphag	Sphagnales	35	6	4
Spla	Splachnales	13		
Tetr	Tetraphidales	3		
Timm	Timmiales	3		
	Byophyte total	1057	98	36

Table 3
Composition of aggregate species in *BRYOATT*; the abbreviation s.l. is short for the Latin *sensu lato* ('in the broad sense').

Group	Aggregate	Component segregates
H	*Phaeoceros laevis* s.l.	*P. laevis, P. carolinianus*
L	*Anastrophyllum joergensenii* s.l.	*A. alpinum, A. joergensenii*
L	*Calypogeia neesiana* s.l.	*C. integristipula, C. neesiana*
L	*Chiloscyphus polyanthos* s.l.	*C. pallescens, C. polyanthos*
L	*Conocephalum conicum* s.l.	*C. conicum, C. salebrosum*
L	*Fossombronia pusilla* s.l.	*F. maritima, F. pusilla*
L	*Metzgeria fruticulosa* s.l.	*M. fruticulosa, M. temperata*
L	*Plagiochila asplenioides* s.l.	*P. asplenioides, P. britannica, P. porelloides*
L	*Plagiochila spinulosa* s.l.	*P. killarniensis, P. spinulosa*
M	*Aloina aloides* s.l.	*A. aloides, A. ambigua*
M	*Bryum caespiticium* s.l.	*B. caespiticium, B. kunzei*
M	*Bryum dichotomum* s.l.	*B. dichotomum* (including *B. dunense*), *B. dyffrynense, B gemmiferum, B. gemmilucens*
M	*Ceratodon purpureus* s.l.	*C. conicus, C. purpureus*
M	*Cratoneuron filicinum* s.l.	*C. filicinum, Callialaria curvicaulis*
M	*Dichodontium pellucidum* s.l.	*D. flavescens, D. pellucidum*
M	*Dicranum fuscescens* s.l.	*D. flexicaule, D. fuscescens*
M	*Ditrichum flexicaule* s.l.	*D. flexicaule, D. gracile*
M	*Drepanocladus revolvens* s.l.	*D. cossonii, D. revolvens*
M	*Fissidens pusillus* s.l.	*F. gracilifolius, F. pusillus*
M	*Fissidens viridulus* s.l.	*F. gracilifolius, F. limbatus, F. pusillus, F. viridulus*
M	*Grimmia donniana* s.l.	*G. arenaria, G. donniana*
M	*Hedwigia ciliata* s.l.	*H. ciliata, H. stellata*
M	*Hymenostylium recurvirostrum* s.l.	*H. insigne, H. recurvirostrum*
M	*Microbryum starckeanum* s.l.	*M. davallianum, M. starckeanum*
M	*Pseudoleskeella catenulata* s.l.	*P. rupestris, P. catenulata*
M	*Racomitrium canescens* s.l.	*R. canescens, R. elongatum, R. ericoides*
M	*Rhynchostegiella tenella* s.l.	*R. litorea, R. tenella*
M	*Schistidium apocarpum* s.l.	*S. apocarpum, S. atrofuscum, S. confertum, S. crassipilum, S. dupretii, S. elegantulum, S. flaccidum, S. frigidum, S. papillosum, S. pruinosum, S. robustum, S. strictum, S. trichodon*
M	*Schistidium rivulare* s.l.	*S. platyphyllum, S. rivulare*
M	*Seligeria trifaria* s.l.	*S. patula, S. trifaria*
M	*Sphagnum denticulatum* s.l.	*S. denticulatum, S. inundatum*
M	*Sphagnum imbricatum* s.l.	*S. affine, S. austinii*
M	*Sphagnum recurvum* s.l.	*S. angustifolium, S. fallax, S. flexuosum*
M	*Sphagnum subsecundum* s.l.	*S. denticulatum, S. inundatum, S. subsecundum*
M	*Syntrichia ruralis* s.l.	*S. ruraliformis, S. ruralis*
M	*Ulota crispa* s.l.	*U. bruchii, U. crispa*

Native/alien status

Species of uncertain status are classified as 'Native or alien'. Introduced species have been classified as archaeophytes or neophytes (Preston, Pearman & Hall, 2004). Both archaeophytes and neophytes are introduced species which are present in the wild as naturalized populations, that is they are spreading vegetatively or reproducing effectively by spores. An archaeophyte is a plant that became naturalized before AD 1500. A neophyte is one that became naturalized after that time.

Compared with vascular plants, among which introduced species are much more numerous than native species, the number of alien bryophytes is very low (Table 4). Only the two *Sphaerocarpos* species have been indicated as archaeophytes. This is because they seem to have been present in Britain for a long time, but can hardly have existed before agriculture opened up suitable habitat. Other archaeophytes will, in the absence of any evidence, either be classified as 'Native or alien', or, if there is currently no evidence that they are introductions, simply as 'Native'.

Table 4
Bryophyte native status in main groups; values are the number of species in each group, excluding varieties and subspecies.

Code	Explanation	Hornworts	Liverworts	Mosses	Total
AN	Alien neophyte		8	13	21
AR	Archaeophyte		2		2
N	Native	2	283	724	1009
NA	Native or alien	2	4	19	25
Total		4	297	756	1057

Size and life history attributes

Length

Every bryophyte taxon has a length measurement, which is to some extent an indication of size. Typically, the length is the height of the leafy shoot in acrocarpous mosses or the length of the shoot or thallus in pleurocarpous mosses and liverworts. For liverworts with roughly circular thalli, such as *Sphaerocarpos* spp., *Petalophyllum ralfsii* and some *Riccia* spp., the 'length' is in reality a diameter. For mosses that lack a stem, such as *Acaulon* spp. and *Ephemerum* spp., the length refers to the height of the plant when viewed from the side, including the leaves. (A similar problem arises with many ferns, the plant height in *PLANTATT* being deemed to be roughly equal to leaf length.) With *Buxbaumia*, it was not really possible to measure the length of the leafy shoot, and, for that genus only, the length refers to the length of the capsule. In *Tetrodontium brownianum*, the length refers to the length of the protonemal flaps, which normally overtop the perichaetial leaves.

The great majority of lengths were derived from floras, especially the standard floras by Paton (1999) and Smith (2004). Paton (1999) provides measurements for almost all liverworts, but Smith (2004) sometimes omits lengths, especially for the pleurocarpous species. Where measurements were lacking from British and Irish floras, they were taken especially from those for Italy (Cortini Pedrotti, 2001, 2006 [2005]), the Netherlands (Touw & Rubers, 1989) and European Russia (Ignatov & Ignatova, 2003, 2004). The published volumes for Spain (Guerra, Cano & Ros, 2006) and Sweden (Hallingbäck *et al.*, 2006) were also consulted, together with notices of newly-found species such as *Anastrophyllum alpinum* (Long *et al.*, 2006), *Conocephalum salebrosum* (Szweykowski, Buczkowska & Odrzykoski, 2005), *Cinclidotus riparius* (Blockeel, 1998) and *Tortella bambergeri* (Bosanquet, 2006).

Published measurements for some species varied widely between authors. Some of the differences can no doubt be attributed to the plants growing better in some environments than others. However, a commoner source of difference is the tendency to select extreme measurements in some cases and not in others. When William Wilson (1855) gave measurements for *Fissidens polyphyllus* he said that the stems are 'from three inches [8 cm] to a foot [30 cm] or more in length'. The upper limit is very rarely achieved, and is not the normal maximum size of the species. Smith (2004) gave a limit of 20 cm but Störmer (1969) had never found it longer than 13.5 cm in Norway. In this case, we have given 15 cm as the limit, suspecting that Störmer, who had made a special effort to measure the plant, examined specimens of more typical size. In many other cases, we have given an average of the lengths quoted by several authors.

Although values for length are inevitably somewhat vague, they are unlikely to be wrong by more than a factor of 1.5. Given that they vary from 0.9 mm (*Microbryum rectum*) to 500 mm (*Fontinalis antipyretica),* they do undoubtedly give an indication of size.

Table 5

Size and life history attributes. Species counts exclude aggregates and infraspecific taxa; counts of primary life-form are in the column N1=, counts of secondary life-form are in N2=.

Attribute or code	N1=	N2=	Explanation
(a) Length	**Len**		Length or diameter, mm (plant height if stemless)
(b) Annual or not	**Per**		Primary and secondary type of perennation
A	42		Annual; includes regeneration from tubers etc.
AP	30		Annual or perennial, more often annual
PA	50		Perennial or annual, more often perennial
P	935		Perennial
(c) Life form	**LF1**	**LF2**	Primary and secondary life form
Ac		4	Aquatic colonial (formless loose colonies)
At	10	8	Aquatic trailing (attached to substrate)
Cu	104	6	Cushion (dome-shaped colonies)
De	7	3	Dendroid (with stolons and erect shoots)
Fa	7	8	Fan (branches in plane on vertical substrate)
Le	3		Lemnoid (floating on the water)
Mr	98	31	Mat, rough (creeping, lateral branches erect)
Ms	196	43	Mat, smooth (creeping, branches lying flat)
Mt	24	6	Mat, thalloid (creeping, thalli forming a layer)
Sc	22	46	Solitary creeping (creeping solitary shoots)
St	19	5	Solitary thalloid (rosette forming patch not mat)
Tf	292	131	Turf (vertical stems with little or no branching)
Thread	5	4	Thread (solitary thread-like creeping stems)
Tp	19	6	Turf, protonemal (persistent protonema)
Ts	49	33	Turf, scattered (scattered vertical shoots)
Tuft	114	37	Tuft (loose cushions, not dome-shaped)
We	88	31	Weft (intertwining branched layers)

Annuals and perennials

Four categories are recognized, annual, perennial, and two intermediate categories (Table 5). No distinction is made between annuals regenerating from spores and those regenerating from vegetative propagules, including dormant buds, tubers, gemmae or bulbils. The essence of annuality is that species should regenerate from a propagule or perennating organ that is much smaller than the growing plant. Thus a bryophyte annual can in principle be rather like a vascular hemicryptophyte. A few bryophytes such as *Gongylanthus ericetorum* do indeed regenerate in this way.

Most strictly annual bryophytes are plants of disturbed ground, regenerating from spores. However, many normally annual bryophytes can be facultatively perennial if the ground is not disturbed; these are indicated as AP (annual or perennial), meaning that they are normally annual but sometimes perennial. Plants that are normally perennial but can complete their life cycle in a year are indicated PA (perennial or annual). The large majority of bryophytes are perennial.

The standard floras give some indication of whether or not bryophytes are annuals. Paton (1999) gives information on this for some genera (e.g. *Riccia, Fossombronia*) in which case her attribution is followed. Smith (2004) indicates annuals as 'ephemeral', but gives this information only for a few obviously annual genera or species (e.g. *Ephemerum, Funaria, Fissidens exilis*).

Life-form

A system of life-forms was set out by Mägdefrau (1982) and has been developed and used by various authors, especially by Bates (1998) and by Kürschner and his co-workers (Kürschner & Parolly, 1998; Kürschner, Tonguc, & Yayintas, 1998; Kürschner, 2002). Bates (1998) distinguished life-forms from growth-forms, using the criterion that the life-form is about the organization of shoots into colonies. He did not include the open-turf life-form of short-lived bryophytes (the 'annuals' of Mägdefrau, 1982), which include *Acaulon, Buxbaumia, Diphyscium* and *Ephemerum*, on the grounds that they represent a life-strategy in which little resource is invested into long-term colony organization. We have not followed him in this, because we required a scheme that could include all species.

In total, 17 life-forms are recognized in *BRYOATT* (Tables 5, 6). For the purposes of *BRYOATT*, size does not need to be categorized within life-form, because shoot length is given as a separate column. Thus tall turfs do not need to be distinguished from short turfs, nor small cushions from large ones.

The primary life-form is listed in column LF1. Many species (about 40%) have secondary life-forms which are listed in column LF2. In general the secondary life-form is less frequent than the primary one. However, in some species, they may be equally frequent – for example in *Plagiochila porelloides*, which has turf-like shoots growing out of a matted weft.

Vegetative propagules

The occurrence and frequency of vegetative propagules is given for tubers, gemmae, bulbils, deciduous branches and leaves (Table 7). Information on the occurrence of tubers is taken from Preston (2004), with some updating. Details of the other organs are taken from the standard floras and other relevant publications. 'Branches' includes both caducous but otherwise unmodified branches (as in *Campylopus introflexus* and *Microlejeunea ulicina*), and branches which are morphologically modified (*Dicranum flagellare, Pellia endiviifolia*). Similarly, 'leaves' includes the presence of caducous but otherwise unmodified leaves (*Dicranodontium denudatum, Frullania fragilifolia*), modified leaves (*Campylopus fragilis, Syntrichia laevipila*) and fragmenting leaves, including species such as *Dicranum tauricum* which shed their leaf tips. The table excludes three aquatic species which spread vegetatively by fragmentation of the whole plant (*Riccia fluitans, R. rhenana* and *Ricciocarpos natans*) and *Gymnocolea inflata*, which has caducous perianths.

Table 6
Life-forms in BRYOATT; abbreviations follow Table 4.

Name	Description	Examples
Shoots not forming part of an organized colony		
Solitary creeping (Sc)	Solitary or scattered, crawling over or through substrate; if more crowded would generally be a mat	*Calypogeia suecica, Fossombronia wondraczekii*
Solitary thalloid (St)	Solitary thalloid rosette, forming a small patch rather than the more extensive growth of a thalloid mat	*Anthoceros agrestis, Cryptothallus, Petalophyllum, Riccia glauca*
Turf, protonemal (Tp)	Scattered vertical shoots from persistent protonema; can approach turf form if dense	*Buxbaumia, Ephemerum, Pogonatum aloides* (usually), *Tetrodontium brownianum*
Turf, scattered (Ts)	Scattered vertical shoots, normally lacking protonema; can approach turf form if dense	*Acaulon, Aloina, Haplomitrium, Pterygoneurum, Seligeria*
Thread	Thread-like, with thread-like, variously-oriented stems that crawl through or over substrate or vegetation	*Blepharostoma* (usually), *Cephaloziella* spp. (usually), *Platydictya*
Lemnoid (Le)	Floating on the water and budding	*Ricciocarpos, Riccia fluitans*
Shoots forming part of an organized colony		
Turf * (Tf)	Many loosely or closely packet vertical stems with limited branching	*Atrichum, Barbula, Fissidens, Polytrichum, Sphagnum* (mostly)
Tuft	Tufts, forming loose cushions not necessarily of central origin	*Aulacomnium androgynum, Splachnum, Tortula subulata*
Cushion (Cu)	Dome-shaped colonies formed by variously-oriented shoots with a central origin	*Andreaea, Dicranoweisia, Grimmia, Gymnomitrion,* several *Orthotrichum* spp.
Dendroid (De)	Sympodially branching shoots with stolons from which spring erect main shoots bearing branches above	*Climacium, Isothecium alopecuroides, Thamnobryum alopecurum*
Mat, rough (Mr)	Shoots creeping substratum, having numerous erect lateral branches	*Brachythecium velutinum, Homalothecium sericeum*
Mat, smooth (Ms)	Shoots that creep over substratum, having leafy branches that generally lie flat	*Frullania dilatata, Plagiothecium, Pseudotaxiphyllum elegans*
Mat, thalloid (Mt)	Shoots that creep over substratum, composed of a layer of thalli	*Conocephalum conicum, Metzgeria furcata, Reboulia*
Weft * (We)	Loosely intertwining, usually richly branched layers	*Hylocomium, Pleurozium, Ptilidium, Trichocolea*
Fan (Fa)	Shoots arising from vertical bark or rock, branching repeatedly in horizontal plane	*Homalia, Leptodon smithii, Neckera complanata* (usually), *Porella platyphylla* (usually)
Aquatic trailing (At)	Aquatic attached to substrate and trailing in the water	*Cinclidotus, Fontinalis, Porella pinnata*
Aquatic colonial (Ac)	Aquatic, forming rather formless loose colonies not anchored to the substrate (a secondary life-form)	*Drepanocladus aduncus, Sphagnum cuspidatum, S. denticulatum* (when aquatic)

* Many liverworts have a weft-like base from which shoots appear as a turf; thus *Plagiochila porelloides* is classified as LF1=Tf, LF2=We.

In many mosses, protonema-gemmae are frequent or abundant, but information on their occurrence and frequency is inadequate and so we have not included them in this compilation. They are undoubtedly much more common than the early review by Whitehouse (1987) had suggested.

Table 7
Occurrence and frequency of vegetative propagules.

Attribute or code	N=	Explanation
(a) Tubers	**Tub**	
F	37	Frequent or common
O	6	Occasional
R	6	Rare
U	18	Found in GB or Ireland, frequency unknown
X	15	Not in Britain or Ireland but found elsewhere
(b) Gemmae	**Gem**	
F	131	Frequent or common
O	20	Occasional
R	15	Rare
X	7	Not in Britain or Ireland but found elsewhere
(c) Bulbils	**Bul**	
F	17	Frequent or common
O	2	Occasional
R	1	Rare
(d) Branches	**Bra**	
F	24	Frequent or common
O	12	Occasional
R	3	Rare
X	2	Not in Britain or Ireland but found elsewhere
(e) Leaves	**Lvs**	
F	23	Frequent or common
O	9	Occasional
R	2	Rare

Sexual reproduction and spores

The column labelled *Sex* gives information on whether species are monoecious or dioecious, or (in a few cases) have not been observed to produce sex organs (Table 8). Data on the sexuality of liverworts were mostly taken from Paton (1999) and on mosses from Smith (1978; 2004).

The column labelled *Fr* gives information on sporophyte frequency and derives from the same main sources. For liverworts, Paton's (1999) 'fairly frequent' and 'fairly common' are counted here as 'frequent'; 'common' is sometimes counted as 'frequent' and sometimes as 'abundant', depending on our experience of the species. We describe a species as fruiting abundantly if most well-grown colonies in the majority of the British and Irish range can be expected to fruit in most years. Most mosses indicated by Smith (1978; 2004) as fruiting commonly were coded as 'A' but some were coded as 'F'. Again, we have applied our own experience in making the distinction.

The months when sporophytes mature are indicated in columns *Spbeg, Spend* (not included in the printed version of BRYOATT). For a species with a single fruiting season, the first and last months of that season are indicated in these two columns. If there are 1-2 months without a record of mature sporophytes between the first and last dates, these are included in the recorded span. Thus a species found fruiting in May, June, July and September will be shown as fruiting in one period, between May and September. However, species with a gap of 3 or more months is treated as having two fruiting periods, so that a species in which mature fruit has been recorded in March, April, May, October and November is treated as March-May, October-November. For the second period, the columns *Spbeg2* and *Spend2* are used.

For liverworts, dates of sporophyte maturity have been taken from Paton (1999) and Holyoak (unpublished manuscript flora of Cornwall). For mosses, dates were taken from Hill (1988), Holyoak (*op. cit.*) and Paton (1969). Dates from Bates (1995) have been accepted for liverworts and *Sphagnum*, but not for mosses unless capsules were described as 'ripe' or 'dehiscing'. We have also added unpublished data from our personal recording in Cambridgeshire.

Minimum and maximum spore sizes are indicated in columns *Sp1* and *Sp2*. Where an approximate size such as '*c.* 15 µm' is given, 15 is given as both minimum and maximum. Where only a minimum or a maximum value is known, only this value is cited, so that a species with spores known to be 'up to 75 µm' has 75 listed as a maximum value. The dimensions of elliptical spores are those of the longer axis. If spores are released both singly and in tetrads (e.g. *Fossombronia incurva*) the dimensions of the single spores are given; where spores are always permanently united in tetrads (e.g. *Cryptothallus, Sphaerocarpos*), the dimensions of the tetrads are given

Dimensions of liverwort spores are taken from Paton (1999) for those genera for which she gives spore measurements; for other genera we have largely followed Damsholt (2002) and Schuster (1966-1992). Spore sizes of mosses are from Smith (1978; 2004) and Nyholm (1986-1998). In filling gaps we have used a range of other publications, of which Crum & Anderson (1981) and Cortini Pedrotti (2001, 2006 [2005]) have been the most useful. The most serious remaining gap is for the species of Lejeuneaceae, for which we have failed to find an informative source.

Table 8

Sexuality, sporophytes and spore size.

Attribute or code	N=	Explanation
(a) Oeciousness	**Sex**	
D	609	Dioecious
D(M)	4	Normally dioecious, rarely monoecious
MD	25	Monoecious or dioecious
M(D)	8	Normally monoecious, rarely dioecious
M	395	Monoecious
Nil	16	Gametangia not known
(b) Sporophytes	**Fr**	
A	265	Abundant
F	189	Frequent
O	140	Occasional
R	248	Rare
X	151	Not in Britain or Ireland but found elsewhere
Nil	64	Sporophytes not known
(c) Ripe sporophyte [Incomplete data, not in printed version]	**Spbeg**	Month beginning of ripe sporophyte
	Spend	Month end of ripe sporophyte
	Spbeg2	Month beginning of second period
	Spend2	Month end of second period
(d) Spore diameter	**Sp1**	Minimum spore size (μm)
	Sp2	Maximum spore size (μm)

Geographic attributes

Occurrence in Britain, Ireland and the Channel Islands

The British Bryological Society, through its vice-county recording scheme, keeps a record of the occurrence of bryophyte species in vice-counties (Blockeel & Long, 1998). For each vice-county, a species may either be not recorded, recorded but not since 1949, or recorded from 1950 onwards. Counts of species in territories of the British Isles (Table 9) can be derived directly from these records. For these counts, Wales consists of vice-counties 35 and 41-52. Scotland consists of vice-counties 72-112. England and the Isle of Man comprise the remaining British vice-counties. Northern Ireland consists of the six counties H33 and H36-40; the remaining Irish vice-counties are in the Republic.

Table 9
Numbers of bryophyte species recorded in territories of the Britain, Ireland and the Channel Islands. Values are the number of species in each group, excluding varieties and subspecies. For the purposes of this enumeration, Isle of Man records have been included with those for England.

Territory	Code	Hornwort	Liverwort	Moss	Total
(a) Records 1950 onwards					
England	E	4	249	630	883
Wales	W	4	217	561	782
Scotland	S	4	259	643	906
Irish Republic	IR	3	220	531	754
Northern Ireland	NI	3	175	409	587
Channel Islands	CI	1	75	212	288
(b) Not recorded since 1949					
England	(E)		1	19	20
Wales	(W)		4	18	22
Scotland	(S)			20	20
Irish Republic	(IR)		3	15	18
Northern Ireland	(NI)		2	45	47
Channel Islands	(CI)	1	1	20	22

European distributions – biogeographic elements

The categorization of taxa to biogeographic elements (Table 10) follows Hill & Preston (1998), with additions for newly recognized taxa. The element is made up of two components, E1 and E2. Non-native species have also been assigned to elements, based on their geographical distribution in Europe about the year 2007. We are well aware that elements may change if the species subsequently expand to new limits.

The Hyperoceanic eastern limit 0 is used only in the combinations 70 (Hyperoceanic Temperate) and 80 (Hyperoceanic Southern-temperate). Species categorized as 80 occur in Macaronesia; those categorized as 70 have similar distributions in Europe but are absent from Macaronesia. The Mediterranean-Atlantic major biome appears only in the combinations 91 (Mediterranean-Atlantic) and 92 (Submediterranean-Subatlantic).

European natives can be expected to change their distributions as a result of warmer winters. Indeed, there is already some penetration of oceanic species such as *Lepidozia cupressina* and *Orthotrichum pulchellum* to new localities in central Europe (Frahm & Klaus, 2001). We have not attempted to alter any categories as a result of these recent changes, but they may present difficulties in future unless distributions are characterized by climatic limits rather than by geographical ones.

Table 10
Major biomes and eastern limits used to specify biogeographic elements in Europe.

Attribute and codes	N=	Explanation
(a) E1		**Biogeographic element, major biome**
1	72	Arctic-montane (main distribution in tundra or above tree-line in temperate mountains)
2	131	Boreo-arctic montane (in tundra and coniferous forest zones)
3	23	Wide-boreal (from temperate zone to tundra)
4	205	Boreal-montane (main distribution in coniferous forest zone)
5	171	Boreo-temperate (in conifer and broadleaf zones)
6	18	Wide-temperate (from Mediterranean region to coniferous forest zone)
7	225	Temperate (in broadleaf forest zone)
8	115	Southern-temperate (in Mediterranean region and broadleaf forest zones)
9	97	Mediterranean-Atlantic (in Mediterranean region, and extending north in Atlantic zone of temperate Europe)
(b) E2		**Biogeographic element, eastern limit category**
0	58	Hyperoceanic, with a western distribution in atlantic zone
1	137	Oceanic (in atlantic zone of Europe, not or scarcely reaching east to Sweden, Germany or S Spain)
2	145	Suboceanic (extending east to Sweden, C Europe or Italy)
3	262	European (extending to more continental parts of Europe but not to Siberia)
4	18	Eurosiberian (eastern limit between 60°E and 120°E)
5	14	Eurasian (extending across Asia to east of 120°E)
6	423	Circumpolar (in Europe, Asia and N America)

Counts of occurrence in 10-km squares in Britain and Ireland

For each taxon, the number of 10-km squares (hectads) in Britain, Ireland and the Channel Islands is enumerated (Table 11). Only squares with post-1949 records have been counted, so that *Helodium blandowii* and *Paludella squarrosa*, not found in Britain since the 19th century, have a zero count there; *P. squarrosa* has a recent record from Ireland, where it has a count of 1. Counts were based on data in the database of the British Bryological Society at the Biological Records Centre in July 2007.

Climatic means

Climatic values for plants were calculated as the mean climate of the 10-km squares where they occur in Britain, Ireland and the Channel Islands, averaging over the squares enumerated for the counts. For these means, as for the counts, only post-1949 records were included. Climate data for 10-km squares were taken from baseline climate summaries of the UK Climate Impacts Programme (Hulme & Jenkins, 1998). These baseline summaries were constructed by interpolation of daily weather measurements from individual met stations, averaged over the 30-year period 1961-1990 (Barrow, Hulme & Jiang, 1993).

Table 11
Counts of squares, means of temperature and precipitation, and maximum altitudes.

Attribute	Min	Max	Explanation
(a) Counts			Counts of 10-km squares
GB	0	2351	Great Britain and Isle of Man
IR	0	416	Ireland
CI	0	11	Channel Islands
(b) Climatic means			Mean values for 10-km squares
Tjan	-1.9	8.0	January mean temperature (°C)
Tjul	9.9	16.7	July mean temperature (°C)
Prec	638	2748	Annual precipitation (mm)
(c) Maximum altitude			Maximum in Britain and Ireland
Alt	0	1344	Maximum altitude (m)

Maximum altitude

It would have been preferable to give separate maximum altitudes for Britain and Ireland. However, there was not enough information to do this for many species in Ireland, and maximum altitudes are for both islands taken together. Maximum altitudes were drawn from several sources, notably the database of the British Bryological Society, Paton's (1999) flora (liverworts), manuscript lists by M.F.V. Corley, D.G. Long and G.P. Rothero, and personal observations, especially by S.D.S.B. Wherever possible, we have attempted to support our maxima with an actual record, complete with finder and date. However, for 175 species, the maximum altitude is taken from the most recent BBS atlas (Hill, Preston & Smith, 1991-1994). These records have a locality, but details of the finder and date were not collected. Likewise for about 100 liverworts, the maximum altitude given by Paton (1999) does not have a supporting locality.

One species, *Timmia megapolitana*, is recorded from the lowest maximum altitude of 0 m, where it is regularly inundated by tidal fresh water. Five species, *Andreaea rothii, Brachythecium rutabulum, Ceratodon purpureus, Kiaeria blyttii* and *Racomitrium sudeticum*, are recorded from the maximum possible altitude, 1344 m, at the top of Ben Nevis. A further 19 species are recorded from nearby at 1340 m. The biogeographic elements of all of these except for *B. rutabulum* are in major biomes that include the boreal or arctic zones. The occurrence of *B. rutabulum* at this altitude is anomalous.

Habitat indicator values

Ellenberg indicator values

Ellenberg defined seven major scales, of which five are presented here. The two that are omitted, T (temperature) and K (continentality), correspond quite closely to the major biome and eastern limit categories used for European distributions by Hill & Preston (1998) and incorporated here in the biogeographic elements. The five remaining scales have values defined in the tables that follow. The values are based on those of Ellenberg *et al.* (1991), as modified by Hill *et al.* (1999). A few example species are given for each value, by way of explanation.

Indicator values for bryophytes found in plant communities with vascular plants were calculated by a computer program called INDEXT (Hill *et al.*, 2000). Starting with the indicator values of vascular plants associated in quadrats, we calculated a mean value for each quadrat, and then used regression to suggest new values for bryophytes.

This process gave initial values for only the 361 bryophytes recorded with vascular plants in at least five quadrats. For the remainder, it was necessary to use published associates. Associates were obtained especially from Paton (1999) for liverworts and Hill, Preston & Smith (1991-1994) for mosses. Other important sources were Paton (1969) and Wigginton (1995). With newly-reported species, the original notice in the British literature was used.

The main difficulty in building up a set of bryophyte indicator values was that many species are found on rocks, bark or rotten wood. These typically have few associates that occur in terrestrial habitats along with vascular plants. Thus they are poorly connected with Ellenberg values. Calculated values for the 361 species with enough occurrences in quadrats were treated as 'anchor values'. For the remainder, an iterative process was needed, first fitting values for those species whose listed associates had anchor values and then moving on to the others. At the end of the process, values were critically reviewed in the light of personal experience and compared with unpublished Dutch values supplied by Dr Henk Siebel. Values were adjusted if necessary, and finally put forward for publication here.

We have also included a column to indicate the tolerance of species to heavy metals. There has been little systematic study of bryophytes on sites in Britain or Ireland that are rich in heavy metals. Our classification is therefore a first attempt and one which we expect could be improved with further fieldwork. Our main sources of data have been the floras of areas with old heavy-metal mines, notably the Isle of Man (Paton, 1971), North Wales (Hill, 1988) and Carmarthenshire (Bosanquet, Graham & Motley, 2005). D.T. Holyoak's draft accounts of the Cornish bryophytes have been particularly useful, and we have also been fortunate in having access to unpublished lists compiled by N.G. Hodgetts for Halkyn Mountain (one of the few lists available for sites that are both rich in heavy metals and highly calcareous) and by R.D. Porley for polluted river gravels in Northumberland. We have also consulted lists of species growing in the *Festuca ovina–Minuartia verna* plant community (Rodwell, 2000) and associated with *Ditrichum plumbicola* (Crundwell, 1976). S.D.S.B. has added some observations from sites in South and Mid Wales. We have, unfortunately, been unable to find any studies of the bryophytes of disused lead mines in Derbyshire and Yorkshire.

Light values (L)

The range of Ellenberg values for light (Table 12) is extended to allow for *Cryptothallus mirabilis,* which lives in darkness.

Table 12
Ellenberg values for light (L).

Code	N=	Explanation
0	1	Plant in darkness (*Cryptothallus mirabilis*)
1	8	Plant in deep shade (*Calypogeia arguta, Fissidens serrulatus, Gyroweisia tenuis, Schistostega pennata*)
2	27	Between 1 and 3 (*Aphanolejeunea microscopica, Scapania umbrosa, Eucladium verticillatum, Plagiothecium latebricola, Seligeria calycina, Tetrodontium brownianum*)
3	67	Shade plant, mostly less than 5% relative illumination, seldom more than 30% illumination when trees are in full leaf (*Calypogeia fissa, Conocephalum conicum, Saccogyna viticulosa, Fissidens viridulus, Heterocladium heteropterum, Plagiothecium nemorale, Thamnobryum alopecurum*)
4	106	Between 3 and 5 (*Cephalozia bicuspidata, Lejeunea cavifolia, Plagiochila porelloides, Atrichum undulatum, Fissidens taxifolius, Polytrichum formosum, Rhynchostegium confertum*)
5	154	Semi-shade plant, rarely in full light, but generally with more than 10% relative illumination when trees are in leaf (*Diplophyllum albicans, Lophocolea bidentata, Radula complanata, Anomodon viticulosus, Bryoerythrophyllum recurvirostrum, Dicranoweisia cirrata, Leucobryum glaucum, Plagiomnium undulatum, Rhytidiadelphus loreus*)
6	238	Between 5 and 7 (*Cololejeunea minutissima, Fossombronia pusilla, Leiocolea turbinata, Brachythecium rutabulum, Dicranum scoparium, Eurhynchium hians, Orthotrichum affine, Polytrichum commune, Sphagnum squarrosum*)
7	283	Plant generally in well lit places, but also occurring in partial shade (*Anthelia julacea, Gymnocolea inflata, Marchantia polymorpha, Riccia sorocarpa, Andreaea rupestris, Barbula convoluta, Funaria hygrometrica, Racomitrium lanuginosum, Sphagnum capillifolium, Weissia controversa*)
8	156	Light-loving plant rarely found where relative illumination in summer is less than 40% (*Cladopodiella fluitans, Odontoschisma sphagni, Aloina aloides, Bryum pseudotriquetrum, Campylium stellatum, Grimmia pulvinata, Polytrichum juniperinum, Sphagnum papillosum*)
9	17	Plant in full light, found mostly in full sun (*Petalophyllum ralfsii, Bryum algovicum, Grimmia laevigata, Hennediella heimii, Polytrichum piliferum, Tortella flavovirens*)

Moisture values (F)

Moisture (F from the German *Feuchtigkeit*) is on a scale of 1 to 12 (Table 13).

Table 13
Ellenberg values for moisture (F).

Code	N=	Explanation
1	20	Indicator of extreme dryness, restricted to situations that often dry out for some time (*Grimmia donniana, G. laevigata, G. pulvinata, Hedwigia stellata, Syntrichia intermedia*)
2	31	Between 1 and 3 (*Campyliadelphus chrysophyllus, Campylopus pilifer, Pleurochaete squarrosa, Racomitrium fasciculare, R. heterostichum, Tortula muralis*)
3	47	Dry-site indicator, more often found on dry substrata than on moist places (*Aloina aloides, Andreaea rothii, Brachythecium albicans, Didymodon vinealis, Homalothecium sericeum, Microbryum davallianum, Syntrichia ruralis*)
4	108	On well-drained terrestrial substrata (*Barbula convoluta, Ceratodon purpureus, Fissidens dubius, Trichostomum crispulum*) or on bark or rock with some shelter (*Cololejeunea minutissima, Metzgeria furcata, Radula complanata, Orthotrichum affine, Rhynchostegiella tenella*)
5	229	On moderately moist soils (*Barbilophozia floerkei, Bryum bicolor, Dicranum scoparium, Hypnum jutlandicum, Rhytidiadelphus squarrosus*) or on bark or rock in moderately humid places (*Frullania tamarisci, Metzgeria fruticulosa, Anomodon viticulosus, Cryphaea heteromalla, Ulota bruchii*)
6	228	On moist soils (*Diplophyllum albicans, Lophocolea bidentata, Atrichum undulatum, Brachythecium rutabulum, Dicranum majus, Polytrichum formosum, Sphagnum quinquefarium*) or rock or bark in humid places (*Colura calyptrifolia, Plagiochila porelloides, Scapania gracilis, Homalia trichomanoides, Isothecium myosuroides, Racomitrium aquaticum, Tetraphis pellucida*)
7	135	On constantly moist or damp, but not permanently waterlogged substrata (*Calypogeia fissa, Conocephalum conicum, Fossombronia pusilla, Scapania nemorea, Bryum pallens, Fissidens adianthoides, Polytrichum commune, Sphagnum capillifolium*)
8	132	Between 7 and 9 (*Cephalozia connivens, Hygrobiella laxifolia, Odontoschisma sphagni, Pellia epiphylla, Brachythecium rivulare, Campylopus atrovirens, Pohlia wahlenbergii, Sphagnum palustre*)
9	102	In waterlogged sites, either in streams and flushes (*Chiloscyphus polyanthos, Trichocolea tomentella, Bryum pseudotriquetrum, Dicranella palustris, Philonotis fontana, Rhynchostegiella teneriffae, Sphagnum teres*) or on bogs (*Cladopodiella fluitans, Kurzia pauciflora, Mylia anomala, Sphagnum denticulatum, S. fallax*)
10	18	In pools and by streams that may intermittently lack water (*Nardia compressa, Scapania undulata, Calliergon cordifolium, Rhynchostegium riparioides, Sphagnum cuspidatum, S. pulchrum*)
11	4	On surface of still water (*Ricciocarpos natans*) or regularly submerged in running water, though sometimes at or above normal water level (*Amblystegium fluviatile, Rhynchostegium alopecuroides*)
12	3	Normally submerged (*Fontinalis* spp., *Octodiceras fontanum*)

Reaction (R)

Reaction (Table 14) refers to environmental acidity, typically measured by pH.

Table 14
Ellenberg values for reaction (R).

Code	N=	Explanation
1	30	Indicator of extreme acidity, never found on weakly acid or basic substrata (*Calypogeia neesiana, Gymnocolea inflata, Odontoschisma sphagni, Riccardia latifrons, Campylopus brevipilus, Sphagnum austinii, S. compactum, S. tenellum*)
2	141	Between 1 and 3 (*Barbilophozia floerkei, Cephalozia bicuspidata, Diplophyllum albicans, Mylia taylorii, Scapania gracilis, Andreaea rothii, Campylopus atrovirens, Grimmia donniana, Polytrichum commune, Racomitrium fasciculare, R. heterostichum, Rhytidiadelphus loreus, Sphagnum fallax*)
3	137	On acid substrata, often on base-poor mineral soils or in acid flushes (*Calypogeia fissa, Marsupella emarginata, Saccogyna viticulosa, Aulacomnium palustre, Calliergon stramineum, Dicranum majus, D. scoparium, Hedwigia stellata, Orthodontium lineare, Sphagnum palustre*)
4	122	Between 3 and 5 (*Calypogeia arguta, Frullania tamarisci, Lophocolea bidentata, Pellia epiphylla, Scapania undulata, Calliergon cordifolium, Dicranella palustris, Dicranoweisia cirrata, Isothecium myosuroides, Philonotis fontana*)
5	163	On moderately acid soils (*Anthoceros* spp., *Fossombronia pusilla, Trichocolea tomentella, Atrichum undulatum, Fissidens bryoides, Pleuridium* spp., *Rhytidiadelphus squarrosus*) or rock or bark (*Lejeunea lamacerina, Metzgeria furcata, Pohlia cruda, Schistidium rivulare, Ulota bruchii*)
6	163	On basic soil (*Conocephalum conicum, Brachythecium rutabulum, Bryum pseudotriquetrum, Eurhynchium hians, Plagiomnium undulatum*) in basic waters (*Fontinalis antipyretica, Rhynchostegium riparioides*) or on basic rock or bark (*Frullania dilatata, Plagiochila porelloides, Radula complanata, Cryphaea heteromalla, Isothecium alopecuroides, Orthotrichum affine*)
7	198	On strongly basic substrata, sometimes on siliceous rocks or soil (*Lunularia cruciata, Pellia endiviifolia, Amblystegium serpens, Barbula convoluta, Bryum bicolor, Calliergonella cuspidata, Ctenidium molluscum, Didymodon fallax, Fissidens taxifolius, Homalothecium sericeum, Microbryum davallianum*)
8	70	Between 7 and 9 (*Leiocolea turbinata, Porella platyphylla, Aloina aloides, Anomodon viticulosus, Campyliadelphus chrysophyllus, Didymodon rigidulus, D. vinealis, Grimmia pulvinata, Palustriella commutata* var. *commutata, Orthotrichum anomalum, Syntrichia intermedia, Tortula muralis*)
9	33	On substrata with free calcium carbonate, mainly chalk and limestone (*Cephalozia baumgartneri, Eucladium verticillatum, Pleurochaete squarrosa, Seligeria calcarea, Tortella nitida*)

Nitrogen (N)

Nitrogen values (Table 15) are in fact a general indication of fertility. N values for vascular plants are on a scale from 1 to 9, but the two highest values, 8 and 9, correspond to conditions where bryophytes are crowded out by vascular plants.

Table 15
Ellenberg values for nitrogen (N).

Code	N=	Explanation
1	152	Indicator of extremely infertile sites; almost all are calcifuges (*Cephaloziella connivens, Diplophyllum albicans, Mylia anomala, Nardia compressa, Odontoschisma sphagni, Andreaea rothii, Campylopus atrovirens, Grimmia donniana, Hedwigia stellata, Polytrichum piliferum, Racomitrium fasciculare, R. heterostichum, Sphagnum papillosum*), but there are a few exceptions (*Anthelia* spp., *Aloina brevirostris, Blindia acuta*)
2	403	Indicator of infertile sites; these include calcifuges (*Barbilophozia floerkei, Cephalozia bicuspidata, Scapania gracilis, S. undulata, Dicranum scoparium, Sphagnum denticulatum, S. palustre*), middling species (*Aneura pinguis, Porella obtusata, Campylium stellatum, Pterogonium gracile, Thuidium delicatulum*) and calcicoles (*Cololejeunea calcarea, Campyliadelphus chrysophyllus, Ctenidium molluscum, Fissidens dubius, Homalothecium lutescens*)
3	184	Indicator of moderately infertile sites; N=3 species, like N=2 species, include a range of calcifuges (*Calypogeia fissa, Dicranum tauricum, Isothecium myosuroides, Philonotis fontana, Polytrichum formosum*), middling species (*Radula complanata, Brachythecium albicans, Bryum pseudotriquetrum, Weissia controversa*) and calcicoles (*Aloina ambigua, Didymodon fallax, Neckera crispa, Trichostomum crispulum*)
4	170	Between 3 and 5; these plants are found mainly in the lowlands, but include calcifuges (*Fossombronia pusilla, Pellia epiphylla, Orthodontium lineare, Mnium hornum, Pseudotaxiphyllum elegans*) as well as species of more basic substrates (*Cololejeunea minutissima, Plagiochila porelloides, Grimmia pulvinata, Homalothecium sericeum, Rhytidiadelphus squarrosus, Syntrichia ruralis, Ulota bruchii*)
5	88	Indicator of moderately fertile sites; these are almost without exception lowland species, with a few calcifuges (*Atrichum undulatum, Calliergon cordifolium, Fissidens bryoides, Plagiothecium curvifolium, P. denticulatum*), but most are tolerant of basic conditions (*Conocephalum conicum, Barbula convoluta, Brachythecium rivulare, Fissidens taxifolius, Orthotrichum affine, Plagiomnium undulatum*)
6	48	Between 5 and 7; these are mostly plants of eutrophic lowlands (*Riccia cavernosa, R. glauca, Amblystegium serpens, Brachythecium rutabulum, Bryum rubens, Dicranella staphylina, Leskea polycarpa, Pohlia melanodon, Tortula acaulon*), but Splachnaceae are on upland dung and carcases (*Splachnum* spp., *Tetraplodon* spp.)
7	12	Plant often found in richly fertile places (*Lunularia cruciata, Bryum argenteum, B. bicolor, Eurhynchium speciosum, Funaria hygrometrica, Leptodictyum riparium*)

Salt tolerance (S)

Values for salt tolerance (Table 16) start at zero, corresponding to no tolerance of salt.

Table 16
Ellenberg values for salt tolerance (S).

Code	N=	Explanation
0	1013	Absent from saline sites; if in coastal situations, only accidental and non-persistent if subjected to saline spray or water (96% of the flora)
1	19	Slightly salt-tolerant species, rare to occasional on saline soils but capable of persisting in the present of salt (includes dune and dune-slack species where the ground water is fresh but where some inputs of salt spray are likely) (*Fossombronia maritima, Frullania dilatata, F. microphylla, F. tamarisci, Petalophyllum ralfsii, Porella obtusata, Radula lindenbergiana, Riccia glauca, Brachythecium mildeanum, Bryum algovicum, B. dyffrynense, Campylopus fragilis, Ceratodon purpureus, Drepanocladus lycopodioides, D. sendtneri, Eurhynchium praelongum, Microbryum starckeanum, Scleropodium tourettii, Syntrichia ruraliformis, Tortula acaulon* var. *pilifera*)
2	12	Species occurring in both saline and non-saline situations, for which saline habitats are not strongly predominant (*Cololejeunea minutissima, Fossombronia angulosa, Frullania teneriffae, Amblystegium serpens, Archidium alternifolium, Bryum mamillatum, Campyliadelphus elodes, Drepanocladus aduncus, Glyphomitrium daviesii, Myurium hochstetteri, Tortula modica, Trichostomum brachydontium*)
3	6	Species most common in coastal sites but possibly or certainly capable of occurring in sites that do not receive salt spray (*Bryum warneum, Drepanocladus polygamus, Sanionia orthothecioides, Tortula wilsonii, Ulota phyllantha, Weissia perssonii*)
4	5	Species of salt meadows and upper saltmarsh, subject to at most only very occasional tidal inundation, or of cliffs receiving some salt spray (*Bryum calophyllum, Bryum marratii, Tortella flavovirens, Tortula atrovirens, Tortula viridifolia*)
5	2	Species of the upper edge of saltmarsh and obligate halophytes of cliffs receiving regular salt spray (*Hennediella heimii, Schistidium maritimum*)

Heavy-metal tolerance (HM)

Values for metal tolerance (Table 17) start at zero, corresponding to no tolerance of heavy metals.

Table 17
Indicator values for heavy-metal tolerance (HM).

Code	N=	Explanation
0	916	Species that are absent from substrates with moderate or high concentrations of heavy metals (87% of the flora)
1	71	Species that are recorded on substrates with moderate or high concentrations of heavy metals but only rarely. They are much more frequent elsewhere and may have occurred on rocks or soil that were locally lacking high metal content. Many are very common plants *(Lophocolea bidentata, Barbula convoluta, Bryum capillare, Calliergonella cuspidata, Eurhynchium praelongum, Hypnum cupressiforme, Mnium hornum, Plagiomnium undulatum)*
2	47	Species that are occasional or frequent on substrates with moderate or high concentrations of heavy metals, and within particular regions may be restricted to such sites, but do not occur as dominants over large areas and in British Isles as a whole they are much more frequent in other habitats. A few of the rarer species either definitely *(Grimmia donniana)* or probably *(Ditrichum lineare, Hymenostylium recurvirostrum, Microbryum starckeanum)* have tolerant genotypes, but many commoner ones may not *(Barbula unguiculata, Dicranella heteromalla, Dicranum scoparium, Didymodon fallax, Didymodon insulanus, Polytrichum juniperinum, Rhytidiadelphus squarrosus, Scleropodium purum)*
3	15	Species that are frequent and often abundant on substrates with moderate or high concentrations of heavy metals, sometimes occurring as dominants over large areas, but are also frequent in other habitats. The plants on polluted sites may be tolerant genotypes *(Cephaloziella integerrima, Cephaloziella stellulifera, Diplophyllum albicans, Gymnocolea inflata, Jungermannia gracillima, Nardia scalaris, Scapania compacta, Bryum pallens, Ceratodon purpureus, Dicranella varia, Dicranoweisia cirrata, Pohlia annotina, P. nutans, Schistidium crassipilum, Weissia controversa var. controversa)*
4	2	Species that are much more frequent on substrates with moderate or high concentrations of heavy metals than on unpolluted substrates, but are sometimes present on non-polluted sites *(Bryum pallescens, Pohlia andalusica, Weissia controversa var. densifolia)*
5	6	Species that in the British Isles are confined to substrates with moderate or high concentrations of heavy metals *(Cephaloziella massalongi, Cephaloziella nicholsonii, Ditrichum cornubicum, D. plumbicola, Grimmia atrata, Scopelophila cataractae)*

Substrates and habitats

Our treatment of the habitats of bryophytes departs in several ways from the corresponding section of *PLANTATT*. We have classified each bryophyte in two ways, recognising the major *habitat* such as coastal cliff, broad-leaved woodland or arable land, and the *substrate* on which the species occurs, such as rock, rotting wood or soil. Whereas substrates are relatively unimportant for British vascular plants, most of which are rooted in soil, they are clearly much more relevant to the ecology of a poikilohydrous group such as the bryophytes. Clearly both the habitat in our restricted use of the term and the substrate are part of the habitat of the species in its broadest sense.

To classify species into habitats, we have used the EUNIS habitat classification system (Davies, Moss & Hill, 2004; also available as http://eunis.eea.europa.eu/habitats.jsp). This is a hierarchical classification of European habitats and we have chosen to use level 2 of the hierarchy, so that coastal cliff is classified as habitat B3. B is the first level of the hierarchy and comprises coastal habitats; at level 2 it splits into three categories, B1 coastal dunes, B2 coastal shingle and B3 coastal rock cliffs, ledges and shores. On the whole the EUNIS system was not too difficult to apply to the bryophytes; a few cases of difficulty are discussed below. For substrates, we have devised our own simple substrate classification.

We have attempted to list all the habitats and substrates in which a species may be encountered, rather than (as in *PLANTATT*) simply the most characteristic habitat(s). We have used a simple scale to indicate the frequency with which they occur in each class (see below).

Substrate classes

Species have been allocated to one or more substrate classes (Table 18).

EUNIS habitat classes

Some of the EUNIS habitats are not represented in Britain or Ireland (e.g. F7, Spiny Mediterranean heaths and H6, Recent volcanic features) and others, although they occur in our area, do not support bryophytes (e.g. A5, Sublittoral sediment). We have also excluded some habitats which do support bryophytes but have a very strong overlap with others or are of rather marginal interest. The habitats classes we have used are listed in Table 19 and the excluded habitats in Table 20. The explanation of the habitat class concentrates on the features of relevance to the bryologist.

Table 18
Substrate classes.

Code	Name	N=	Notes
RH	Rock, hard	601	Includes drystone walls when made of hard rock
RS	Rock, soft	228	Includes chalk, soft sandstones and schists, tufa etc.
RW	Rock, worked	264	Includes building stone, roofing slates, brick, mortar, concrete, asphalt etc., but drystone walls built of unworked rocks and stones count as RH or RS
SR	Soil on rock	352	Thin layer of soil over rock; includes soil over natural, worked or artificial rock
SO	Soil	722	Includes mineral, sandy, gravelly, humus-rich and peaty soils; pure peats, sands and gravels are treated separately
PT	Peat	179	Includes relatively shallow peat over mineral soil
GS	Gravel or sand	275	
DW	Decorticated wood	203	Includes decorticated logs, rotting wood and worked wood (fence posts etc.)
DV	Decaying vegetation	105	Includes leaf litter, thatch, decaying vascular plant tussocks (e.g. *Carex paniculata*, *Molinia caerulea*) etc.
DA	Decaying animal	9	Decaying animal matter, including bones, dung etc.
BR	Bryophyte	79	Growing amongst or through other bryophytes (including *Sphagnum*)
EN	Epiphytic on non-woody substrates	23	Includes epiphytic occurrences on lichens, other bryophytes and fern fronds, and on the leaves of flowering plants
EW	Epiphytic on living wood	274	On bark on the trunks, branches, stems and exposed roots of vascular plants (including the trunks of tree ferns)
AQ	Floating on water	5	

Table 19
EUNIS habitat classes.

Code	Name	Explanation	N
A	**Marine habitats**		
A2	Littoral sediment	Saltmarshes in the intertidal zone	62
B	**Coastal habitats**		
B1	Coastal dunes and sandy shores	Sandy shores, shifting and stable sand dunes, moist and humid dune slacks, machair and grassland, heathland and woodland on dunes	185
B2	Coastal shingle	Includes scrub and woodland on shingle as well as open shingle	20
B3	Rock cliffs, ledges and shores	Includes rocky shores, rocky cliffs with halophytes and vegetated soft cliffs	269
C	**Inland surface waters**		
C1	Surface standing waters	Aquatic communities in lakes, reservoirs, ponds and canals; dune-slack pools; bog pools; wet phase of temporary ponds	25
C2	Surface running waters	Aquatic communities in rivers, springs, wet phase of temporary water-courses, films of water flowing over rocky watercourse margins	38
C3	Littoral zone of inland surface waters	The frequently inundated zone, including beds of emergents (*Glyceria fluitans*, *Phragmites* etc), low-growing amphibious vegetation (*Eleocharis acicularis*, *Littorella* etc), lake and river shingles, ephemeral vegetation of periodically inundated shores and areas in the spray zone of waterfalls; the occasionally flooded zone by rivers has been excluded	295
D	**Mires, bogs and fens**		
D1	Raised and blanket bogs		119
D2	Valley mires, poor fens and transition mires	Weakly to strongly acidic mires, often with *Calliergon, Drepanocladus* and *Sphagnum*, and soft water bryophyte springs with *Philonotis fontana* etc.	153
D4	Base-rich fens and calcareous spring mires	Base-rich mires, springs with calcareous or eutrophic water, basic montane flushes	97
E	**Grasslands and lands dominated by forbs, mosses or lichens**		
E1	Dry grasslands	Includes swards on rock debris, decomposed rock surfaces, rock edges with annuals and succulents, dry acidic and neutral grassland, inland dune grassland, calcareous grassland, grasslands rich in lichens and mosses on soils rich in heavy metals	178
E2	Mesic grasslands	Mesotrophic and eutrophic pastures, hay meadows, improved grassland, sports fields and lawns	22
E3	Seasonally wet and wet grasslands	Includes moist or wet eutrophic, mesotrophic and oligotrophic grasslands, and *Juncus effusus* meadows	126
E4	Alpine and subalpine grasslands	Includes snow-patch grassland, moss- and lichen-dominated snow patch communities and exposed moss- and lichen-dominated mountain summits, ridges and plateaux as well as montane grassland	112

Code	Name	Explanation	N
E7	Sparsely wooded grasslands	Includes parkland	62
F	**Heathland, scrub and tundra**		
F3	Temperate scrub	Temperate thickets and scrub, including *Corylus, Crataegus, Prunus, Rubus fruticosus* and *Ulex* scrub	104
F4	Temperate shrub heathland	Wet and dry heaths, usually dominated by Ericaceae but including *Molinia caerulea*-dominated communities	245
F9	Riverine and fen scrubs	Includes willow carr, fen scrub with *Rhamnus, Frangula* etc. and boreo-alpine willow scrub	110
FA	Hedgerows		143
G	**Woodland, forest habitats and other wooded land**		
G1	Broadleaved deciduous woodland	Includes semi-natural broadleaved woodland, poplar plantations and orchards, including species growing on rocks in woodland but excluding woodland rides	410
G1R	Rides in broadleaved deciduous woodland	Rides and forest roads in G1	94
G3	Coniferous woodland	Includes conifer plantations and semi-natural Caledonian pine forests, including species growing on rocks in such woodland but excluding woodland rides	126
G3R	Rides in coniferous woodland	Rides and forest roads in G3	47
H	**Inland unvegetated or sparsely vegetated habitats**		
H2	Screes		195
H3	Inland cliffs, rock pavements and outcrops	Includes sea-cliffs free from saline influence, inland cliffs, limestone pavements and disused quarries	650
H5	Miscellaneous inland habitats with very sparse or no vegetation	Includes block slopes, clay, silt, sand, gravel and rocky soils, including open or bryophyte-dominated soil banks by tracks or well above the water level on the sides of ditches, streams and rivers, inland dunes and burnt and trampled areas	271
I	**Regularly or recently cultivated agricultural, horticultural and domestic habitats**		
I1	Arable land and market gardens	Includes cultivated fields and fallow and recently abandoned arable land	110
I2	Cultivated areas of parks and gardens	Includes actively cultivated and recently abandoned parks and gardens	95
J	**Constructed, industrial and other artificial habitats**		
J1	Buildings of cities, towns and villages		52
J2	Low density buildings	Includes scattered residential buildings, agricultural buildings, fences, field walls and rural churchyards	315
J3	Extractive industry sites	Active mines and opencast sites, including sand and gravel workings, and recently abandoned extraction sites and quarries	282
J4	Transport networks and other constructed hard-surface areas	Roads, railways (including railway ballast), car parks and pavements	61

Excluded EUNIS habitats

The following habitats (Table 20) are represented in Britain and have associated bryophytes but are not sufficiently significant to be reported on.

Table 20
Main EUNIS habitat classes occurring in Britain or Ireland and supporting bryophytes but excluded from the dataset.

Code	Name	Comment
A1	Littoral rock and other hard substrata	Includes rocks within the splash zone; can be accommodated in B3
D5	Sedge and reed beds, normally without free-standing water	Bryologically rather insignificant
E5	Woodland fringes and clearings and tall forb habitats	Includes subalpine *Cicerbita alpina* etc. tall-herb communities, herbaceous woodland-edge communities, bracken fields and lowland tall-herb communities in eutrophic places and on abandoned land, a heterogeneous group of habitats with few bryophytes and those well represented in other habitats
F2	Arctic, alpine and subalpine scrub habitats	Includes areas of snow-patch dwarf willow scrub in Scottish Highlands, and dwarf or prostrate wind-pruned ericaceous vegetation, dwarf juniper and *Dryas* heaths; only occurs over restricted areas and bryophytes can be accommodated in other habitats (e.g. E4)
FB	Shrub plantations	Includes low-stem orchards and vineyards; bryologically insignificant
G2	Broadleaved evergreen wood	Represented by small areas of bryologically insignificant *Ilex aquifolium* woodland in Britain
G4	Mixed deciduous and coniferous woodland	A frequent and bryophyte-rich habitat, but we have treated the broadleaved and coniferous components separately
G5	Lines of trees, small anthropogenic woodlands, recently felled woodland, early stage woodland and coppice	Includes regrowth stages of coppice woodland without standards, early stages of plantations, Christmas tree and other tree nurseries, *Arctium*, *Rubus* and scrub communities in clearings, clear felled and burnt areas, a bryologically heterogeneous set of habitats which are covered by other classes
J5	Highly artificial man-made waters and associated structures	Bryophyte-poor habitats with all species also occurring under C, Inland surface waters
J6	Waste deposits	Includes habitats such as rubbish tips which are bryologically insignificant

Difficulties in applying the EUNIS classification

One of the major difficulties arises from the structural complexity of woodland habitats. We have arbitrarily chosen to code species on rocks in woodland as occurring in the woodland habitat G1 or G3, although in practice almost all are also coded as growing on inland rocks H3 as well, but we have invented our own subcategories of G1 and G3 for species on rides, tracks and non-metalled roads in woodland. Species growing on scattered trees (such as those in lines along a riverbank but above the flood level, on the edge of a gorge, or along a driveway) are also difficult to deal with and have tended to be coded as woodland, hedgerow or parkland species (if they also occur in these habitats).

The second major difficulty has been the treatment of the many bryophytes that occur on open soil on crumbling banks, such as ditch, stream and river banks above the water level, trackside and laneside banks and small banks in pastures. These have been coded under H5 which we have probably interpreted more broadly than the authors of the EUNIS classification intended.

Frequency classes

The occurrence in habitats and on substrates has been scored using the frequency classes in Table 21.

Table 21
Frequency classes used for substrates and habitats.

Class	Explanation
1	A rare habitat or substrate for the species
2	An occasional habitat or substrate for the species
3	A normal habitat or substrate for the species

Class 1 includes numerous chance or casual occurrences, and when using *BRYOATT* for analyses it is probably best to disregard occurrences at frequency class 1.

Sources of habitat and substrate information

The information on habitat and substrates was initially compiled from Hill *et al.* (1991) and Paton (1999) for liverworts and Hill *et al.* (1992; 1994) for mosses; data for mosses not treated in the latter were taken from Smith (2004). We then consulted a number of floras which were published after the compilation of the accounts in the *Atlas of Bryophytes*, notably Bates (1995), Bosanquet *et al.* (2005), Rothero (2002), Wigginton (1995) and D.T. Holyoak's draft accounts of the habitat of Cornish bryophytes. We have also amended some of the entries in the light of our own field experience.

Taxon name	ML	Ord	Stat	Len	Per	LF1	LF2	Tub	Gem	Bul	Bra	Lvs	Sex	Fr	Sp1	Sp2	E	W	Sc	IR	Ni	Cl	Elem	GBno	IRno	Clno	T.Jan	T.Jul	Prec	Alt	L	F	R	N	S	HM
Acaulon muticum	M	Pott	N	2	A	Ts								M	A	30	50	E	W	S			CI	83	137		2	4.1	15.7	839	490	7	5	5	4	0	0
Acaulon muticum var. mediterraneum	M	Pott	N	2	A	Ts								M	A	30	30	E						91	6			6.0	16.0	1031	100	7	5	5	4	0	0
Acaulon muticum var. muticum	M	Pott	N	2	A	Ts								M	A	30	50	E	W		IR	(NI)	CI	73	12			5.7	15.8	966	490	7	5	5	4	0	0
Acaulon triquetrum	M	Pott	N	1.5	A	Ts								M	A	30	30	E						92	5			4.8	16.2	848	120	9	2	9	3	0	0
Achrophyllum dentatum	M	Hook	AN	35	P	Mr								D	X	12	18	E						70	1			6.8	16.2	1110	50	2	8	6	3	0	0
Acrobolbus wilsonii	L	Jung	N	25	P	Ms	Tf					O	M	R	20	22			S	IR			80	18	9		3.4	13.1	1976	490	5	6	3	2	0	0
Adelanthus decipiens	L	Jung	N	40	P	Tf	We						D	X			E	W	S	IR	NI		80	102	45		3.3	13.3	1943	610	4	6	3	2	0	0
Adelanthus lindenbergianus	L	Jung	N	100	P	Tuft			X				D	X	13	16			S	IR			41	1	6		3.8	13.4	1576	800	6	6	2	2	0	0
Aloina aloides s.l.	M	Pott	N	5	P	Ts							D	A	18	22	E	W	S	IR	NI	CI	92	483	55	3	3.9	15.5	896	460	8	3	8	3	0	0
Aloina aloides s.l.	M	Pott	N	5	P	Ts							D	A	14	22	E	W	S	IR	NI	CI	83	519	61	4	3.9	15.5	886	460	8	3	8	3	0	0
Aloina ambigua	M	Pott	N	5	P	Ts							D	A	14	18	E	W		IR	(NI)	CI	83	85	4		3.9	16.0	738	220	8	4	7	3	0	0
Aloina brevirostris	M	Pott	N	2	P	Ts							M(D)	A	18	22			S				26	21			3.4	15.7	696	225	8	3	9	1	0	0
Aloina rigida	M	Pott	N	2	P	Ts							D	A	14	16	E	W	S				43	37	1		3.2	15.4	754	500	8	8	8	2	0	0
Amblyodon dealbatus	M	Spla	N	20	P	Tuft	Ts						M	A	40	40	E	W	S	IR	NI		43	67	16		2.9	13.1	1346	870	8	8	7	2	0	0
Amblystegium confervoides	M	Hypn	N	20	P	Mr							M	F	8	10	E	W	S	IR	NI		73	32	4		3.5	15.3	1030	150	3	5	9	4	0	0
Amblystegium fluviatile	M	Hypn	N	150	P	Mr	At						M	R	12	18	E	W	S	IR	NI	CI	53	371	14	1	3.3	14.5	1135	380	6	11	5	4	0	0
Amblystegium humile	M	Hypn	N	35	P	Mr							M	R	14	16	E	W	S	IR	NI		76	69	2		3.7	16.1	722	107	7	9	7	7	0	0
Amblystegium radicale	M	Hypn	N	30	PA	Mr							M	A	10	18	E	W	S				73	10			4.7	14.8	1179	120	5	9	7	5	0	0
Amblystegium serpens	M	Hypn	N	30	PA	Mr	We						M	A	8	15	E	W	S	IR	NI	CI	56	1944	221	8	3.6	15.0	987	580	5	6	7	6	2	0
Amblystegium tenax	M	Hypn	N	60	P	Mr	We						M	F	16	20	E	W	S	IR	NI	CI	76	494	18	1	3.5	15.0	985	440	4	9	6	4	0	0
Amblystegium varium	M	Hypn	N	40	P	Mr							M	O	10	16	E	W	S	IR	NI	CI	76	224	20	1	3.7	15.7	846	380	5	9	7	7	0	0
Amphidium lapponicum	M	Dicr	N	35	P	Tuft	Tf						M	A	8	12	E	W	S	IR			26	70	1		1.2	12.0	2099	1150	9	7	2	2	0	0
Amphidium mougeotii	M	Dicr	N	80	P	Tuft	Tf						D	R	10	12	E	W	S	IR	NI		46	745	107		2.7	13.2	1555	1180	6	5	7	2	0	0
Anastrepta orcadensis	L	Jung	N	80	P	Tuft	Sc		F				D	X		10	E	W	S	IR	NI		42	277	24		2.1	12.3	2036	1170	7	4	2	2	0	0
Anastrophyllum alpinum	L	Jung	N	120	P	We	Tf						D	X	11	13			S				41	12			1.4	11.1	2142	990	5	5	2	2	0	0
Anastrophyllum donnianum	L	Jung	N	120	P	We	Tf						D	R					S				41	57			0.7	11.1	2307	1060	5	6	2	2	0	0
Anastrophyllum hellerianum	L	Jung	N	8	P	Ms			F				D	X	9	12	E	W			NI		43	45	2		1.6	12.4	2120	360	4	7	6	2	0	0
Anastrophyllum joergensenii s.l.	L	Jung	N	120	P	We	Tf						D	X	11	13			S				41	21			0.8	10.9	2059	990	5	6	2	1	0	0
Anastrophyllum joergensenii s.str.	L	Jung	N	90	P	We	Tf						D	Nil					S				41	7			-0.7	10.2	1929	920	7	6	2	1	0	0
Anastrophyllum minutum	L	Jung	N	35	P	We	Tf		F				D	R	12	14	E	W	S	IR	NI		26	219	30		2.0	12.5	1738	1070	4	7	3	2	0	0
Anastrophyllum saxicola	L	Jung	N	50	P	We	Tf						D	X	12	14			S				46	5			0.0	11.4	1397	700	5	6	3	2	0	0
Andreaea alpestris	M	Andr	N	10	P	Cu	Tf						M	O	22	26			S				16	6			-1.0	10.5	1678	1335	7	4	2	1	0	0
Andreaea alpina	M	Andr	N	60	P	Cu	Tf						M	O	26	38			S	IR	NI		41	199	28		1.9	12.2	2053	1300	5	3	3	1	0	0
Andreaea blyttii	M	Andr	N	25	P	Cu	Tf						D	O	13	19			S				16	10			-1.1	10.3	1908	1190	7	6	2	1	0	0
Andreaea frigida	M	Andr	N	40	P	Cu	Tf						M	A	25	35			S				43	4			-1.5	10.3	2006	1200	6	5	2	1	0	0
Andreaea megistospora	M	Andr	N	10	P	Cu	Tf						M	A	50	90	E	W	S	IR	(NI)		70	19	4		2.1	12.3	2211	1100	8	3	2	1	0	0
Andreaea mutabilis	M	Andr	N	10	P	Cu							M	A	12	21	E	W	S				41	30			0.5	11.5	2031	1300	7	5	2	1	0	0
Andreaea nivalis	M	Andr	N	60	P	Cu	Tf						D	O	24	33			S				13	18			-0.4	10.7	2098	1340	7	3	2	1	0	0
Andreaea rothii	M	Andr	N	25	P	Cu	Tf						M	A	36	52	E	W	S	IR	NI		53	254	40		2.7	13.2	1731	1344	8	3	3	2	1	0
Andreaea rothii subsp. falcata	M	Andr	N	25	P	Cu	Tf						M	A	36	52	E	W	S	IR	NI		53	181	35		2.7	13.2	1757	800	8	3	2	1	0	0
Andreaea rothii subsp. rothii	M	Andr	N	25	P	Cu	Tf						M	A	26	32	E	W	S				52	28	14		3.0	13.5	1538	800	8	3	2	1	0	0
Andreaea rupestris	M	Andr	N	30	P	Cu	Tf						M	A	26	32	E	W	S	IR	NI		26	208	16		2.0	12.6	1817	1330	7	3	2	1	0	0
Andreaea rupestris var. papillosa	M	Andr	N	30	P	Cu	Tf						M	A	13	19	(E)	W	S				16	2			2.5	12.9	2575	500	7	3	2	1	0	0
Andreaea rupestris var. rupestris	M	Andr	N	30	P	Cu	Tf						M	A	26	32	E	W	S				26	152	14		2.0	12.6	1842	1110	7	3	2	1	0	0
Andreaea sinuosa	M	Andr	N	10	P	Cu							D	A	13	19			S				11	5			-0.8	10.5	1645	1200	6	5	2	1	0	0
Aneura pinguis	L	Metz	N	60	P	Mt	St						D	F	18	25	E	W	S	IR	NI	CI	36	1495	227	2	3.3	14.2	1220	1070	8	9	6	2	0	2

Taxon name	RH	RS	RW	SR	SO	PT	GS	DW	DV	DA	BR	EN	EW	AQ	A2	B1	B2	B3	C1	C2	C3	D1	D2	D4	E1	E2	E3	E4	E7	F3	F4	F9	FA	G1	G1R	G3	G3R	H2	H3	H5	I1	I2	J1	J2	J3	J4
Acaulon muticum		3		3			3																												2				3	3					3	
Acaulon muticum var. mediterraneum		3		3																																			3	3						
Acaulon muticum var. muticum		3		3			3				3																								2				3	3	3				3	
Acaulon triquetrum					3																																					3				
Achrophyllum dentatum	3																				3																									
Acrobolbus wilsonii	1			3	1					2							2				3																	2	3							
Adelanthus decipiens	3			3	3		1			2	1						2				2																		3							
Adelanthus lindenbergianus				1		3																					2				3							3								
Aloina aloides			3	3	3		3									3																						3	3			3		3		3
Aloina aloides s.l.			3	3	3		3									3																							3			3		3		3
Aloina ambigua				3	3		3									3																						3	3			3		3		3
Aloina brevirostris				3																																			3							
Aloina rigida				3	3		3																															2	3			3		3		3
Amblyodon dealbatus	3																				2			3														2								
Amblystegium confervoides	3	3														3																								3						
Amblystegium fluviatile	3	3		3									3		3					3	3						3																			
Amblystegium humile	2		2	3									3		1						3						3			3																
Amblystegium radicale	3	3		3			3		3				3		3						3									3	3	3														
Amblystegium serpens	3	3					3		3				3		3						3									3	3	3	3		1						3					
Amblystegium tenax	3						3		2				3		1						3				3	3						3		2					1							
Amblystegium varium	3	3		3											1											3	3			3				2				3							2	
Amphidium lapponicum	3	3			3																													2				3								
Amphidium mougeotii	3	3																2																3				3								
Anastrepta orcadensis	3			3						2			1									2						2		3	3			3	3			3								
Anastrophyllum alpinum	3			3						2																				3	3			3				3								
Anastrophyllum donnianum	3			3			3						1		1												3			3	3			2	3			1								
Anastrophyllum hellerianum			1	1																										3				3				1								
Anastrophyllum joergensenii s.l.	3			3			3													3	3	2											3	3				3								
Anastrophyllum joergensenii s.str.	2			3	2		3													3	3	2												2				2								
Anastrophyllum minutum	2			3	3		1				2		1							3	3	3								3	3		3	3				3								
Anastrophyllum saxicola	3	3		3			3													3	3							3										3								
Andreaea alpestris	3			3																3	3						3											3								
Andreaea alpina	3																			3	3																									
Andreaea blyttii	3																										3																			
Andreaea frigida	3						3														3																									
Andreaea megistospora	3					3	3													3	3																	3								
Andreaea mutabilis	3	1		1	1			3												3	3										3			2	3			1								
Andreaea nivalis	3																			3	3																									
Andreaea rothii	3			3	3															3	3										3							3						3	3	
Andreaea rothii subsp. falcata	3			3	2	2														3	3																									
Andreaea rothii subsp. rothii	3			3	3	3			1				1								3												3					3								
Andreaea rupestris	3	3		1							2										3							1		3				3				3	3	3				3		
Andreaea rupestris var. papillosa	3			1																	3																	3	3	3						
Andreaea rupestris var. rupestris	3			1																	3						1											3	3	3						
Andreaea sinuosa	3			3		3			2												3						3		3	3	3							2	3							3
Aneura pinguis	3	3	3	3	3		3	2	2	2			3		3						3	3	3	3	3	3	3	3	3	3	3			2	2			2	3							3

Taxon name	ML	Ord	Stat	Len	Per	LF1	LF2	Tub	Gem	Bul	Bra	Lvs	Sex	Fr	Sp1	Sp2	E	W	Sc	IR	NI	CI	Elem	GBno	IRno	Clno	T.Jan	T.Jul	Prec	Alt	L	F	R	N	S	HM
Anoectangium aestivum	M	Pott	N	73	P	Tuft	Tf						D	R	12	16	E	W	S	IR	NI		43	305	33		2.2	12.5	1922	1180	6	7	7	2	0	0
Anomobryum julaceum	M	Brya	N	50	P	Tf	Tuft						D	O	10	18	E	W	S	IR	NI		46	439	75		2.4	12.7	1744	1100	7	7	4	2	0	1
Anomobryum julaceum var. concinnatum	M	Brya	N	50	P	Tuft	Tf						D	X			E	W	S	IR	NI		43	59	11		2.4	12.9	1652	1100	7	6	6	2	0	0
Anomobryum julaceum var. julaceum	M	Brya	N	50	P	Tf	Tuft						D	O	10	18	E	W	S	IR	NI		46	417	70		2.3	12.7	1752	950	7	7	4	2	0	0
Anomodon attenuatus	M	Hypn	N	50	P	Mr							D	X	10	15			S				56	1			1.5	13.2	968	150	5	5	7	4	0	0
Anomodon longifolius	M	Hypn	N	60	P	Mr							D	X	16	18	E	W	S				55	6			2.6	14.6	1023	250	5	5	7	4	0	0
Anomodon viticulosus	M	Hypn	N	120	P	Mr							D	R	14	18	E	W	S	IR	NI	CI	56	740	90	1	3.6	15.1	1029	460	5	5	8	5	0	0
Anthelia julacea	L	Jung	N	40	P	We	Ms						D	O	12	16	E	W	S	IR	NI		16	202	34		1.9	12.1	2040	1340	5	9	3	1	0	0
Anthelia juratzkana	L	Jung	N	6	P	Ms	Sc						M	F	16	21		W	S	IR	NI		16	67	7		1.1	11.6	2066	1340	7	7	3	1	0	0
Anthoceros agrestis	H	Anth	NA	15	A	St							M	A	42	62	E	W	S	IR	NI		73	118	5		3.8	15.5	937	226	7	7	5	4	0	0
Anthoceros punctatus	H	Anth	N	30	AP	St	Mt						M	A	42	62	E	W	S	IR	NI	CI	91	146	28	4	4.7	14.9	1152	300	7	5	4	3	0	0
Antitrichia curtipendula	M	Hypn	N	200	P	We	Mr						D	R	34	36	E	W	S	IR	NI		53	230	9		2.0	12.5	1764	900	6	4	5	2	0	0
Aongstroemia longipes	M	Dicr	N	10	P	Tuft	Ts						D	R	15	20			S	IR			46	11	1		1.6	12.4	1847	520	8	6	5	3	0	0
Aphanolejeunea microscopica	L	Pore	N	6	P	Ms	Thread	F					M	R	20	30	E	W	S	IR	NI		80	181	46		2.9	12.9	1969	610	2	8	4	2	0	0
Aphanorhegma patens	M	Funa	N	2.5	A	Ts	Tf						M	A	26	32	E	W	S	IR	NI		74	228	22		3.9	15.7	830	230	7	8	7	7	0	0
Aplodon wormskjoldii	M	Spla	N	60	A	Tuft							M	A	10	15	E		S				16	6			-0.2	11.4	1586	869	8	7	3	2	0	0
Apometzgeria pubescens	L	Metz	N	35	P	We	Mt						D	X	19	23	E	W	S		NI		46	178	4		1.7	12.9	1457	1000	4	5	8	3	0	0
Archidium alternifolium	M	Arch	N	20	PA	Tf	Ts	X					M	F	127	262	E	W	S	IR	NI	CI	83	480	59	2	3.8	14.3	1280	460	7	8	4	3	2	2
Arctoa fulvella	M	Dicr	N	30	P	Cu							M	A	18	28	E	W	S	IR			13	54	4		1.3	11.8	2203	1340	7	7	2	1	0	0
Athalamia hyalina	L	Marc	N	70	P	Mt							D	F	45	55			S				16	1			-0.8	11.1	1125	530	7	6	7	2	0	0
Atrichum angustatum	M	Poly	N	30	P	Tf	Mt	X					D	R	12	14	E	(W)	(S)	IR	NI	CI	73	17	1		3.8	16.2	800	137	6	7	4	3	0	0
Atrichum crispum	M	Poly	AN	70	P	Tf		F					D	X	17	32	E	W					72	143	7		3.0	14.2	1483	450	6	8	3	2	0	0
Atrichum tenellum	M	Poly	N	15	P	Tf	Ts	X					D	R	20	25	E	W	S	IR	NI		56	44	7		3.0	13.9	1388	460	7	8	4	3	0	0
Atrichum undulatum	M	Poly	N	70	P	Tf	Mr	X					M(D)	A	16	20	E	W	S	IR	NI	CI	56	2087	283	3	3.3	14.6	1121	1000	4	6	5	5	0	0
Atrichum undulatum var. gracilisetum	M	Poly	N	70	P	Tf							M	A			(E)						56							175	4	6	5	5	0	0
Atrichum undulatum var. undulatum	M	Poly	N	70	P	Tf							M(D)	A	16	20	E	W	S	IR	NI	CI	56	479	12		3.6	15.1	1091	1000	4	6	5	5	0	0
Aulacomnium androgynum	M	Brya	N	25	P	Tuft		F					D	R	9	11	E	W	S	IR	NI		73	993	3		3.3	15.5	812	450	5	6	3	4	0	0
Aulacomnium palustre	M	Brya	N	90	P	Tf	Tuft	O					D	O	11	14	E	W	S	IR	NI	CI	36	1359	215	2	3.1	14.0	1263	975	7	8	3	2	0	1
Aulacomnium turgidum	M	Brya	N	100	P	Tf	Tuft						D	X	9	11	(E)		S				16	33			0.7	11.1	2395	100	7	4	4	1	0	0
Barbilophozia atlantica	L	Jung	N	30	P	We	Mr	F					D	Nil			E	W	S	IR			42	126	1		2.2	13.3	1480	900	6	5	2	2	0	0
Barbilophozia attenuata	L	Jung	N	30	P	Mr		F					D	X	10	14	E	W	S	IR	NI	CI	46	509	28	1	2.7	13.7	1391	600	4	5	3	2	0	0
Barbilophozia barbata	L	Jung	N	50	P	Ms							D	X	15	15	E	W	S	IR	NI		46	296	4		1.9	12.8	1637	1150	5	3	2	0	0	2
Barbilophozia floerkei	L	Jung	N	60	P	We	Mr						D	R	13	16	E	W	S	IR	NI		46	638	30		2.2	13.1	1482	1250	5	2	2	0	0	2
Barbilophozia hatcheri	L	Jung	N	40	P	We	Mr	F					D	R	14	16	E	W	S	IR	NI		26	144			1.1	12.3	1287	1050	6	3	2	0	0	0
Barbilophozia kunzeana	L	Jung	N	50	P	Ms	Sc	F					D	X	10	14	E	W	S	(IR)	NI	CI	26	14			1.4	12.9	1231	1250	6	5	2	0	0	0
Barbilophozia lycopodioides	L	Jung	N	50	P	Ms							D	X	12	14	E		S				26	44			0.1	11.0	2011	1200	6	4	2	0	0	0
Barbilophozia quadriloba	L	Jung	N	50	P	Ms	Tf	X					D	X			E		S				16	11			-0.4	11.3	1835	1175	6	7	5	2	0	0
Barbula convoluta	M	Pott	N	18	PA	Tf		F					D	O	8	10	E	W	S	IR	NI	CI	66	2009	313	3	3.6	14.8	1032	580	7	4	7	3	0	1
Barbula convoluta var. convoluta	M	Pott	N	25	PA	Tf		F					D	O	8	10	E	W	S	IR	NI	CI	66	1483	262	3	3.6	14.8	1053	510	7	4	5	2	0	0
Barbula convoluta var. sardoa	M	Pott	N	10	P	Tf							D	O	8	10	E	W	S	IR	NI	CI	66	569	64	3	4.0	15.5	970	510	7	5	5	3	0	0
Barbula unguiculata	M	Pott	N	25	P	Tf		X					D	F	10	14	E	W	S	IR	NI	CI	66	1948	266	3	3.6	14.9	1012	580	7	5	7	5	0	2
Bartramia halleriana	M	Brya	N	100	P	Tuft							M	A	20	24	E	W	S	IR	(NI)		43	100	1		1.7	12.6	2146	730	4	6	4	2	0	2
Bartramia ithyphylla	M	Brya	N	40	P	Tuft	Tf						M	A	34	40	E	W	S	IR	NI		26	366	12		2.1	12.8	1610	1170	6	4	6	4	0	0
Bartramia pomiformis	M	Brya	N	65	P	Tuft	Tf						M	A	20	26	E	W	S	IR	NI		56	829	45		2.9	13.8	1406	900	6	4	4	2	0	0
Bartramia stricta	M	Brya	N	30	P	Tuft							M	A	26	32	(E)	W	S	IR	NI	CI	91	3		2	3.8	14.9	1084	245	9	3	5	3	0	0
Bazzania pearsonii	L	Jung	N	70	P	We	Tf						D	Nil			S		IR				41	44	11		2.2	12.0	2035	1000	5	6	2	2	0	0

Taxon name	RH	RS	RW	SR	SO	PT	GS	DW	DV	DA	BR	EN	EW	AQ	A2	B1	B2	B3	C1	C2	C3	D1	D2	D4	E1	E2	E3	E4	E7	F3	F4	F9	FA	G1	G1R	G3	G3R	H2	H3	H5	I1	I2	J1	J2	J3	J4
Anoectangium aestivum	3	3																			3			2										2				3						3		
Anomobryum julaceum	3	3	2	3																	3			2														3	1							1
Anomobryum julaceum var. concinnatum		3	3	3																				3														3								
Anomobryum julaceum var. julaceum	3				3																3			2									3					3	1							1
Anomodon attenuatus	3						3					3																					3					3								
Anomodon longifolius	3																																					3								
Anomodon viticulosus	3	3	3	2			1					3									2		2										3	3				3	3				3			
Anthelia julacea	3				3							3									3	3																3								
Anthelia juratzkana		3	3	3	3																	3						3										3		3	3			3		
Anthoceros agrestis	2				3	2	2										3							2		3								2				2	3		3	3			3	2
Anthoceros punctatus	3				1	1	1					3			1	1					3		1			1		3					3					3	3			1				3
Antitrichia curtipendula					3	3											3				3																	3	3							3
Aongstroemia longipes	3				3							3	2				3				3												3		2			3	3	2			3			
Aphanorhegma patens																										2								2				3	2							
Aplodon wormskjoldii								3														3																								
Apometzgeria pubescens	3	3	1	2			1					1									3												3					3						3		
Archidium alternifolium		3	3				3								3		3				3			3									3	3	3			3	3	3				3		
Arctoa fulvella	3				1																						1												3								
Athalamia hyalina					3																																									
Atrichum angustatum					3	1																						2						3		3								1		
Atrichum crispum					3	3																														2				1						
Atrichum tenellum					3	3															1													2		2				3					1	
Atrichum undulatum					3	3															3				3				3	3			3	3				3	3	1	2	1	3		
Atrichum undulatum var. gracilisetum					3																											3	3													
Atrichum undulatum var. undulatum		3			3	3	3					3									3				3		3		3	3		3	3	3		3		3	3	1	2	3	1	3		
Aulacomnium androgynum					3	3	3														3		3	2	3	3				3	3		3	2	2			2	2	2		3	2	2		
Aulacomnium palustre		3	3	2	3	2	1					3					2																1	1		1		2	2	2	1			2	2	
Aulacomnium turgidum					3																					3																				
Barbilophozia atlantica	3	2	2	2	3	3	3		2												3										3		3	3		3		3	3	2	3			3		
Barbilophozia attenuata	3	3	3	3	3	3	3					3									3	1								3	3		3	3		3		3	3	3		3	3			
Barbilophozia barbata	3	3	3		3	1	1					1			2								2	2		2					2		2	2		2		3	3			3	3			
Barbilophozia floerkei	2	3	3		3	3	1								3								3	2				3			3		3	3		2		3	3			2	3			
Barbilophozia hatcheri	3	3	3		3	3	2					1																			3		3	3				3	3			3				
Barbilophozia kunzeana					3	3	1															3	3	3		3	3			3	3							3	3							
Barbilophozia lycopodioides	3	3	3		3				3													3	3			3					2							3								
Barbilophozia quadriloba		3	3		3				3															3														3								
Barbula convoluta	2	2	3	3			3						3	3		3								3		3												3	3	3	3	3	3	3	3	2
Barbula convoluta var. convoluta	2	2	3	3			3						3	3		3								3		3												3	3	3	3	3	3	3	3	2
Barbula convoluta var. sardoa	2	2	3	3			3						3	3		3								3														3	3	3	3	3	3	3	3	2
Barbula unguiculata		2	3	3	3	3	2				2		3			1	3		1					3		3										3		3	3	3	3	3	3	3	3	1
Bartramia halleriana	3	3																															1	2				3								
Bartramia ithyphylla	3	3	2	2	2	2										3	3																3	3				3	3			2				
Bartramia pomiformis	3	3	3	3	3	3	1										3																1	3				3	3			3	3	3	3	2
Bartramia stricta	3	3	3		3																																	3				3	3	3	3	3
Bazzania pearsonii	3	3			3												3								3	3				3									3	3							

37

Taxon name	ML	Ord	Stat	Len	Per	LF1	LF2	Tub	Gem	Bul	Bra	Lvs	Sex	Fr	Sp1	Sp2	E	W	Sc	IR	NI	Cl	Elem	GBno	IRno	Clno	TJan	TJul	Prec	Alt	L	F	R	N	S	HM
Bazzania tricrenata	L	Jung	N	90	P	We	Tf						D	X	16	20	E	W	S	IR	NI		43	283	56		2.4	12.5	1986	1220	5	6	2	2	0	0
Bazzania trilobata	L	Jung	N	100	P	We	Ms				O		D	R	12	17	E	W	S	IR	NI	Cl	72	382	41	2	3.0	13.5	1678	900	4	6	2	2	0	0
Blasia pusilla	L	Blas	N	25	PA	St	Mt		F				D	F	35	55	E	W	S	IR	NI		56	459	63		2.5	13.2	1457	1040	6	8	4	4	0	1
Blepharostoma trichophyllum	L	Jung	N	15	P	Thread	Ms		F				M	F	10	14	E	W	S	IR	NI		26	414	33		2.3	12.9	1686	1205	4	8	5	5	0	0
Blindia acuta	M	Grim	N	20	P	Tf	Tuft						D	F	18	20	E	W	S	IR	NI		26	671	92		2.6	12.8	1606	1205	7	9	5	1	0	0
Blindia caespiticia	M	Grim	N	15	P	Cu							M	A	10	12	E	W	S				13	2			-1.0	10.6	1963	1175	4	5	7	1	0	0
Brachydontium trichodes	M	Grim	N	2	P	Tf							M	A	10	12	E	W	S	IR	NI		72	86	3		2.2	13.6	1480	1000	3	6	4	2	0	0
Brachythecium albicans	M	Hypn	N	80	P	Mr	We						D	A	12	14	E	W	S	IR	NI	Cl	56	1281	55	10	3.7	15.2	935	705	8	6	3	3	0	0
Brachythecium erythrorrhizon	M	Hypn	N	40	P	Mr							D	X	14	20	E		S				46	1			3.6	12.4	993	10	8	4	7	2	0	0
Brachythecium glaciale	M	Hypn	N	40	P	Mr							M	R	12	16	E		S				16	16			-0.6	10.7	2069	1200	5	6	3	4	0	0
Brachythecium glareosum	M	Hypn	N	80	P	Mr							D	R	14	20	E	W	S	IR	NI	(Cl)	55	370	24		3.3	15.0	1014	1065	7	4	8	3	0	1
Brachythecium mildeanum	M	Hypn	N	80	P	Mr	We						M	O	12	18	E	W	S	IR	(NI)	Cl	76	234	14	1	4.2	15.5	923	370	8	6	6	4	1	1
Brachythecium plumosum	M	Hypn	N	60	P	Mr							M	F	16	24	E	W	S	IR	NI	Cl	56	1173	157	2	3.0	13.7	1366	1205	5	8	4	3	0	1
Brachythecium populeum	M	Hypn	N	55	P	Mr							M	F	12	20	E	W	S	IR	NI	Cl	76	823	61	2	3.5	14.6	1168	580	5	5	6	5	0	0
Brachythecium reflexum	M	Hypn	N	65	P	Mr							M	R	12	16	E		S				46	18			-0.1	11.0	2070	1080	5	6	3	4	0	0
Brachythecium rivulare	M	Hypn	N	120	P	Mr							D	O	16	20	E	W	S	IR	NI	Cl	56	1722	154	7	3.3	14.4	1162	960	6	8	6	5	0	1
Brachythecium rutabulum	M	Hypn	N	120	P	Mr	We						M	A	16	24	E	W	S	IR	NI	Cl	73	2330	376	7	3.5	14.7	1058	1344	6	6	6	6	0	0
Brachythecium salebrosum	M	Hypn	N	70	P	Mr							M	O	12	18	E	W	S				36	63			3.5	16.1	668	300	5	6	6	5	0	0
Brachythecium starkei	M	Hypn	N	85	P	Mr							M	O	12	15	E		S				46	5			-0.5	10.8	1832	1050	6	7	2	2	0	0
Brachythecium trachypodium	M	Hypn	N	50	P	Mr							M	X	10	12	E		S				16	1			1.2	12.0	2360	1090	6	6	7	2	0	0
Brachythecium velutinum	M	Hypn	N	50	P	Mr	Tf						M	F	13	16	E	W	S	IR	NI	Cl	76	1290	15	5	3.5	15.3	907	580	4	5	6	5	0	1
Breutelia chrysocoma	M	Brya	N	100	P	We	Ts						D	R	24	30	E	W	S	IR	NI		70	669	185		2.9	13.1	1607	760	7	4	4	2	0	0
Bryoerythrophyllum caledonicum	M	Pott	N	30	P	Tuft							Nil	Nil					S				41	13		9	0.7	11.5	2428	1130	7	9	7	2	0	0
Bryoerythrophyllum ferruginascens	M	Pott	N	32	P	Tf		F					Nil	Nil			E	W	S		NI		44	181	22		2.1	12.6	1880	1075	7	6	7	2	0	0
Bryoerythrophyllum recurvirostrum	M	Pott	N	28	P	Tf	Tuft	X					M	A	14	20	E	W	S	IR	NI	Cl	56	1545	186	3	3.4	14.6	1117	1180	5	5	7	4	0	1
Bryum algovicum	M	Brya	N	15	P	Tf							M	A	22	36	E	W	S	IR	NI	Cl	56	255	25	1	3.9	14.8	992	460	9	6	7	4	0	0
Bryum alpinum	M	Brya	N	60	P	Tf	Tuft	F					D	R	12	14	E	W	S	IR	NI	Cl	73	603	85	6	3.2	13.3	1564	920	7	8	5	2	0	0
Bryum archangelicum	M	Brya	N	5	P	Cu							M	A	26	30	E		S				16	2	2		2.4	13.8	1043	700	6	6	7	2	0	0
Bryum arcticum	M	Brya	N	5	P	Tf							M	A	20	28	E		S				16	8			-0.3	11.2	1757	1007	6	6	7	2	0	2
Bryum argenteum	M	Brya	N	15	P	Tf	Tuft			F			D	O	8	14	E	W	S	IR	NI	Cl	36	1971	225	9	3.6	14.9	1012	893	8	4	6	7	0	1
Bryum bornholmense	M	Brya	N	15	P	Tf		F					MD	A	10	14	E	W	S	IR	NI	Cl	73	123	5	9	4.0	15.3	1079	535	8	5	3	3	0	0
Bryum caespiticium	M	Brya	N	10	P	Tf	U						D	A	10	14	E	W	S	IR	NI	Cl	56	287	4		3.5	15.6	838	110	7	4	6	5	0	0
Bryum caespiticium s.l.	M	Brya	N	10	P	Tf							D	A	10	18	E	W	S	IR	NI	Cl	56	921	12	1	3.5	15.5	831	270	7	4	6	5	0	0
Bryum calophyllum	M	Brya	N	15	PA	Tf		F					M	A	26	40	E	W	S	IR	NI	Cl	26	12	2		4.1	14.5	1004	10	8	8	7	4	0	1
Bryum canariense	M	Brya	N	50	P	Tf	U						M	O	13	16	E	W			(Cl)		91	28			0.8	11.4	2117	200	9	2	8	2	0	0
Bryum capillare	M	Brya	N	50	P	Tf	Cu			F			D	A	12	15	E	W	S	IR	NI	Cl	56	2246	347	4	3.5	14.7	1080	900	6	4	7	4	0	1
Bryum creberrimum	M	Brya	N	40	P	Tf							M	A	14	16	E	W	S	IR			56	18	1		3.2	14.8	920	380	7	5	6	4	0	0
Bryum cyclophyllum	M	Brya	N	80	PA	Tf				F			D	X	14	14	(E)				NI		46	6			2.3	13.2	1645	250	7	8	6	4	0	0
Bryum dichotomum	M	Brya	N	15	PA	Tf	F						D	O	8	16	E	W	S	IR	NI	Cl	63	1115	39	6	3.8	15.5	897	440	7	5	7	5	0	1
Bryum dichotomum s.l.	M	Brya	N	15	PA	Tf	U			F			D	O	8	18	E	W	S	IR	NI	Cl	63	1889	245	9	3.6	14.9	1013	440	7	5	7	7	0	1
Bryum dixonii	M	Brya	N	10	P	Tf	Tuft			O		O	Nil	Nil			E						42	20			0.8	11.4	2117	850	6	7	6	2	0	0
Bryum donianum	M	Brya	N	10	P	Tf							D	R	12	14	E	W	S	IR		Cl	91	152	12	5	5.0	15.7	1013	300	6	3	8	3	0	0
Bryum dyffrynense	M	Brya	N	20	P	Tf			F				D	O	12	14	E	W					71	9	3		4.6	15.2	1017	10	8	6	7	1	0	0
Bryum elegans	M	Brya	N	40	PA	Tuft	R						D	R	12	15	E	W	S	IR	NI		43	34	2		1.3	12.8	1482	915	7	3	8	3	0	1
Bryum gemmiferum	M	Brya	N	15	PA	Tf	U		F				D	O	12	18	E	W	S	IR	NI	Cl	72	378	16		3.6	15.7	796	350	7	7	6	6	0	0
Bryum gemmilucens	M	Brya	NA	10	PA	Tuft	Ts			F			Nil	Nil	14	18	E						73	19			3.6	16.1	679	60	7	5	5	5	0	0

Taxon name	RH	RS	RW	SR	SO	PT	GS	DW	DV	DA	BR	EN	EW	AQ	A2	B1	B2	B3	C1	C2	C3	D1	D2	D4	E1	E2	E3	E4	E7	F3	F4	F9	FA	G1	G1R	G3	G3R	H2	H3	H5	I1	I2	J1	J2	J3	J4
Bazzania tricrenata	2												1											3							3		3	3				3	3						3	
Bazzania trilobata	3	1								2	2		2											3							3		3	3	1			3	3		2			3		
Blasia pusilla				2	3	2	3	1			3									2				3	3	3		3		2	2		2		2				3	3	2				3	
Blepharostoma trichophyllum				3	3		2	3		3		2								3		3	3							3	3		3					3	3				3			1
Blindia acuta	3	3													2		3		3			3	3															3	3			1				
Blindia caespiticia	3	3																																				3							3	
Brachydontium trichodes	1	3										1				3	3																1	2									3			3
Brachythecium albicans		2		3			3	3						3	3	3						3	3			3				3	2								3		2	3		2	3	3
Brachythecium erythrorrhizon	3						3	3								3																							2								1
Brachythecium glaciale	3							3				1								2			3										2					2		2				3		
Brachythecium glareosum	2	1			3		3	3				1			3	3						3	3			3							2		2			2	3					3	3	3
Brachythecium mildeanum				3	3		3								3											3									2			3	1							3
Brachythecium plumosum	3		3		1							3								3		3	3										2					2	1			3		1		1
Brachythecium populeum	3	3	3		3			1				3															3			3	3	3	3					3	3		3			3	1	
Brachythecium reflexum								3																														3								
Brachythecium rivulare	3	3		3	3		2	3				3			2					3		3			2	3				3	3	3	2			3		3			2			2	3	3
Brachythecium rutabulum	3	3		3	3		3	3				3			3	3						3			3	3	3	3		3	3	3	3			3		3	2		2		3	3	3	3
Brachythecium salebrosum	2			2	2		2	2				2								3						2		2		2			3			3										
Brachythecium starkei	3				3																							3											3							
Brachythecium trachypodium	3								3																														3							
Brachythecium velutinum	3	3		3	3		3	3				3								3		3	3		3	3				3		3	3			3						3		3	3	3
Breutelia chrysocoma					3	2	2																3							3	3		1														
Bryoerythrophyllum caledonicum		3																		3															1									2		
Bryoerythrophyllum ferruginascens	3	3	3		3									3	3			2		3							2											3	2	2				3	3	3
Bryoerythrophyllum recurvirostrum	3	3	3	2	2		3				3				3					3		3											3					3	2			3	3	3	1	
Bryum algovicum		3	3	3	3		3	3							3					3																		3	3	3			2	3		
Bryum alpinum	3	3			3		3	3							3					3															2			3	3			3	3	1		
Bryum archangelicum	3																3																					3								
Bryum arcticum				3																																		3								
Bryum argenteum	3	3	3	3	3		3	2							1	3				2		2									3		3	2				2	3	2	2	2	3	3	3	3
Bryum bornholmense		1	3	3	3	3	3								3		2			3		2									3		1	1				1	3	3				3	1	
Bryum caespiticium	3	3	2	3	3		3	3							3					3		3									2		3	2				3	3				3	3	3	2
Bryum caespiticium s.l.	3	3		3	3		3	3							2	3				3		3									2							3	3				3	3	3	2
Bryum calophyllum					3		3	3							3		3			3																										
Bryum canariense		3					1								1	2																															
Bryum capillare	3	3	3	3	3		3	3				3			2	3	3			2		2							3	3	3	3	3			2		3	3		3	3	3	3	3	3
Bryum creberrimum	2	2	2	2	3		2	3							2																		3					3	2		2		3	2		
Bryum cyclophyllum					3															3					2																					
Bryum dichotomum	3	3	3	3	3		3	1							2	3				3											1				2				3	3	3	3		3	3	3
Bryum dichotomum s.l.	3	3	3	3	3		3	3							2	3				3											1				2				3	3	3	3		3	3	3
Bryum dixonii	3	3			3		3																2																3	3					2		
Bryum donianum				3	3		2									3																	3	2				3	3		1			3	2	2
Bryum dyffrynense				3			3													3																									2	
Bryum elegans	3	2	2	2			2								2					3															2				3		3						
Bryum gemmiferum	2			3	3											3				3														2				2	3		3	3			3	3
Bryum gemmilucens	2	2			3															3															3							3					

39

Taxon name	ML	Ord	Stat	Len	Per	LF1	LF2	Tub	Gem	Bul	Bra	Lvs	Sex	Fr	Sp1	Sp2	E	W	Sc	IR	NI	Cl	Elem	GBno	IRno	Clno	TJan	TJul	Prec	Alt	L	F	R	N	S	HM
Bryum gemmiparum	M	Brya	N	30	P	Tf		X		F			D	X	12	14	E	W		IR			91	5	1		3.5	14.5	1307	150	7	9	5	4	0	0
Bryum imbricatum	M	Brya	N	10	P	Tf							M	A	16	30	E	W	S	IR	NI	Cl	56	296	30	2	3.5	14.4	1155	730	8	5	7	4	0	2
Bryum intermedium	M	Brya	N	25	P	Tf							M	A	18	24	E	W	S	IR	(NI)		75	80	1		3.5	15.2	951	310	8	6	7	4	0	0
Bryum klinggraeffii	M	Brya	N	5	AP	Tf		F					D	R	8	12	E	W	S	IR	NI	Cl	73	683	46		3.7	15.6	835	350	8	6	6	6	0	0
Bryum knowltonii	M	Brya	N	10	P	Tf							M	F	20	26	E	W		IR			43	19	1		3.9	15.2	848	60	7	7	7	4	0	0
Bryum kunzei	M	Brya	N	10	P	Tuft							D	X		18	E	W					92	15			4.7	15.8	873	270	8	2	8	2	0	0
Bryum lawersianum	M	Brya	N	5	P	Tf							M	A	26	32			(S)				42							1070	6	6	7	2	0	0
Bryum mamillatum	M	Brya	N	5	PA	Tf							M	A	36	42	E						43	1			3.8	15.8	661	2	8	7	7	5	2	0
Bryum marratii	M	Brya	N	5	P	Tuft	Ts						M	O	26	32	E	W	S	IR	(NI)		43	13	5		4.2	14.2	1115	10	7	9	7	4	4	0
Bryum mildeanum	M	Brya	N	25	P	Cu							D	X			E	W	S				43	16			1.6	12.5	1922	850	6	7	6	2	0	0
Bryum moravicum	M	Brya	N	40	P	Tuft		U					D	X	9	13	E	W	S	IR			76	567	1		3.4	15.7	802	950	5	5	5	5	0	0
Bryum muehlenbeckii	M	Brya	N	70	P	Tuft	Tf	F					D	X	12	14		W	S				43	11			-0.2	10.9	1920	900	7	8	5	2	0	0
Bryum neodamense	M	Brya	N	80	PA	Tf							D	R	14	20	E	W	S	IR	(NI)		46	5	19		4.4	14.7	1025	75	8	7	7	3	0	0
Bryum pallens	M	Brya	N	60	P	Tf	Ts		O			O	D	R	16	26	E	W	S	IR	NI		36	1115	167		3.1	14.0	1247	1180	7	7	6	4	0	3
Bryum pallescens	M	Brya	N	40	P	Tuft	Tf						M	A	18	26	E	W	S	IR	NI	Cl	56	129	21	2	3.8	14.0	1156	1205	7	5	6	4	0	4
Bryum pseudotriquetrum	M	Brya	N	100	P	Tf	Tuft	F	R				D(M)	O	12	25	E	W	S	IR	NI	Cl	36	1540	245	5	3.2	14.1	1245	1170	8	9	6	3	0	0
Bryum pseudotriquetrum var. bimum	M	Brya	N	100	P	Tf	Tuft	F	R				M	A	15	25	E	W	S	IR	NI	Cl	36	90	12	1	3.6	15.2	984	75	8	9	6	3	0	1
Bryum pseudotriquetrum var. pseudotriquetrum	M	Brya	N	100	P	Tf	Tuft	F	R				D	O	12	18	E	W	S	IR	NI		36	679	70		3.1	14.0	1264	580	8	8	6	3	0	0
Bryum radiculosum	M	Brya	N	10	P	Cu	Tf	F					D	F	10	14	E	W	S	IR	NI	Cl	92	688	28	8	4.0	15.5	951	305	6	3	8	5	0	0
Bryum riparium	M	Brya	N	30	PA	Tuft	Tf	F					D	Nil			E	W	S	IR	(NI)		70	54	8		2.4	12.7	1942	760	6	8	5	2	0	0
Bryum rubens	M	Brya	N	15	AP	Tf		F					D	O	8	10	E	W	S	IR	NI	Cl	73	1418	82	8	3.7	15.3	927	450	8	5	6	6	0	0
Bryum ruderale	M	Brya	NA	8	PA	Tf		F					D	X	9	11	E	W	S	IR	NI	Cl	73	726	43	2	3.9	15.5	915	370	7	4	7	6	0	1
Bryum salinum	M	Brya	N	15	P	Tf							M	A	18	36	E		S	IR			23	7	2		4.0	13.8	1135	10	8	8	7	4	0	0
Bryum sauteri	M	Brya	N	4	AP	Tf		F					D(M)	X	16	20	E	W	S	IR	NI		73	245	18	3	4.3	14.9	1119	525	6	8	5	5	0	0
Bryum schleicheri	M	Brya	N	87	P	Cu	Tf						D	X	16	20	E	W	S	IR	NI	Cl	46	2			2.3	13.9	1417	230	7	9	6	4	0	0
Bryum stirtonii	M	Brya	N	40	P	Tf							D	R	12	14	E		S				46	5			-0.5	11.2	1411	1170	6	6	7	4	0	0
Bryum subapiculatum	M	Brya	N	10	PA	Tf		F					D	O	10	12	E	W	S	IR	NI	Cl	73	677	25	3	3.7	15.2	965	470	8	4	5	5	0	0
Bryum tenuisetum	M	Brya	N	10	P	Tf		F					D(M)	F	12	16	E	W	S	IR			53	64	2	2	3.7	14.5	1300	350	8	3	6	3	0	0
Bryum torquescens	M	Brya	N	25	PA	Tf	Cu						M(D)	A	10	16	E	W	S	IR	NI		91	38	2		4.6	15.8	894	110	8	3	7	3	0	0
Bryum turbinatum	M	Brya	N	30	P	Tf	Tuft						D	F	16	20	(E)	(W)	(S)	(IR)			45				0.7	11.7	1836	210	8	7	7	4	0	0
Bryum uliginosum	M	Brya	N	30	PA	Tf							M	F	22	30	(E)		S	IR	(NI)		46	1	3		2.1	13.9	1236	150	7	6	4	2	0	0
Bryum valparaisense	M	Brya	AN	9	A	Tp							D	X	10	10	(E)						80	1			7.4	15.7	1077	12	7	5	5	2	0	0
Bryum violaceum	M	Brya	N	7	AP	Tf		F					D	X	9	11	E	W	S	IR	NI	Cl	73	566	25	1	3.7	15.5	827	300	8	4	6	6	0	0
Bryum warneum	M	Brya	N	10	PA	Tf							M	O	25	45	E	W	S	IR			43	18	3		4.1	14.9	1003	5	8	8	8	4	3	0
Bryum weigelii	M	Brya	N	107	P	Tf	Tuft						D	X	12	15	E	W	S	(IR)			26	68			0.7	11.7	1836	1070	7	9	5	3	0	0
Buxbaumia aphylla	M	Buxb	N	8	PA	Sc	We						D	A	10	13	E	W	S	IR	NI		46	27			2.1	13.7	996	275	5	6	2	2	0	0
Buxbaumia viridis	M	Buxb	N	9	A	Tp	Sc						D	A	10	10	E	W	S	S			43	6			0.7	12.3	1008	350	4	7	2	2	0	0
Callialaria curvicaulis	M	Hypn	N	100	P	Mr	We						D	Nil					(S)				15				1.4	11.8	2208	1060	6	7	3	0	0	0
Calliergon cordifolium	M	Hypn	N	150	P	Tf							M	R	10	16	E	W	S	IR	NI		56	606	48	9	3.5	14.7	1066	910	5	10	4	5	0	0
Calliergon giganteum	M	Hypn	N	200	P	Tf							D	R	16	20	E	W	S	IR	NI		26	328	69		3.2	14.1	1141	910	7	10	6	3	0	0
Calliergon sarmentosum	M	Hypn	N	120	P	Tf							D	A	14	20	E	W	S	IR	NI		26	403	41		2.4	12.6	1764	1200	8	9	5	2	0	0
Calliergon stramineum	M	Hypn	N	100	P	Sc							D	A	12	16	E	W	S	IR	NI		26	664	46		2.8	13.8	1338	1280	7	9	3	2	0	0
Calliergon trifarium	M	Hypn	N	95	P	Ms							D	X	12	16	E		S	IR			26	54	3		1.4	11.8	2208	960	8	9	6	2	0	0
Calliergonella cuspidata	M	Hypn	N	120	P	We							D	O	16	24	E	W	S	IR	NI	Cl	76	2337	416	9	3.4	14.5	1108	900	7	7	7	4	0	1
Calomnion complanatum	M	Rhiz	AN	10	P	Tp							D	X	16	24				IR			70	1			5.0	14.4	1403	20	4	8	5	0	0	0
Calypogeia arguta	L	Jung	N	20	P	Ms	Sc			F			D	R			E	W	S	IR	NI	Cl	92	1064	170	8	3.7	14.6	1218	610	1	7	4	4	0	0

Taxon name	RH	RS	RW	SR	SO	PT	GS	DW	DV	DA	BR	EN	EW	AQ	A2	B1	B2	B3	C1	C2	C3	D1	D2	D4	E1	E2	E3	E4	E7	F3	F4	F9	FA	G1	G1R	G3	G3R	H2	H3	H5	I1	I2	J1	J2	J3	J4
Bryum gemmiparum	3																				3																		3	3		1		2	3	
Bryum imbricatum	3	3	2																						1														3	3		1	2	3		
Bryum intermedium	2	2																																					3	3		1	2	2		
Bryum klinggraeffii				2	3										1						3																			3	3					
Bryum knowltonii						3										3					3																		3						2	
Bryum kunzei	3	2		2	3	3												2					3		3														3							
Bryum lawersianum					3																																		3							
Bryum mamillatum						3										3																														
Bryum marratii	3				3	3	3									3					3																		3							
Bryum mildeanum	3			3	3	3	3								3	3					3																		3							
Bryum moravicum	2			3	2	2		2						3							3									3	3	3							1	1						
Bryum muehlenbeckii	3					3										3								3			3												3							
Bryum neodamense	3					3	3									3					3		3	3											3				3	3						
Bryum pallens	3			3	3	3	3									3					3		3	3									3						3	3			3	3	3	
Bryum pallescens	3			3	3	3	3	1	3							3					3		3				3												3	2			3	3	3	3
Bryum pseudotriquetrum	3		3		3	3	3								1	3	3		3		3		3		3					2									3			1		1	3	
Bryum pseudotriquetrum var. *bimum*	3		3		3	3	3														3		3																3						3	
Bryum pseudotriquetrum var. *pseudotriquetrum*	3				3	3	3									3					3		3																3						3	
Bryum radiculosum	3	3		3	3	3															3				3														3	1	2		3	3	3	1	1
Bryum riparium	3					3																																		2						
Bryum rubens				2	3	2	3	1							1	1					2				3	3				2			3	1		2			3	3	3	3	3	3		
Bryum ruderale				2	3	3									1	1							2											1			1		3	3	3	3	3	3		
Bryum salinum					3										3	3																							3	3						
Bryum sauteri					3	3																	3							3			3	1	3				3	3						
Bryum schleicheri	3				3	3																3	3																			2					
Bryum stirtonii	1					3															1		3		3						3			1	3				3	3				2		
Bryum subapiculatum				2	3	3											3				3				3					3	3				1				3	1						
Bryum tenuisetum					3																3									3																
Bryum torquescens	2		2		3	3										3									3														2			2		2		
Bryum turbinatum					3	3	2									3					3		3	3																						
Bryum uliginosum					3	3										3					3		3																3							
Bryum valparaisense					3																3		3	3			2	1				2		2					3	3						
Bryum violaceum						3										3					2		3	3			3							2							3	2				
Bryum warneum							3									3					3		3														1				3	2			1	
Bryum weigelii					3	3		2	2																										1	3								3		
Buxbaumia aphylla					3	3		2																											1									3		
Buxbaumia viridis								3																											3											
Callialaria curvicaulis	3				3												3				3		3																3							
Calliergon cordifolium					3				3												3		3				3							3												
Calliergon giganteum					3	2										2		3	3		3	3	3				3					2														
Calliergon sarmentosum	3				3	3										3					3		3	3															3							
Calliergon stramineum		3			3	3										2				2	2		3	3			2	1				2		2					3	3		3				
Calliergon trifarium		3			3	3															3	3	3				3																			
Calliergonella cuspidata			2	2	3	3		2				1			3	3	3				3	3	3		3	3				3		3	3	2	3	1			3	3		3	3	3	3	1
Calomnion complanatum			2	2									3														3													3		3				
Calypogeia arguta	3				3	3			2							3					2		2							3	3	3	3	3	1		1		3	3					3	

41

Taxon name	ML	Ord	Stat	Len	Per	LF1	LF2	Tub	Gem	Bul	Bra	Lvs	Sex	Fr	Sp1	Sp2	E	W	Sc	IR	NI	CI	Elem	GBno	IRno	Cno	TJan	TJul	Prec	Alt	L	F	R	N	S	HM
Calypogeia azurea	L	Jung	N	50	P	Ms	Sc						M	X	12	16	E	W	S	IR	NI		52	82	16		1.9	12.6	1658	1000	3	7	3	1	0	0
Calypogeia fissa	L	Jung	N	30	P	Ms	Sc						M	F	9	14	E	W	S	IR	NI	CI	72	1589	254	2	3.4	14.4	1201	850	3	7	3	3	0	0
Calypogeia integristipula	L	Jung	N	30	P	Sc	Ms						M	R	10	13	E		S	(IR)	NI		56	70	4		2.7	14.2	1183	850	3	7	2	1	0	0
Calypogeia muelleriana	L	Jung	N	30	P	Ms	Sc						M	F	10	16	E	W	S	IR	NI	CI	56	1154	191	1	3.1	14.0	1293	920	3	7	2	1	0	0
Calypogeia neesiana	L	Jung	N	25	P	Sc	Ms						M	R	10	14	E	W	S	IR	NI		56	118	24		2.3	12.9	1467	760	3	7	1	1	0	0
Calypogeia neesiana s.l.	L	Jung	N	30	P	Sc	Ms						M	R	10	14	E	W	S	IR	NI		56	174	27		2.4	13.4	1365	850	3	7	1	1	0	0
Calypogeia sphagnicola	L	Jung	N	30	P	Sc	Thread						M	R	10	12	E	W	S	IR	NI		26	141	51		3.1	13.7	1335	670	8	9	1	1	0	0
Calypogeia suecica	L	Jung	N	15	P	Sc							MD	R	9	11			S		NI		43	20	4		2.3	12.3	2131	300	3	7	2	2	0	0
Calyptrochaeta apiculata	M	Hook	AN	30	P	Tf			O				D	X			E						81	2	1		5.4	15.5	1036	30	5	5	6	5	0	0
Campyliadelphus chrysophyllus	M	Hypn	N	50	P	We	Mr						D	R	14	14	E	W	S	IR	NI	(CI)	56	516	58		3.7	15.1	981	950	8	2	8	2	0	1
Campyliadelphus elodes	M	Hypn	N	70	P	We	Mr						D	R	12	17	E	W	S	IR	NI		73	88	29		4.0	14.9	994	380	8	9	7	3	2	0
Campylium stellatum	M	Hypn	N	100	P	We	Mr						D	R	12	20	E	W	S	IR	NI	CI	56	1277	191	3	3.2	14.0	1270	1070	8	8	6	2	0	1
Campylium stellatum var. protensum	M	Hypn	N	60	P	We	Mr						D	R	16	20	E	W	S	IR	NI		56	459	32		3.2	14.4	1203	850	7	8	6	3	0	0
Campylium stellatum var. stellatum	M	Hypn	N	100	P	We							D	R	12	18	E	W	S	IR	NI	CI	56	1108	176	3	3.1	13.8	1328	1070	8	9	6	2	0	0
Campylophyllum calcareum	M	Hypn	N	30	P	Mr							D	R	10	16	E	W	S	IR	(NI)		73	102	1		3.3	15.7	799	500	2	5	8	4	0	0
Campylophyllum halleri	M	Hypn	N	40	P	Mr							M	O	10	13			S				26	4			-0.9	10.8	1864	1030	7	5	7	2	0	0
Campylopus atrovirens	M	Dicr	N	130	P	Tuft	Tf				F	F	D	X			E	W	S	IR	NI		70	566	157		3.0	13.0	1680	940	8	2	1	1	0	0
Campylopus atrovirens var. atrovirens	M	Dicr	N	130	P	Tuft	Tf					F	D	X			E	W	S	IR	NI		70	95	3		3.0	13.1	1986	860	8	8	2	1	0	0
Campylopus atrovirens var. falcatus	M	Dicr	N	130	P	Tuft						F	D	Nil			(E)		S	IR	NI		70	30	6		3.4	12.7	1943	460	8	8	2	1	0	0
Campylopus brevipilus	M	Dicr	N	50	P	Tuft					F	F	D	R	11	13	E	W	S	IR	NI	CI	71	248	57	2	4.2	13.9	1290	550	8	8	1	1	0	0
Campylopus flexuosus	M	Dicr	N	57	P	Tuft		U				F	D	O	10	17	E	W	S	IR	NI	CI	72	1476	249	2	3.3	14.2	1255	800	6	6	2	1	0	2
Campylopus fragilis	M	Dicr	N	45	P	Tuft	Tf	U				F	D	O	9	20	E	W	S	IR	NI	CI	72	623	114	2	3.5	13.8	1450	760	7	5	3	2	1	0
Campylopus gracilis	M	Dicr	N	80	P	Tuft						F	Nil	Nil			E	W	S	IR	NI		42	107	29		2.6	12.5	2018	900	7	8	2	1	0	0
Campylopus introflexus	M	Dicr	N	50	AN	Tuft	Tf					F	D	F	10	14	E	W	S	IR	NI	CI	72	1420	238	2	3.6	14.8	1094	640	7	5	2	4	0	2
Campylopus pilifer	M	Dicr	N	50	P	Tuft						F	D	R	13	17	E	W	S	IR	NI	CI	81	24	18	9	5.5	15.2	1277	100	8	7	4	2	0	0
Campylopus pyriformis	M	Dicr	N	25	P	Tf	Tuft	U			R	O	D	O	8	17	E	W	S	IR	NI	CI	72	1312	182	8	3.3	14.4	1191	910	6	5	2	2	0	0
Campylopus schimperi	M	Dicr	N	70	P	Tuft					O	F	D	X					S	IR			16	24	2		1.5	11.6	2108	900	6	5	4	1	0	0
Campylopus setifolius	M	Dicr	N	130	P	Tuft	Tf				R	F	D	Nil			E	W	S	IR	NI		70	65	47		3.4	13.2	1892	800	6	9	2	1	0	0
Campylopus shawii	M	Dicr	N	110	P	Tf						F	D	X			E	W	S	IR			80	55	8		3.7	12.8	1853	455	8	9	1	1	0	0
Campylopus subulatus	M	Dicr	N	30	PA	Tuft		U					D	R			E	W	S	IR	NI	CI	72	74	5	1	3.2	13.4	1847	850	8	7	4	2	0	0
Campylostelium saxicola	M	Grim	N	2	P	Ts							M	A	7	10	E	W	S	IR	NI		72	30	6		3.0	14.2	1384	680	3	6	5	2	0	0
Catoscopium nigritum	M	Brya	N	40	P	Cu	Tf						D	F	40	45	E	W	S	IR	NI		26	33	7		2.8	12.8	1331	550	9	8	2	1	0	0
Cephalozia ambigua	L	Jung	N	7	P	Ms	Tf						D	X	11	12			S				16	5			-1.9	10.0	1532	1200	4	7	2	1	0	0
Cephalozia bicuspidata	L	Jung	N	30	P	Ms	Sc		F				M	F	12	15	E	W	S	IR	NI	CI	56	1606	219	6	3.3	14.2	1220	1220	4	7	2	2	0	1
Cephalozia catenulata	L	Jung	N	10	P	Ms	Tf		F				D	O	9	12	E	W	S	IR	NI		53	106	41		3.3	13.4	1673	500	3	7	1	1	0	0
Cephalozia connivens	L	Jung	N	15	P	Ms	Sc		O				M	F	12	15	E	W	S	IR	NI	CI	53	534	138		3.3	14.2	1274	670	6	8	1	1	0	0
Cephalozia hibernica	L	Jung	N	15	P	Ms	Sc		F				D	Nil			E	W	S	IR			80		5		4.5	14.1	1393	45	3	7	2	2	0	0
Cephalozia leucantha	L	Jung	N	10	P	Ms	Sc		F				D	O	8	10	E	W	S	IR	NI		46	127	31		2.9	12.7	1617	1000	9	8	1	1	0	0
Cephalozia loitlesbergeri	L	Jung	N	30	P	Ms	Sc		F				M	F	9	12	E	W	S	IR			43	42	8		2.3	12.9	1513	700	7	9	1	1	0	0
Cephalozia lunulifolia	L	Jung	N	30	P	Ms	Sc		F				D	O	8	12	E	W	S	IR	NI		56	535	56		3.2	14.0	1350	650	5	8	2	2	0	0
Cephalozia macrostachya	L	Jung	N	30	P	Ms	Sc		F				MD	F	10	15	E	W	S	IR	NI		42	76	11		3.6	14.9	1101	300	7	8	1	1	0	0
Cephalozia macrostachya var. macrostachya	L	Jung	N	25	P	Ms	Sc		F				D	R	10	15	E	W	S	IR	NI		42	18	2		3.8	14.9	1113	275	7	8	1	1	0	0
Cephalozia macrostachya var. spiniflora	L	Jung	N	35	P	Ms			F				MD	Nil			E	W	S	IR			42	3			2.9	13.6	968	300	7	8	1	1	0	0
Cephaloziella baumgartneri	L	Jung	N	7	P	Sc	Ms		F				M	F	11	14	E	W					91	59	9		2.6	13.1	1531	1080	4	8	8	2	0	0
Cephaloziella calyculata	L	Jung	N	4	P	Sc			F				M	R	12	12	E	W					81	11	11		5.9	15.7	1090	230	7	3	6	1	1	1

Taxon name	RH	RS	RW	SR	SO	PT	GS	DW	DV	DA	BR	EN	EW	AQ	A2	B1	B2	B3	C1	C2	C3	D1	D2	D4	E1	E2	E3	E4	E7	F3	F4	F9	FA	G1	G1R	G3	G3R	H2	H3	H5	I1	I2	J1	J2	J3	J4
Calypogeia azurea	3	1		3	3	3	1		3	3												3	3							3	3	3	3	1				3	3	3				3		
Calypogeia fissa	1	2		3	3	3	3		3	3						1		3	1			3	3				3			3	3	3	3	3	2			3	3	3	3				3	
Calypogeia integristipula	2	3		3	3			3	3	3												3	3								3		3	3		3		3	3	3					3	
Calypogeia muelleriana		3		3	3	3	3		3	3								3				3	3				3				3	3	2	3	3			3	3	3						
Calypogeia neesiana				2	3		2		2	2												3									3		2	2				3	2							
Calypogeia neesiana s.l.	2	3		3	3	3	2		2	2								3				3	3							3	3		3	3				3	3	3						
Calypogeia sphagnicola					2					3	3										2	3		2							2																
Calypogeia suecica				1			3																											3		1						3					
Calyptrochaeta apiculata	3	3		3	3		3							3	3		3													3				2	1			3	3	2				2	3	
Campyliadelphus chrysophyllus	3	2			3	3	1	3							3									3	3		3			3	3			2				3	3	2	3					3
Campyliadelphus elodes				3	3									1	3							3	3	3	3	2	3							2					3	3						
Campylium stellatum	3			3	3									2	3							3	3	3	3	2	3							2					3	3	1		1			
Campylium stellatum var. protensum	3			3	3		3								3							3	3	3			3																			3	
Campylium stellatum var. stellatum	3	1		3	3									3			3					3								3			3	3												
Campylophyllum calcareum	3			3	3		2									2	3			3		3	3	3						3	3	3	3	3		3		3	3				2	2		
Campylophyllum halleri	3				3	3								3								3	3	3	3		3			3	3		3	3		3		3	3		1		1	1		1
Campylopus atrovirens	3			3	3		2							2	2							3	3		2			3		3	3	2	2					3	3					1		1
Campylopus atrovirens var. atrovirens	3			3	3																	3	3							3	3							3	3					1		1
Campylopus atrovirens var. falcatus	3			3	3		2								2			3				3	3							3	3	3						3	3							
Campylopus brevipilus	3			3	3									3	2			3		3		3	3				3			3	3							3	3	3						2
Campylopus flexuosus	3	3		3	3				3			3				1		3				3	3		3		3			3	3		3	3		3		3	3	3	3	1		2	3	3
Campylopus fragilis	3	3		3	3		2		2			2				2		3				2	3		2					3	3	2	3	2				3	3		1		3		3	1
Campylopus gracilis	3			3	2																	3	3			2		2		3	3							3	3							
Campylopus introflexus	2	3		3	3		3		3			1				3		3				3	3		3		3		3	3	3	3	3		3		3	3	3	3	3	3	3	3	3	2
Campylopus pilifer	3			3	3		2											3				3																								
Campylopus pyriformis				3	3		3		3			2						3				3	3		3		2			3	3	3	3	3	3			3	3		2	2		2		2
Campylopus schimperi		3		3																				3				3	3																	
Campylopus setifolius	3			3	2		2															3	2								3			2				3	3							
Campylopus shawii	2			3	3																	3	3								3			3												
Campylopus subulatus	1	1	1	3	1		3			3								2			3				1			3	3				2						2	3						3
Campylostelium saxicola		3										2				3					3												2		2					3					1	
Catoscopium nigritum																								3				3																		
Cephalozia ambigua							3																				3																			
Cephalozia bicuspidata	3	3		3	3		1		3	3		2		1	1	3						3	3				3			3	3		3	3	3		3	3	3		2		3	
Cephalozia catenulata	2	2		3		3			3	3												3	3							3	2		3	3					3							
Cephalozia connivens		2			2				2	3		2										3	3				3			3	3	3	2	2				2	2							
Cephalozia hibernica					3				3	3												3	3							3	3		3	3												
Cephalozia leucantha					3				2	3												3	3								2		2	2												
Cephalozia loitlesbergeri				2					2	2												3	3										3	3	2											
Cephalozia lunulifolia	2	3		3	3		3		3	2		2					1					3	3							1	3		3	3	3	2		3	3					3		
Cephalozia macrostachya				3	3		3		3	3		1										3	3							3	3		3	3					3	3				2		
Cephalozia macrostachya var. macrostachya		3			3		3		3	3												3	3								3			3					3	3				3		
Cephalozia macrostachya var. spiniflora		2		3			2		2													3	3							3	3			3												
Cephalozia pleniceps	2			2	2		1	2		3		2										3	3				3			3	3		2	3		2		3	2							
Cephaloziella baumgartneri		3		2																		3																	3						3	3
Cephaloziella calyculata		3		3																		3									3														3	3

Taxon name	ML	Ord	Stat	Len	Per	LF1	LF2	Tub	Gem	Bul	Bra	Lvs	Sex	Fr	Sp1	Sp2	E	W	Sc	IR	NI	CI	Elem	GBno	IRno	CIno	TJan	TJul	Prec	Alt	L	F	R	N	S	HM
Cephaloziella dentata	L	Jung	N	8	P	Sc			F				D	Nil			E						82	2			6.7	15.8	970	75	7	6	4	2	0	0
Cephaloziella divaricata	L	Jung	N	10	P	Ms	Sc		F				D	O	6	9	E	W	S	IR	NI		56	802	82	8	3.4	14.5	1207	1200	7	5	2	2	0	2
Cephaloziella elachista	L	Jung	N	12	P	Thread	Ms		F				M	F	9	11	E	W	S	IR			43	11	1		3.5	15.2	892	120	7	8	2	1	0	0
Cephaloziella hampeana	L	Jung	N	12	P	Thread	Sc		F				M	F	8	11	E	W	S	IR	NI		53	455	78		3.4	14.2	1265	1175	6	6	2	2	0	2
Cephaloziella integerrima	L	Jung	N	4	P	Sc	Ms		F				M	R	6	10	E			IR			42	9	2		5.5	15.3	1235	250	7	5	4	1	0	3
Cephaloziella massalongi	L	Jung	NA	6	P	Ms	Sc		F				D	X	9	10	E	W		IR			52	14	3		5.2	15.1	1387	670	6	6	3	1	0	5
Cephaloziella nicholsonii	L	Jung	NA	15	P	Ms	Sc		F				M	Nil			E	(W)					72	16			5.7	15.5	1271	275	6	6	3	1	0	5
Cephaloziella rubella	L	Jung	N	8	P	Ms	Sc		F				D	F	6	9	E	W	S	IR	NI	CI	56	124	6	1	3.1	14.7	1085	900	6	5	2	2	0	2
Cephaloziella spinigera	L	Jung	N	5	P	Thread	Ms		F				M	F	7	10	E	W	S	IR			26	23	6		3.4	14.2	1260	600	7	6	2	2	0	2
Cephaloziella stellulifera	L	Jung	N	8	P	Ms	Sc		F				M	F	9	12	E	W	S	IR		CI	92	90	9	7	5.2	15.3	1165	400	7	5	5	1	0	3
Cephaloziella turneri	L	Jung	N	7	P	Ms			F				M	F			E	W	S	IR		CI	91	26	1	1	5.4	15.7	1098	215	4	6	3	2	0	0
Ceratodon conicus	M	Dicr	NA	10	P	Tf							D	O	11	13	E						92	7			3.5	16.2	658	210	7	3	8	2	0	0
Ceratodon purpureus	M	Dicr	N	35	PA	Tf					R		D	A	10	14	E	W	S	IR	NI	CI	36	2030	244	3	3.4	14.6	1078	1344	7	4	5	3	1	3
Ceratodon purpureus s.l.	M	Dicr	N	35	PA	Tf							D	A	10	14	E	W	S	IR	NI	CI	36	2301	282	9	3.4	14.6	1085	1344	7	5	5	3	1	3
Cheilothela chloropus	M	Dicr	NA	10	P	Tf							D	X	8	12	E					CI	91	6		9	5.0	16.3	902	35	9	2	8	2	0	0
Chenia leptophylla	M	Pott	AN	3	A	Ts						F	D	X	15	20	E						81	6			6.5	16.2	896	110	7	5	5	4	0	0
Chiloscyphus pallescens	L	Jung	N	60	P	Tf	Ms						M	F	14	22	E	W	S	IR	NI		56	678	59		3.5	14.6	1201	850	6	9	6	4	0	0
Chiloscyphus polyanthos	L	Jung	N	30	P	At	Ms						M	F	14	21	E	W	S	IR	NI		56	1176	140	4	3.3	14.2	1230	1040	6	9	5	4	0	0
Chiloscyphus polyanthos s.l.	L	Jung	N	60	P	At	Tf						M	F	14	22	E	W	S	IR	NI		56	1480	172	4	3.3	14.3	1191	1040	6	9	6	4	0	0
Cinclidium stygium	M	Brya	N	80	P	Tf							M	R	25	35	E	(W)	S	IR	NI		46	44	6	4	1.8	13.0	1458	970	7	9	6	4	0	0
Cinclidotus fontinaloides	M	Pott	N	120	P	At							D	F	18	20	E	W	S	IR	NI		83	572	141		3.4	14.5	1135	580	7	8	7	4	0	0
Cinclidotus riparius	M	Pott	NA	50	P	At							D	X	12	20	E			(IR)			74	4			3.4	15.7	752	80	7	8	7	4	0	0
Cirriphyllum cirrosum	M	Hypn	N	83	P	Mr							D	X	18	20	E		S				16	5			0.3	11.1	2499	1170	5	5	7	3	0	0
Cirriphyllum piliferum	M	Hypn	N	125	P	We	Mr						D	R	12	16	E	W	S	IR	NI		56	1287	104	2	3.5	14.9	1043	1010	4	6	6	6	0	1
Cladopodiella fluitans	L	Jung	N	80	P	We	Sc						D	R	15	22	E	W	S	IR	NI		46	157	32		3.4	14.1	1411	600	8	9	1	1	0	0
Cladopodiella francisci	L	Jung	N	8	P	We			F				D	R	12	18	E	W	S	IR	NI		43	70	5		3.6	14.7	1212	500	6	7	2	2	0	0
Climacium dendroides	M	Hypn	N	100	P	De							D	R	16	24	E	W	S	IR	NI		36	846	156		3.0	14.0	1208	914	7	7	5	3	0	2
Cololejeunea calcarea	L	Pore	N	5	P	Mr			F				M	F	12	20	E	W	S	IR	NI		52	250	31		2.2	12.8	767	825	3	6	7	2	0	0
Cololejeunea minutissima	L	Pore	N	4	P	Ms			F				M	F	17	17	E	W	S	IR	NI	CI	80	225	66	7	4.8	15.3	1107	245	6	4	6	4	2	0
Cololejeunea rossettiana	L	Pore	N	5	P	Mr	Sc		F				M	F			E	W	S	IR	NI		92	68	15		3.6	14.8	1078	400	3	5	7	3	0	0
Colura calyptrifolia	L	Pore	N	5	P	Mr			F				D	X			E	W		IR			80	149	71		3.6	13.6	1738	610	4	6	4	2	0	0
Conardia compacta	M	Hypn	N	20	P	Mr			F				D	X	11	15	E	W	S				46	26			3.4	14.2	1065	350	1	6	8	4	0	1
Conocephalum conicum s.l.	L	Marc	N	110	P	Mt		O					D	O	53	97	E	W	S	IR	NI	CI	56	1706	190	2	3.4	14.6	1140	1000	3	8	7	5	0	1
Conocephalum conicum s.str.	L	Marc	N	110	P	Mt							D	O	53	97	E	W	S	IR	NI		73	49		2	4.2	15.3	1082	550	3	7	6	5	0	1
Conocephalum salebrosum	L	Marc	N	90	P	Mt	Fa						M	A	15	18	E	W	S	IR	NI	CI	56	697	155	5	3.1	15.4	1055	505	3	6	5	5	0	1
Conostomum tetragonum	M	Brya	N	20	P	Cu							M	A	18	18	E	W		IR			16	52			0.1	11.1	2200	1335	5	5	2	1	0	0
Coscinodon cribrosus	M	Grim	N	10	P	Cu							D	F	10	12	E	W	S				56	39			3.4	14.1	1413	915	7	2	3	1	0	1
Cratoneuron filicinum	M	Hypn	N	60	P	We	Mr						D	O	12	14	E	W	S	IR	NI		66	772	18		3.7	15.1	1016	950	6	8	7	5	0	2
Cratoneuron filicinum s.l.	M	Hypn	N	120	P	We	Mr						D	O	12	14	E	W	S	IR	NI	CI	66	1870	272	5	3.5	14.6	1081	1060	6	7	7	5	0	2
Cryphaea heteromalla	M	Hypn	N	100	P	Fa	Mr						M	A	15	18	E	W	S	IR	NI	CI	92	697	155	5	4.1	15.4	1184	360	5	6	6	4	0	1
Cryphaea lamyana	M	Hypn	N	40	P	St							D	F	38	52	E	W		IR			81	12			4.8	15.4	915	90	0	8	3	3	0	1
Cryptothallus mirabilis	L	Metz	N	60	P	Mr							D	X	13	15	E	W		IR			43	73	8		3.1	14.2	1341	320	0	3	7	3	0	1
Ctenidium molluscum	M	Hypn	N	80	P	We							D	R	13	15	E	W	S	IR	NI	CI	53	1623	317	2	3.3	14.2	1216	1205	7	5	7	2	0	2
Ctenidium molluscum var. condensatum	M	Hypn	N	20	P	Mr	We						D	X			E	W	S	IR	NI		53	130	15		2.1	12.5	1795	1070	7	7	7	5	0	2
Ctenidium molluscum var. molluscum	M	Hypn	N	100	P	Mr	We						D	R	13	15	E	W	S	IR	NI	CI	53	1155	266	5	3.2	14.1	1246	940	7	7	6	5	0	2
Ctenidium molluscum var. robustum	M	Hypn	N	100	P	We							D	Nil			(E)	W	S	IR	(NI)		53	12			1.6	12.1	1924	790	6	8	7	7	0	0

Taxon name	RH	RS	RW	SR	SO	PT	GS	DW	DV	DA	BR	EN	EW	AQ	A2	B1	B2	B3	C1	C2	C3	D1	D2	D4	E1	E2	E3	E4	E7	F3	F4	F9	FA	G1	G1R	G3	G3R	H2	H3	H5	I1	I2	J1	J2	J3	J4
Cephaloziella dentata	3																								3						3									3						
Cephaloziella divaricata		3					3			2			2			3		3				3		3	3						3			1	1	1		3	3	3				3	3	3
Cephaloziella elachista									2	3												3	3								2														3	3
Cephaloziella hampeana			3	3	3	3	3			3						3		3				3	2				3				3			2				3	3						3	3
Cephaloziella integerrima			1	3		1	1																								3				2				3				1	3	3	3
Cephaloziella massalongi	3	2	3	3				2	2																																			3	3	
Cephaloziella nicholsonii	3	2	3					2	2																																			3	3	
Cephaloziella rubella					3	3	3	3	3	3						3		3				3									3			3					3	3				3		
Cephaloziella spinigera				2	2	2	3	1	3	3												3									2			3											2	3	
Cephaloziella stellulifera			3	3	3	3	3		3				1									3			3						3									3				2	3	
Cephaloziella turneri		3		3	3	3												3												3										3				3	3	
Ceratodon conicus	2	3	3	3	3	3	3	3	3			3			2	2	3	3	2	3	2	3			3			3		3	3	3	3	3	3	3	3		3	3	3	3	3	3	3	3
Ceratodon purpureus	3	3	3	3	3	3	3	3	1			3			2	3	3	3	2	3	3	3			3			3		3	3	3	3	3	3	3	3		3	3	3	3	3	3	3	3
Ceratodon purpureus s.l.			3		3			1	1													3	3		3																						
Cheilothela chloropus																		3																						3	3						
Chenia leptophylla	2	2		3		3										2							3				3				3			3				2		3						
Chiloscyphus pallescens	3	2		3	3	3	3	3								2			2	3		3									3	3		2	3				3	3							
Chiloscyphus polyanthos	3		1	3	1	1	3	3										3	2	3		3	3								3	3		2	2					3							
Chiloscyphus polyanthos s.l.	3	3		3	3	3	3	3								2		3	2	3		3	3							3	3			2					3							
Cinclidium stygium					3																	3	3																		3	3					
Cinclidotus fontinaloides	3						3					2							3		3		3															3							1
Cinclidotus riparius	3	3																	3		3																	3							
Cirriphyllum cirrosum	3	1	2																																			3								
Cirriphyllum piliferum	2		3		3														3			2				2	3		3	3	1	3	3	3				1				2		2		
Cladopodiella fluitans						3				3			3	3					3		3									3	3															
Cladopodiella francisci					3	2	3			1									3		3									3	3		3	3				2		2				2		
Climacium dendroides	3					3	3						1		3	3					3	3	2		3	3					2		3	3		2		2	3						3	
Cololejeunea calcarea	3									3			1																				3	3					3							
Cololejeunea minutissima	2		2	2									3				3	2												3	3	2		3												
Cololejeunea rossettiana	3	2	3			1		1					3				3													3	3		3	3	3			3	3						3	
Colura calyptrifolia	3												2		2		3														3			3			3		3							
Conardia compacta	3				3																								3																	
Conocephalum conicum s.l.	3	3	3	3	3	1	2						1			3	2		3			3									3		2	2										3		
Conocephalum conicum s.str.	3	3	3	3	3								1			3	2		3			3									3			3												
Conocephalum salebrosum	3	3	3										3			3	3		3			3																	3							
Conostomum tetragonum	3			2	3													3									3																			
Coscinodon cribrosus	2	3	3	1											3							3				3											1	3					3			
Cratoneuron filicinum	2	2	3	3	3	3	3						2	3	3	3			3			3					3				3		3	2						2					3	2
Cratoneuron filicinum s.l.	2	2	3	3	3	3	3						2	3	3	3			3			3					3				3		3	2						2					3	2
Cryphaea heteromalla	2	2																										3		3												3				
Cryphaea lamyana	3												3																		3		3													
Cryptothallus mirabilis	3		3	2	3	3	1	2								3															2	3	3	3	3		1							3			
Ctenidium molluscum	3	3	3	3	3	3							2			3	3		3			3	3			3					3		3	3				3	3					3		
Ctenidium molluscum var. condensatum	3		3	3	3												1		3				3																3	3							
Ctenidium molluscum var. molluscum	3	3	3	3	3					2			2			3	3		3			3	3								3		3					3	3					3	3	
Ctenidium molluscum var. robustum	3		3	3	3												3		3																				3								

Taxon name	ML	Ord	Stat	Len	Per	LF1	LF2	Tub	Gem	Bul	Bra	Lvs	Sex	Fr	Sp1	Sp2	E	W	Sc	IR	NI	Cl	Elem	GBno	IRno	Clno	TJan	TJul	Prec	Alt	L	F	R	N	S	HM
Ctenidium procerrimum	M	Hypn	N	140	P	Mr							D	Nil					S				16	3			-1.2	10.6	1526	1068	6	6	7	2	0	0
Cyclodictyon laetevirens	M	Hook	N	80	P	Mr							M	R	12	16	E		S	IR			80	3	19		4.8	14.2	1366	330	2	8	6	3	0	0
Cynodontium bruntonii	M	Dicr	N	30	P	Cu		U					M	F	15	19	E	W	S	IR	NI	Cl	73	228	11	1	2.9	13.9	1381	700	5	5	3	3	0	0
Cynodontium fallax	M	Dicr	N	40	P	Cu							M	A	18	23			(S)				45							500	5	5	3	1	0	0
Cynodontium jenneri	M	Dicr	N	40	P	Cu							M	A	18	24	E	W	S	IR			42	47	1		1.4	12.3	1600	730	5	5	3	1	0	0
Cynodontium polycarpon	M	Dicr	N	40	P	Cu							M	A	20	25	E	W	S				43	5			0.8	12.1	1705	880	5	5	3	1	0	0
Cynodontium strumiferum	M	Dicr	N	40	P	Cu							M	A	18	24	E		S				26	11			-0.4	11.1	1358	700	5	5	3	1	0	0
Cynodontium tenellum	M	Dicr	N	30	P	Cu							M	A	16	20			S				26	14			0.2	11.6	1262	700	5	5	3	1	0	0
Daltonia splachnoides	M	Hook	N	10	P	Mr							M	A	16	16			S	IR	NI		80	7	15		3.5	13.5	1703	460	5	8	5	2	0	0
Dialytrichia mucronata	M	Pott	N	30	P	Tuft	Tf		R				D	O	14	16	E	W			NI		91	189			4.0	16.1	836	125	6	5	5	5	0	0
Dichodontium flavescens	M	Dicr	N	70	P	Tf			O				M	R	10	24	E	W	S	IR	NI		43	22	6		3.1	13.9	1520	490	5	9	3	2	0	0
Dichodontium pellucidum	M	Dicr	N	70	P	Tf			O				M	O	10	22	E	W	S	IR	NI		26	939	132		2.9	13.7	1362	900	6	8	6	2	0	2
Dichodontium pellucidum s.l.	M	Dicr	N	70	P	Tf			O				M	O	10	24	E	W	S	IR	NI		26	1185	166		2.9	13.7	1346	1170	6	8	6	2	0	2
Dicranella cerviculata	M	Dicr	N	20	P	Tf	Ts						D	A	16	22	E	W	S	IR	NI		46	220	17		3.2	14.8	1013	380	7	6	2	2	0	0
Dicranella crispa	M	Dicr	N	10	P	Tf	Ts						MD	A	16	20	E	(W)	S	IR	NI		26	36	5		2.9	13.8	1222	550	6	6	5	4	0	0
Dicranella grevilleana	M	Dicr	N	8	P	Tf	Tuft	U					MD	F	12	22			S	IR			46	9	3		1.3	12.1	1826	750	6	7	5	3	0	1
Dicranella heteromalla	M	Dicr	N	30	P	Tf	Tuft						D	A	12	17	E	W	S	IR	NI	Cl	56	2139	270	3	3.4	14.6	1121	1100	4	5	3	3	0	0
Dicranella palustris	M	Dicr	N	90	P	Tf	Tuft	F					D	R	16	22	E	W	S	IR	NI		43	795	113		2.5	13.1	1521	1100	7	9	4	2	0	0
Dicranella rufescens	M	Dicr	N	8	PA	Tf	Ts	O					D	O	12	16	E	W	S	IR	NI	Cl	56	681	61	1	3.2	14.1	1301	580	7	6	3	2	0	0
Dicranella schreberiana	M	Dicr	N	10	AP	Tf	Ts	F					D	F	12	16	E	W	S	IR	NI	Cl	56	1023	88	1	3.6	15.2	923	490	7	6	6	6	0	0
Dicranella staphylina	M	Dicr	NA	10	A	Tf		F					D	X			E	W	S	IR	NI	Cl	73	1087	68	3	3.7	15.3	898	490	8	5	6	6	0	1
Dicranella subulata	M	Dicr	N	20	P	Tuft	Tf	U					D	A	16	20	E	W	S	IR	NI		26	135	9		2.3	13.0	1634	1000	7	5	3	2	0	0
Dicranella varia	M	Dicr	N	10	PA	Tf		O					D	A	14	18	E	W	S	IR	NI	Cl	56	1448	209	2	3.6	14.9	1011	580	7	5	7	4	0	3
Dicranodontium asperulum	M	Dicr	N	75	P	Tuft							D	X			E	W	S	IR	NI		42	32	4		1.2	11.7	2116	850	5	6	2	2	0	0
Dicranodontium denudatum	M	Dicr	N	50	P	Tuft						F		D	R	10	15	E	W	S	IR	NI		43	272	40		2.4	13.0	1862	950	4	6	3	2	0	0
Dicranodontium uncinatum	M	Dicr	N	110	P	Tuft							D	F	14	18	E		S	IR			42	72	8		2.0	12.1	2210	750	5	6	2	2	0	0
Dicranoweisia cirrata	M	Dicr	N	30	P	Cu	Tf						M	A	12	20	E	W	S	IR	NI	Cl	73	1720	37	1	3.4	15.1	985	700	5	4	4	4	0	3
Dicranoweisia crispula	M	Dicr	N	30	P	Cu	Tf		F				M	A	12	20	E	W	S				26	49	9		0.9	11.6	2049	1335	5	4	3	1	0	0
Dicranum bergeri	M	Dicr	N	100	P	Tuft							D	R	20	24	E		S	IR			26	18	3		2.5	13.8	974	350	8	8	1	1	0	0
Dicranum bonjeanii	M	Dicr	N	108	P	Tuft	Tf				O		D	R	18	20	E	W	S	IR	NI	Cl	56	699	55		3.2	14.2	1208	1000	7	7	3	2	0	0
Dicranum elongatum	M	Dicr	N	60	P	Tuft							D	X	16	23	(E)		S				16	1			-0.8	11.1	1125	1150	8	5	2	3	0	0
Dicranum flagellare	M	Dicr	N	50	P	Tuft	Tf		F				D	R	14	16	E	W					56	35			3.4	16.0	816	380	4	4	3	3	0	0
Dicranum flexicaule	M	Dicr	N	80	P	Tuft	Tf						D	X	15	18	E		S				26	9			0.5	11.4	2187	610	7	4	2	1	0	0
Dicranum fuscescens	M	Dicr	N	75	P	Tuft	Tf						D	O	18	24	E	W	S	IR	NI		26	155	8		2.4	13.2	1648	1000	6	5	2	2	0	0
Dicranum fuscescens s.l.	M	Dicr	N	80	P	Tuft	Tf						D	O	15	24	E	W	S	IR	NI		26	562	53		2.3	13.0	1556	1205	6	5	2	2	0	0
Dicranum leioneuron	M	Dicr	N	65	P	Tuft	Tf				O		D	X	18	25	E	W	S				46	12			2.3	13.5	1468	800	7	8	2	1	0	0
Dicranum majus	M	Dicr	N	108	P	Tuft	Tf						D	O	14	26	E	W	S	IR	NI	Cl	56	1175	121	3	3.1	13.9	1357	1080	4	6	3	3	0	0
Dicranum montanum	M	Dicr	N	30	P	Cu	Tf		O				D	X	14	18	E	W	S	IR			56	210			3.3	15.7	826	300	5	4	3	3	0	0
Dicranum polysetum	M	Dicr	N	133	P	Tuft	Tf						D	X	15	27	E						46	42			3.2	15.3	779	110	5	5	3	2	0	0
Dicranum scoparium	M	Dicr	N	90	P	Tuft	Tf						D	O	12	22	E	W	S	IR	NI	Cl	36	2176	376	2	3.4	14.4	1150	1220	6	5	3	2	0	2
Dicranum scottianum	M	Dicr	N	75	P	Cu							D	O	25	30	E	W	S	IR	NI	Cl	80	195	59	1	3.5	13.5	1672	430	3	5	3	2	0	0
Dicranum spurium	M	Dicr	N	67	P	Tuft							D	R	14	24	E		S				43	45			2.7	14.8	910	490	6	5	3	2	0	0
Dicranum subporodictyon	M	Dicr	N	50	P	Cu							D	Nil					S		NI		70	6			1.6	11.6	2761	250	7	8	2	1	0	0
Dicranum tauricum	M	Dicr	N	40	P	Tuft	Tf						D	R	14	18	E	W	S	IR	NI	Cl	73	347			3.2	15.4	823	450	4	4	3	3	0	0
Didymodon acutus	M	Pott	N	20	P	Tf	Ts						D	R	9	12	E	W	S	IR	(NI)	(Cl)	86	73	4		4.0	15.6	901	600	8	3	8	2	0	1
Didymodon cordatus	M	Pott	N	10	P	Tf			F				D	Nil			E			IR			83	1			5.9	16.0	1092	70	9	2	7	4	0	0

Taxon name	RH	RS	RW	SR	SO	PT	GS	DW	DV	DA	BR	EN	EW	AQ	A2	B1	B2	B3	C1	C2	C3	D1	D2	D4	E1	E2	E3	E4	E7	F3	F4	F9	FA	G1	G1R	G3	G3R	H2	H3	H5	I1	I2	J1	J2	J3	J4
Ctenidium procerrimum	3																																						3							
Cyclodictyon laetevirens	3										2					3																							3							
Cynodontium bruntonii	3		1																															3					3							
Cynodontium fallax	3																																						3							
Cynodontium jenneri	3		1		2																													2					3			1				
Cynodontium polycarpon	3																																					3	3							
Cynodontium strumiferum	3																																					3	3							
Cynodontium tenellum	3		1																																			3	3					1		
Daltonia splachnoides	3				3		3					3																								3										
Dialytrichia mucronata	2	3			3						3								3															1		3							1		1	2
Dichodontium flavescens	3	3			2		3								3	1			3																				3							
Dichodontium pellucidum	3	2	3		2		3								3	1			3					2														2						2		
Dichodontium pellucidum s.l.	3	2	3		2		3								3	1			3					2														2						2		
Dicranella cerviculata				3	3		3								2						3	3		3														3	3	1					2	
Dicranella crispa	2	3			3	2	2								2																								3	3							
Dicranella grevilleana					3																	2														3		3	3							
Dicranella heteromalla	3	3		3	3	3	3	3			3				2	2			3		3			3			3	3		3	3		3		3		3	1	3	3	3		1			
Dicranella palustris	3				3		3												3	3	3																									
Dicranella rufescens	1		2	3	3				2										3															3	2	3				3	3					
Dicranella schreberiana				3	3														3											3				2						3	3					
Dicranella staphylina				3	3		3												2						3													3	3	3			3			
Dicranella subulata	3			3	3		3	3											3								3											3	3	3			3			
Dicranella varia	2			3	3		3	3							3				3						3									2	2			2	3	3	2	2		2		
Dicranodontium asperulum	3				3														2																				3					2		
Dicranodontium denudatum	3			3	3	2							2						2						3								3	3					3	2	2			2		
Dicranodontium uncinatum	3							3								2	2								3				3	3	3		3						3	3	3					
Dicranoweisia cirrata	3		2					3			3				2	2			3		3									3		3	3	3	1	1		3	3	3	3	3	3	3	3	
Dicranoweisia crispula	3							3																										3				3	3	3						
Dicranum bergeri				3							3											3																	1							
Dicranum bonjeanii			2		3	2	2	1							2	2			3				3		3	2				3		3	2	2		2	1	3	3	3	2			2		
Dicranum elongatum					3	3																						3							1				3							
Dicranum flagellare								3			1																							3												
Dicranum flexicaule	3				3																						3	3											3	3						
Dicranum fuscescens	3				3		3				3																3			1	1		3		3			3	3	3			2	2		
Dicranum fuscescens s.l.	3				3		3				3					3	3										3			1	1		3		3			3	3	3			2	2		
Dicranum leioneuron		1	1		1				3		1				3		3										3			1	1								1	1						
Dicranum majus		3	3	2	3		2	1			2				1				3		3									3	3		3	3		3		3	3	3				2		
Dicranum montanum	1				3		1	3			3																						3	3					1			3				
Dicranum polysetum					3	3																								3	3		3	3		3										
Dicranum scoparium	3	3	3	3	3		3	3		3	3			1	3	3			3		3	3		3					3	3	3	3	3	3		3		3	3	3	3			3	3	
Dicranum scottianum	3	2	2		3						1					3																3	3	3		3			3	3						
Dicranum spurium	3			3															3																	2			3							
Dicranum subporodictyon		1																																3		1			1					2		
Dicranum tauricum	1				3	3		3																															2							
Didymodon acutus	2	3	3		3	3	3	3		3				1	3	3			3		3	3			3			3		3	3	3	3	3		3		3	2	3	3	3		1	3	1
Didymodon cordatus		3			3		3									3		3							3																						

47

Taxon name	ML	Ord	Stat	Len	Per	LF1	LF2	Tub	Gem	Bul	Bra	Lvs	Sex	Fr	Sp1	Sp2	E	W	Sc	IR	NI	CI	Elem	GBno	IRno	Clno	TJan	TJul	Prec	Alt	L	F	R	N	S	HM
Didymodon fallax	M	Pott	N	15	P	Tf							D	O	12	16	E	W	S	IR	NI	CI	86	1570	222	2	3.6	14.8	1034	580	7	4	7	3	0	2
Didymodon ferrugineus	M	Pott	N	25	P	Tf							D	X			E	W	S	IR	NI		53	186	55		3.3	14.1	1241	785	7	4	8	3	0	0
Didymodon glaucus	M	Pott	N	3	P	Tf							D	Nil			E		S	IR			73	1			3.3	15.9	767	185	3	5	9	2	0	0
Didymodon icmadophilus	M	Pott	N	20	P	Tf			F				D	X	10	13	E		S	(IR)	NI		26	10			1.0	11.5	1988	610	7	6	7	2	0	0
Didymodon insulanus	M	Pott	N	50	PA	Tf		R					D	R	8	13	E	W	S	IR	NI	CI	85	1753	214	3	3.6	14.8	1028	580	6	5	6	4	0	2
Didymodon luridus	M	Pott	N	30	P	Tf							D	O	12	16	E	W	S	IR	NI	CI	92	809	19	1	3.9	15.7	850	510	4	4	8	4	0	0
Didymodon maximus	M	Pott	N	80	P	Tf							Nil	Nil						IR			70		5		3.3	13.7	1344	490	6	8	9	2	0	0
Didymodon nicholsonii	M	Pott	N	20	P	Tf		X					D	R	8	15	E	W	S	IR	NI		72	294	13		4.2	15.6	993	370	6	5	7	4	0	0
Didymodon rigidulus	M	Pott	N	10	P	Tuft	Tf		F				D	O	10	12	E	W	S	IR	NI	CI	56	1388	148	1	3.5	14.8	1086	841	5	4	8	4	0	1
Didymodon sinuosus	M	Pott	N	20	P	Tf						F	D	Nil			E	W	S	IR	NI		92	717	39	1	3.8	15.8	849	300	4	6	7	5	0	0
Didymodon spadiceus	M	Pott	N	30	P	Tf							D	O	10	16	E	W	S	IR	NI	CI	73	206	18	2	2.5	13.6	1209	580	6	7	7	4	0	0
Didymodon tomaculosus	M	Pott	NA	6	AP	Ts	Tf						D	Nil			E	W	S	IR	NI		72	17	5		4.3	15.5	872	150	8	6	6	5	0	0
Didymodon tophaceus	M	Pott	N	50	P	Tf			O				D	F	12	16	E	W	S	IR	NI	CI	83	1099	86	3	3.8	15.1	970	580	5	8	8	4	0	2
Didymodon umbrosus	M	Pott	AN	10	P	Tf			F				D	X	11	15	E	W	S	IR			81	64	1		4.0	16.2	728	60	3	6	8	5	0	0
Didymodon vinealis	M	Pott	N	20	P	Tuft	Tf						D	R	8	15	E	W	S	IR	NI	CI	83	818	21	2	3.8	15.8	803	320	6	3	8	4	0	0
Diphyscium foliosum	M	Diph	N	5	P	Tf							D	F	8	13	E	W	S	IR	NI		53	464	45		2.7	13.1	1724	1205	5	3	1	1	0	0
Diplophyllum albicans	L	Jung	N	60	P	Ms	We						D	F	11	15	E	W	S	IR	NI	CI	52	1561	281	6	3.3	14.0	1286	1340	5	2	1	1	0	3
Diplophyllum obtusifolium	L	Jung	N	10	P	Ms			F				D	A	8	12	E	W	S	IR	(NI)		56	130	8		3.2	14.2	1399	480	6	2	2	1	0	0
Diplophyllum taxifolium	L	Jung	N	25	P	Ms			F				D	X	13	15	(E)	W	S	IR	NI		26	31			-0.5	10.7	2006	1130	6	2	1	1	0	0
Discelium nudum	M	Funa	N	2	A	Tp							M	A	20	24	E	W	S	IR	NI		46	89	2		2.4	14.1	1208	520	7	6	3	3	0	0
Distichium capillaceum	M	Dicr	N	63	P	Tuft							M	F	17	22	E	W	S	IR	NI		26	261	22	2	2.1	12.7	1673	1205	6	7	7	2	0	0
Distichium inclinatum	M	Dicr	N	30	P	Tuft	Tf						M	F	30	40	E	W	S	IR	NI		26	79	13		3.4	13.4	1362	950	8	6	7	2	0	1
Ditrichum cornubicum	M	Dicr	NA	5	PA	Tuft	Ts		F				D	Nil			E						71	3			5.4	15.3	1353	260	7	5	4	2	0	5
Ditrichum cylindricum	M	Dicr	N	5	PA	Tuft	Ts		F			F	D	R	12	16	(E)	W	S	IR	NI	CI	56	1048	82	2	3.4	14.7	1065	700	7	5	5	4	0	0
Ditrichum flexicaule	M	Dicr	N	50	P	Tuft							D	X	7	12	E	W	S	IR	(NI)		66	42	1		3.2	14.6	1004	1214	7	3	7	2	0	0
Ditrichum flexicaule s.l.	M	Dicr	N	110	P	Tf	Tuft						D	R	7	12	E	W	S	IR	NI	CI	66	641	99	2	3.2	14.1	1231	1214	7	5	7	2	0	0
Ditrichum gracile	M	Dicr	N	110	P	Tf	Tuft						D	R			E	W	S	IR	NI	CI	56	143	12		3.4	14.5	1221	638	7	5	5	2	0	0
Ditrichum heteromallum	M	Dicr	N	10	P	Tf		R					D	A	12	18	E	W	S	IR	NI		53	686	96	2	2.9	13.7	1447	820	5	6	3	2	0	0
Ditrichum lineare	M	Dicr	N	15	PA	Tuft	Ts		U				D	R	12	16	E	W	S	IR	NI		43	47	2		1.9	12.6	1954	1040	6	3	2	2	0	2
Ditrichum plumbicola	M	Dicr	NA	15	PA	Tuft	Tf		U				Nil	Nil			E	W	S	IR	NI		71	17			2.9	13.5	1645	460	7	6	5	2	0	5
Ditrichum pusillum	M	Dicr	N	10	PA	Ts	Tf		F				D	F	12	15	E	W	S	IR	(NI)		56	28			3.1	13.7	1470	900	7	5	4	3	0	0
Distichium subulatum	M	Dicr	N	6.5	P	Tf			U				M	A	14	18	E	W		IR	NI		91	12			6.1	15.8	1127	40	6	5	5	3	0	0
Ditrichum zonatum	M	Dicr	N	50	P	Cu			U				D	X			E	W	S	IR	NI		13	86	4		1.3	11.9	2161	880	5	4	2	1	0	0
Douinia ovata	L	Jung	N	15	P	Ms							D	F	23	34	E	W	S	IR	NI		71	183	17		2.1	12.5	2011	915	5	6	3	2	0	0
Drepanocladus aduncus	M	Hypn	N	127	P	We	Ac						D	R	16	16	E	W	S	IR	NI	CI	56	689	35	4	3.7	15.2	916	430	7	10	7	6	2	0
Drepanocladus cossonii	M	Hypn	N	80	P	We	Mr						D	R	14	20	E	W	S	IR	NI		26	110	4		3.3	14.0	1323	620	8	8	7	2	1	0
Drepanocladus lycopodioides	M	Hypn	N	143	P	Mr							D	R	12	18	E	W	S	IR	NI		73	27	13		4.1	14.6	1003	520	8	9	7	3	3	0
Drepanocladus polygamus	M	Hypn	N	80	P	Mr	We						M	O	20	24	E	W	S	IR	NI		56	148	22		4.0	14.8	1032	850	9	8	7	3	0	0
Drepanocladus revolvens	M	Hypn	N	100	P	We							M	R	12	16	E	W	S	IR	NI		26	157	14		2.7	13.3	1598	550	8	9	6	2	0	0
Drepanocladus revolvens s.l.	M	Hypn	N	100	P	We	Mr						MD	R	12	20	E	W	S	IR	NI		26	833	154		2.9	13.3	1445	975	8	9	6	2	0	0
Drepanocladus sendtneri	M	Hypn	N	130	P	We	Mr						D	R	16	16	E	W	S	IR	NI		26	40	13		4.5	15.0	1029	30	8	9	8	2	1	0
Drepanolejeunea hamatifolia	L	Pore	N	10	P	Ms	Sc					F	MD	F			E	W	S	IR	NI		80	145	69		3.4	13.2	1906	610	3	7	4	2	0	0
Dumortiera hirsuta	L	Marc	N	120	P	Mt			O				MD	O	34	34	E		S	IR	NI		81	11	26		4.5	14.4	1299	400	2	8	6	5	0	0
Encalypta alpina	M	Enca	N	40	P	Tuft	Tf						M	A	28	40	E	(W)	S	IR	NI		16	18	1		0.2	11.4	2051	1205	5	5	7	3	0	0
Encalypta brevicollis	M	Enca	N	20	P	Tuft							M	A	30	36	E		(S)		NI		26							170	4	5	7	3	0	0
Encalypta ciliata	M	Enca	N	50	P	Tuft	Tf						M	A	30	38	E	W	S	IR	NI		46	91	2		1.4	12.3	1880	1100	4	5	7	3	0	0

Taxon name	RH	RS	RW	SR	SO	PT	GS	DW	DV	DA	BR	EN	EW	AQ	A2	B1	B2	B3	C1	C2	C3	D1	D2	D4	E1	E2	E3	E4	E7	F3	F4	F9	FA	G1	G1R	G3	G3R	H2	H3	H5	I1	I2	J1	J2	J3	J4
Didymodon fallax		1	3	3	3	3	3								2	2		3																2					3	3	3		3	3	3	1
Didymodon ferrugineus		1	3	3	3	3	3								3	3																	2	2					3	3		3	2	3	
Didymodon glaucus	3			3	3																																		3						1	
Didymodon icmadophilus	3	3			2																			1														3	3							
Didymodon insulanus	3	3	3	3		3	3	1				3				3					3								3	3			3	1	3				3	3	2	3	3	3	3	3
Didymodon luridus	3	3	3	3	3							2									3						3		2	3			2	2					3	3				2	2	3
Didymodon maximus																											3											3								
Didymodon nicholsonii	3		3				3	2				3							3																			3		3			3		3	3
Didymodon rigidulus	3		3				3	1				3																													3	3	3		3	1
Didymodon sinuosus	3		3				3					3				3			3										3				3	2					3			3	3	3		
Didymodon spadiceus	3						3					3							3																												
Didymodon tomaculosus			3	3											1	3		3					3		1														3	3	3		3			
Didymodon tophaceus			3	3	3		3												3																3				3	2			3	3	3	
Didymodon umbrosus				3	2		3																						1						1											
Didymodon vinealis	3	3		3	3	3	3					1				3		3	3					3					3				3	2					3	3		3	3	3	2	2
Diphyscium foliosum	3		3	3	3																										2		2	3				3	3	3			1		1	
Diplophyllum albicans	3		3	3	3	3	3	2	2			2						3		3	3						3				3		3	3	3			3	3	3	3		3	3		3
Diplophyllum obtusifolium			3	3	3		3	1										3																1		3			3	3					3	
Diplophyllum taxifolium	3		3	3	3		3					1				3													3					1				3	3							
Discelium nudum				3	3														3																					2						2
Distichium capillaceum	3	3	2	2	2		2								1							3	3		3						2		2	3		3			3	3			2			
Distichium inclinatum	3			3	3		3									3									3						3		3	3					3	3				3	3	
Ditrichum cornubicum				3														3			2				2															3					3	
Ditrichum cylindricum				3	3		3									3					3			3	3								1	1	1				3	3	3	3			3	
Ditrichum flexicaule			3	3	3		3									3		3						3	3														3	3						
Ditrichum flexicaule s.l.	3		3	3	2		2									3		3						3	3														3							
Ditrichum gracile	3		3	3	3		3									3		3						3									3	2	3		3				2			2		3
Ditrichum heteromallum			3	3	3		3					3						3			3										3		2	3	3		3		3	3	3			3		3
Ditrichum lineare			3	1	3																				3														3		1		1	1	2	
Ditrichum plumbicola			3	3	3											3					3		3	3	3														3		3				3	
Ditrichum pusillum			3	3			3														3		3		3								1	1					3	3						
Ditrichum subulatum			3	3																	3		3																3							
Ditrichum zonatum	3		3	3			3					3							3		2			1	3									1					3	3			2			
Douinia ovata	3	2	3	2			1	3	1	1		3									3																		3	3					2	3
Drepanocladus aduncus		2		3	3		3						3		3	3							3				3				3		3			3		3	3	2						
Drepanocladus cossonii				3	3		2									2		3			3		2																3							
Drepanocladus lycopodioides				3	3		3									3					3		3								1								3							
Drepanocladus polygamus			1		3	3	3									3		3			3		3			3							3						3				1	1		2
Drepanocladus revolvens				3	3	3	3									3					3		3																3							
Drepanocladus revolvens s.l.				3	3		3								1	1					3		1																3							
Drepanocladus sendtneri	3			3			3									3		3			3													3					3	3						3
Drepanolejeunea hamatifolia	3	3									3		3																										3	3						
Dumortiera hirsuta	3	3			3							3																											3							
Encalypta alpina	3																																						3							
Encalypta brevicollis	3	3																																					3							
Encalypta ciliata	3	3																																					3							2

49

Taxon name	ML	Ord	Stat	Len	Per	LF1	LF2	Tub	Gem	Bul	Bra	Lvs	Sex	Fr	Sp1	Sp2	E	W	Sc	IR	NI	CI	Elem	GBno	IRno	Clno	TJan	TJul	Prec	Alt	L	F	R	N	S	HM
Encalypta rhaptocarpa	M	Enca	N	20	P	Tuft							M	A	34	50	E	(W)	S	IR	NI		26	45	2		1.6	12.2	1582	1190	7	4	7	3	0	0
Encalypta streptocarpa	M	Enca	N	60	P	Tuft	Tf		F				D	R	10	14	E	W	S	IR	NI		55	998	176		3.2	14.4	1195	760	6	4	8	2	0	1
Encalypta vulgaris	M	Enca	N	20	P	Tuft	Tf						M	A	30	45	E	W	S	IR	NI		76	310	21		3.2	14.9	921	730	7	4	8	3	0	0
Entodon concinnus	M	Hypn	N	100	P	We							D	X	11	14	E	W	S	IR	NI		46	226	40		3.4	14.5	1120	1175	8	4	8	2	0	0
Entosthodon attenuatus	M	Funa	N	5	AP	Ts	Tf						M	A	24	30	E	W	S	IR	NI	CI	91	276	78	2	3.7	13.4	1613	700	7	7	5	3	0	0
Entosthodon fascicularis	M	Funa	N	10	A	Tf							M	A	24	28	E	W	S	IR	(NI)	CI	73	191	9	3	4.5	15.8	910	245	8	6	5	4	0	0
Entosthodon obtusus	M	Funa	N	5	AP	Ts	Tf						M	A	30	38	E	W	S	IR	NI	CI	92	480	99	7	3.4	13.5	1478	787	7	7	5	3	0	0
Ephemerum cohaerens	M	Pott	N	1.5	A	Tp							M	A	60	70	E			IR			73	5	6		3.9	15.3	883	60	7	7	5	5	0	0
Ephemerum hibernicum	M	Pott	N	2.2	A	Tp							M	A	61	69		W		IR			70	2	1		4.1	15.3	1170	140	7	4	6	6	0	0
Ephemerum recurvifolium	M	Pott	N	1.5	A	Tp	Tf						M	A	40	55	E	W					83	107			3.6	16.1	705	270	7	4	8	4	0	0
Ephemerum serratum	M	Pott	N	2.2	A	Tp	Tf						M	A	40	70	E	W	S	IR	NI		73	601	66		3.8	15.2	955	400	6	6	5	4	0	1
Ephemerum serratum var. minutissimum	M	Pott	N	1.8	A	Tp	Tf						M	A	50	65	E	W	S	IR	NI		73	453	46		3.9	15.4	913	300	6	5	5	4	0	1
Ephemerum serratum var. serratum	M	Pott	N	2.2	A	Tp	Tf						M	A	65	90	E	W	S	IR	NI		73	131	15		3.7	14.7	1154	400	7	8	5	5	0	0
Ephemerum sessile	M	Pott	N	2	A	Tp							M	A	60	80	E	W		IR	NI		83	35	8		4.3	15.3	1094	360	7	7	4	4	0	0
Ephemerum spinulosum	M	Pott	N	2.2	A	Tp							M	A	70	110	E	W		IR	NI		71		2		3.9	14.0	1165	200	7	7	6	6	0	0
Ephemerum stellatum	M	Pott	N	1.5	A	Tp							M	A	40	50	E			IR			73	3	2		5.0	16.0	1005	5	7	6	5	4	0	0
Epipterygium tozeri	L	Brya	N	5	P	Ts	Tf	O	F				D	R	14	20	E	W	S	IR	NI	CI	91	249	11	5	4.9	15.5	1091	150	5	6	5	2	0	0
Eremonotus myriocarpus	L	Jung	N	8	P	Ms	Sc						D	R	12	17	E	W	S	IR	NI		13	77	9		1.9	12.2	2176	1220	2	7	9	3	0	0
Eucladium verticillatum	M	Pott	N	30	P	Tuft	Tf						D	X	12	14	E	W	S	IR	NI		83	600	73		3.5	14.6	1115	700	7	6	7	3	0	0
Eurhynchium crassinervium	M	Hypn	N	50	P	Mr							D	O	16	22	E	W	S	IR	NI	CI	73	716	72	1	3.7	15.2	1000	380	4	6	7	5	0	0
Eurhynchium hians	M	Hypn	N	110	P	Mr	We						D	R	12	16	E	W	S	IR	NI	CI	76	1774	192	6	3.6	15.0	991	950	6	6	6	2	0	0
Eurhynchium meridionale	M	Hypn	NA	30	P	Mr							D	X	14	18	E		S	IR	NI		91	3			5.1	16.2	822	160	7	4	9	2	0	0
Eurhynchium praelongum	M	Hypn	N	120	P	Mr	We						D	F	11	13	E	W	S	IR	NI	CI	73	2384	371	7	3.5	14.6	1076	1050	5	6	5	5	1	1
Eurhynchium pulchellum	M	Hypn	N	30	P	Mr							D	X	10	14	E		S	IR	NI		26	5	1		1.8	12.8	1571	800	6	4	7	2	0	0
Eurhynchium pumilum	M	Hypn	N	40	P	Mr							D	F	12	15	E	W	S	IR	NI	CI	92	929	41	6	3.9	15.5	945	580	3	5	7	6	0	0
Eurhynchium schleicheri	M	Hypn	N	60	P	Mr	We						D	R	10	14	E	W	S	IR			92	155	1		3.8	16.0	855	270	5	5	6	4	0	0
Eurhynchium speciosum	M	Hypn	N	130	P	Mr							M	F	16	20	E	W	S	IR	NI		73	253	11	2	4.1	15.8	850	200	5	8	7	7	0	0
Eurhynchium striatulum	M	Hypn	N	50	P	Mr	De						D	R	14	20	E	W	S	IR	NI		92	54	14		4.3	15.4	1080	365	5	4	9	7	0	0
Eurhynchium striatum	M	Hypn	N	150	P	We					R		D	O	12	16	E	W	S	IR	NI	(CI)	73	1667	288	7	3.6	14.7	1100	777	4	6	6	4	0	0
Fissidens adianthoides	M	Hypn	N	78	P	Tuft	Tf						MD	F	18	24	E	W	S	IR	NI	CI	56	1320	229	1	3.3	14.1	1267	950	7	7	6	2	0	0
Fissidens bryoides	M	Dicr	N	20	P	Tf			X				M	A	10	14	E	W	S	IR	NI	CI	76	1748	163	7	3.6	14.9	1057	580	4	5	5	5	0	0
Fissidens celticus	M	Dicr	N	4.6	AP	Ts	Tf						D	Nil			E	W	S	IR	(NI)	(CI)	71	240	17		4.0	14.6	1469	335	3	6	3	3	0	0
Fissidens crassipes	M	Dicr	N	20	P	Ts	Ts						D	F	18	28	E	W	S	IR	NI		83	478	30		3.6	15.7	921	425	5	9	7	7	0	0
Fissidens curnovii	M	Dicr	N	20	P	Tf					R		M	A	9	14	E	W	S	IR	NI	(CI)	81	223	12	1	4.2	15.4	1490	250	5	4	7	7	0	0
Fissidens curvatus	M	Dicr	N	3	P	We							D	O	13	18	E	W		IR	NI	(CI)	92	579	15		5.5	15.5	1140	290	3	5	7	4	0	0
Fissidens dubius	M	Dicr	N	35	P	Tf	Tf		X				MD	F	18	24	E	W	S	IR	NI	CI	73	1046	195	2	3.4	14.3	1268	760	7	4	7	2	0	0
Fissidens exilis	M	Dicr	N	3	AP	Ts							MD	A	10	12	E	W	S	IR	(NI)	(CI)	73	388	6		3.8	15.7	857	290	4	5	5	3	0	0
Fissidens gracilifolius	M	Dicr	N	2.5	P	Tf	Tf						M	A	9	14	E	W	S	IR	NI		83	223	12		3.5	15.7	844	460	1	5	7	4	0	0
Fissidens incurvus	M	Dicr	N	5	P	Tf	Ts						MD	A	12	16	E	W	S	IR	NI		92	579	15		4.0	15.9	814	490	4	5	7	4	0	0
Fissidens limbatus	M	Dicr	N	7	P	Ts	Tf						MD	A	8	18	E	W		IR			91	62	6		4.9	15.3	1143	175	3	5	5	5	0	0
Fissidens mongillonii	M	Dicr	N	25	P	Tf							MD	O	14	18	E	W	S	IR	NI		81	16	3		4.6	15.1	1297	45	6	9	7	6	0	0
Fissidens osmundoides	M	Dicr	N	58	P	Tf	Tf	U					D	O	18	24	E	W	S	IR	NI		26	559	86		2.7	13.0	1650	920	7	7	5	2	0	0
Fissidens polyphyllus	M	Dicr	N	150	P	Tf	Tf	U					MD	X			E	W	S	IR	NI		80	22	5		4.6	14.6	1534	155	2	8	3	2	0	1
Fissidens pusillus	M	Dicr	N	6	P	Ts	Tf						M	A	10	19	E	W	S	IR	NI		83	282	29		3.6	14.9	1102	920	4	6	6	4	0	0
Fissidens pusillus s.l.	M	Dicr	N	6	P	Ts	Tf						M	A	9	19	E	W	S	IR	NI		83	451	37		3.6	15.2	1019	920	3	6	6	4	0	0
Fissidens rivularis	M	Dicr	N	20	P	Tf							M	O	17	20	E	W	S	IR		(CI)	91	53	2		4.2	15.3	1170	230	2	9	5	4	0	0

Taxon name	RH	RS	RW	SR	SO	PT	GS	DW	DV	DA	BR	EN	EW	AQ	A2	B1	B2	B3	C1	C2	C3	D1	D2	D4	E1	E2	E3	E4	E7	F3	F4	F9	FA	G1	G1R	G3	G3R	H2	H3	H5	I1	I2	J1	J2	J3	J4
Encalypta rhaptocarpa	3	3	3	3			3								3	3		3			3				3								3	3					3					3	3	
Encalypta streptocarpa	3	3	3	3	3	3	3								3	3		3			3				3	3							3	3					3		3		3	3	3	1
Encalypta vulgaris	3	3	3	3											3	3		3							3								2	2					3		3		1	3		
Entodon concinnus					3	3	3								3			3			3				3		3											3	3	3				3		
Entosthodon attenuatus			3		3	3	3											3			3						3			3		3			2				3	3						
Entosthodon fascicularis																										3								1					3	3	3					
Entosthodon obtusus				3	3		3											3			3	3	3			3				3				1					2	3			1			
Ephemerum cohaerens																					3																									
Ephemerum hibernicum																					3																									
Ephemerum recurvifolium																									3								1	1	2					3						
Ephemerum serratum				3	3	3												3			3					3							3	1	3					3	3	3		1			
Ephemerum serratum var. minutissimum					3																1					3								1	3					3	3	2		2			
Ephemerum serratum var. serratum					3													3			3																			3	1	1					
Ephemerum sessile					3													1			3									1					2					3	1	1					
Ephemerum spinulosum					3																3																										
Ephemerum stellatum					3																														2					1						
Epipterygium tozeri	2	3		3	3	2												3			3				2	2			2		3		3	3	2				3		2	2	2			
Eremonotus myriocarpus	3	3		3	3					3																									3			3								
Eucladium verticillatum	3	3		3	3								3					3			3												2	2			3		3	1		3		3			
Eurhynchium crassinervium	3	3		3	2		3	1				3						3			3											3	3	3		3			3	1	3		3			
Eurhynchium hians	2	2		3	3		1	1				2						3			3				3	3	3		3	3	3	3	3	3				2	3	3	3	3	2	3		
Eurhynchium meridionale	3	1		3														3			3				3	3	3						1						3							
Eurhynchium praelongum	3	3		3	3		3	3	1			3		3	3		3		3	3		3		3	3	3	3		3	3	3	3	3		3		3	3	3	3	2	3	3		
Eurhynchium pulchellum	3			3	3					1		3		3		3		3			3												3						3	3						
Eurhynchium pumilum	2	2		3	3		3					3						2			3				1				2				3	3				2	2		2		2		3	
Eurhynchium schleicheri	3			3	3							3									3					3			3		3	3	3	3					3							
Eurhynchium speciosum	3	3					1		2			3			1			2			3		2		3								3	3	3								3			
Eurhynchium striatulum	3	3										3													3					3	2		3	3	3				3				3	2		
Eurhynchium striatum	3	3		3	3		3	1				2		2				3			3				3			3	3		2	3	3		3			3	3				2	3	2	
Fissidens adianthoides	3	2		3	3	3	3	1				1		3				3			1			3	3		3			2	3	3	3	2				3	3		3		2	3		
Fissidens bryoides	1	1		3	3			1										3			3				3				3	3	3	3	3	3	2				3	3	2	3				
Fissidens celticus				3														3			3									3				3	1					3				1			
Fissidens crassipes	3			3	2			1				2								3	3																										
Fissidens curnovii	3	2		3	3							2						3			3				3								3		1					1							
Fissidens curvatus				3	3							2									3												3							3							
Fissidens dubius	3	3		3	3	3						2			3			3			3		2	2	3								2	3					3	3		3		3	3		
Fissidens exilis	3	3																			3												3	3						3	3	3					
Fissidens gracilifolius	3	2																3			3				3								3	3						3	3			2	3		
Fissidens incurvus				3	3													3			1												3	3										1			
Fissidens limbatus	2	2		3	3	3						1		3				3			1				3					2	3		3	3					3	3				3		
Fissidens monguillonii	3			3	3				3									3	3		3						3		3						2		1			3					3		
Fissidens osmundoides	3			3	3													3			3		3	3				3						3						3							
Fissidens polyphyllus	3			3	3													2			3																			3					3		
Fissidens pusillus	3	3	2															3			3													3						3				3	3		
Fissidens pusillus s.l.	3	3	2															3			3													3						3					3	3	
Fissidens rivularis	3	1	1															3	3		3																			3						3	

51

Taxon name	ML	Ord	Stat	Len	Per	LF1	LF2	Tub	Gem	Bul	Bra	Lvs	Sex	Fr	Sp1	Sp2	E	W	Sc	IR	NI	CI	Elem	GBno	IRno	Clno	TJan	TJul	Prec	Alt	L	F	R	N	S	HM
Fissidens rufulus	M	Dicr	N	20	P	Tf							D	O	18	22	E	W	S	IR	NI		73	78	9		2.8	14.2	1225	365	5	9	7	4	0	0
Fissidens serrulatus	M	Dicr	N	75	P	Tf							D	X			E	W		IR			91	5	2		4.7	14.8	1480	130	1	8	4	3	0	0
Fissidens taxifolius	M	Dicr	N	20	P	Tf		U					M	O	7	18	E	W	S	IR	NI	CI	83	1995	285	3	3.5	14.8	1075	580	4	5	7	5	0	0
Fissidens taxifolius var. pallidicaulis	M	Dicr	N	30	P	Tf		O					M	F	7	11	E	W	S	IR	NI		81	45	9		3.2	13.4	1760	200	3	8	7	5	0	0
Fissidens taxifolius var. taxifolius	M	Dicr	N	20	PA	Tf							M	O	12	18	E	W	S	IR	NI		83	463	4		3.8	15.4	946	490	4	5	7	5	0	0
Fissidens viridulus	M	Dicr	N	6	P	Tf							MD	A	8	15	E	W	S	IR	NI	CI	66	487	23		4.0	15.6	945	700	3	5	7	6	0	0
Fissidens viridulus s.l.	M	Dicr	N	6	P	Tf							MD	A	8	19	E	W	S	IR	NI	CI	66	1114	98	7	3.7	15.2	1004	920	3	5	7	5	0	0
Fontinalis antipyretica	M	Hypn	N	500	P	At							D	R	10	20	E	W	S	IR	NI	CI	56	1602	287	7	3.3	14.3	1158	880	6	12	6	5	0	0
Fontinalis antipyretica var. antipyretica	M	Hypn	N	500	P	At							D	R	10	20	E	W	S	IR	NI	CI	56	959	136		3.3	14.4	1183	820	6	12	6	5	0	0
Fontinalis antipyretica var. gracilis	M	Hypn	N	400	P	At							D	R			E	W	S	IR	NI		54	88	6		2.4	13.1	1424	760	7	12	6	4	0	0
Fontinalis squamosa	M	Hypn	N	400	P	At							D	R	18	28	E	W	S	IR	NI		72	392	52		3.0	13.7	1409	830	7	12	4	3	0	0
Fontinalis squamosa var. curnowii	M	Hypn	N	400	A	Sc							D	R	18	22	E						71	6			5.7	15.3	1297	180	7	12	4	3	0	0
Fontinalis squamosa var. dixonii	M	Hypn	N	400	P	At							D	Nil			E	W	(S)		NI		71	8			2.2	13.0	2075	490	7	12	4	3	0	0
Fontinalis squamosa var. squamosa	M	Hypn	N	400	P	At							D	R	20	28	E	W	S	IR	NI		72	50	4		4.6	14.9	1262	95	7	12	4	3	0	0
Fossombronia angulosa	L	Foss	N	25	P	Ms							D	F	34	52	E	W	S	IR		CI	91	23	18	6	5.5	15.0	1243	120	6	7	5	4	2	1
Fossombronia caespitiformis	L	Foss	N	10	AP	Sc							M	A	38	56	E	W					91	30		1	4.9	16.0	919	135	7	6	5	4	0	0
Fossombronia crozalsii	L	Foss	N	8	A	Sc							M	F	34	41	E						91	1		3	3.3	15.9	793	150	6	7	5	4	0	0
Fossombronia fimbriata	L	Foss	N	3.5	AP	Sc						F	D	R	24	28	E	W	S	IR			71	16	3		2.1	12.7	1809	360	7	8	5	3	0	0
Fossombronia foveolata	L	Foss	N	15	AP	Sc	Ms						M	A	35	50	E	W	S	IR	NI		53	70	19	3	3.8	14.1	1314	345	7	9	5	3	0	0
Fossombronia husnotii	L	Foss	N	10	PA	Sc	Ms						M	A	42	56	E	W	S	IR		CI	91	34	11	3	5.7	15.5	1120	245	8	4	4	3	0	0
Fossombronia incurva	L	Foss	N	5	P	Sc							D	A	22	32	E	W	S	IR	NI	CI	72	82	25	1	3.5	14.0	1374	500	7	8	5	3	0	0
Fossombronia maritima	L	Foss	N	5	PA	Sc	Ms						M	A	45	64	E	W	S	IR		CI	81	16	3	3	6.2	15.7	1057	90	8	6	4	3	1	0
Fossombronia pusilla	L	Foss	N	15	AP	Sc	Ms						M	A	38	56	E	W	S	IR	NI	(CI)	92	275	20		4.1	15.3	993	460	6	7	5	4	0	0
Fossombronia pusilla s.l.	L	Foss	N	15	AP	Sc	Ms						M	A	38	64	E	W	S	IR	NI	CI	92	629	66	3	3.9	15.2	1020	460	6	7	5	4	0	0
Fossombronia wondraczekii	L	Foss	N	10	AP	Sc							M	A	34	50	E	W	S	IR	NI	CI	73	391	43	3	3.7	14.9	1121	490	7	7	4	3	0	0
Frullania dilatata	L	Pore	N	35	P	Ms	We						D	F	40	60	E	W	S	IR	NI	CI	85	1538	349	9	3.6	14.6	1144	610	6	4	6	4	1	0
Frullania fragilifolia	L	Pore	N	20	P	Ms						F	D	R	35	50	E	W	S	IR	NI	CI	72	411	46	4	3.2	13.4	1649	850	5	5	4	2	0	0
Frullania microphylla	L	Pore	N	30	P	Ms						F	D	F			E	W	S	IR			80	163	35		4.2	13.8	1581	610	5	5	4	2	1	0
Frullania microphylla var. deciduifolia	L	Pore	N	30	P	Ms						R	D	Nil				W					80	2			2.5	13.9	1960	610	5	6	4	2	0	0
Frullania microphylla var. microphylla	L	Pore	N	30	P	Ms						F	D	F			E	W	S	IR		CI	80	47	2		5.4	14.9	1293	610	5	5	4	2	1	0
Frullania tamarisci	L	Pore	N	80	P	Ms	We						D	F	40	56	E	W	S	IR	NI	CI	52	1258	273	7	3.4	13.9	1339	1000	6	5	4	2	1	0
Frullania teneriffae	L	Pore	N	60	P	Ms	Fa						D	F			E	W	S	IR	NI	CI	80	299	131	2	3.8	13.4	1646	700	5	5	4	2	2	0
Funaria hygrometrica	M	Funa	N	30	AP	Tuft	Tf						M	A	16	22	E	W	S	IR	NI	CI	66	1943	216	10	3.5	14.9	1034	715	7	5	6	7	0	1
Funaria muhlenbergii	M	Funa	N	5	P	Tf							M	A	18	28	E	W	(S)	(IR)			92	32			3.1	14.8	1144	390	7	3	9	3	0	0
Funaria pulchella	M	Funa	N	5	P	Tf							M	A	20	28	E	W	S				92	14			4.9	15.6	950	160	7	3	9	3	0	0
Geocalyx graveolens	L	Jung	N	40	P	Sc	Tf						M	F	8	14	E	W		S	NI		43	9	6		3.9	13.2	1723	300	4	6	2	2	0	0
Glyphomitrium daviesii	L	Dicr	N	10	P	Cu	Tuft						D	O	10	16	E	W	S	IR	NI		81	82	15		3.5	12.9	1895	490	7	4	4	2	0	5
Gongylanthus ericetorum	L	Jung	N	10	AP	Sc	Ms						M	X			E					CI	91	5		4	6.9	16.3	878	60	8	4	3	2	0	0
Grimmia alpestris	M	Grim	N	20	P	Cu	Tf						D	X	9	12		W			NI		16	1			2.8	13.6	2097	850	8	1	5	1	0	0
Grimmia anodon	M	Grim	N	15	P	Cu							M	A	8	10	E	(S)					66	2			3.1	14.5	1136	250	9	1	7	1	0	0
Grimmia arenaria	M	Grim	N	10	P	Cu	Tf						M	A	10	16	E	W		S	NI	CI	72	8		7	2.8	13.4	2253	200	6	2	7	2	0	0
Grimmia atrata	M	Grim	N	40	P	Cu	Tuft						D	O	10	16	E	W	S	IR	NI		42	22	1	2	1.4	12.2	1966	950	5	3	2	2	0	5
Grimmia crinita	M	Grim	N	10	AP	Sc	Cu						M	A	10	12	E						92	1			5.7	15.4	1216	150	9	1	8	0	0	0
Grimmia curvata	M	Grim	N	100	P	Tf							D	R	12	16	E	W	S	IR	NI		43	173	19		1.8	12.3	1928	1020	6	5	3	2	0	0
Grimmia decipiens	M	Grim	N	25	P	Cu							M	A	12	14	E	W	S	IR	NI	CI	92	47	6	1	3.5	13.8	1449	550	8	1	4	1	0	0
Grimmia dissimulata	M	Grim	N	20	P	Cu	Tf						D	X	10	15	E		S	IR			83	22	2		3.3	15.8	784	95	7	2	3	0	0	0

Taxon name	RH	RS	RW	SR	SO	PT	GS	DW	DV	DA	BR	EN	EW	AQ	A2	B1	B2	B3	C1	C2	C3	D1	D2	D4	E1	E2	E3	E4	E7	F3	F4	F9	FA	G1	G1R	G3	G3R	H2	H3	H5	I1	I2	J1	J2	J3	J4
Fissidens rufulus	3																																													
Fissidens serrulatus	3	3																3		3	3																		3	3	3	3				
Fissidens taxifolius	3		1	2	3		3						1					3			2			3	3		1		3	3			3	3		1			3	3	3	3	2			
Fissidens taxifolius var. pallidicaulis	3				3																3																	3									
Fissidens taxifolius var. taxifolius	3		1	2	3								1					3						3	3		1		3	3			3	3		1			3	3	3	2	2	1	1	
Fissidens viridulus		2	1	3	3													3				2			2				3	3			3	3					1	3	2	2	2	2	1	
Fissidens viridulus s.l.	3	3	2	3														3	3		3	2			2				3	3			3						3	3	2	2	2	3		
Fontinalis antipyretica	3	3					2	2					3						3	3																											
Fontinalis antipyretica var. antipyretica	3	3					2	2					3	1					3	3																											
Fontinalis antipyretica var. gracilis	3	1																	1	3																											
Fontinalis squamosa	3	2			2		2						3						2	3													3						3								
Fontinalis squamosa var. curnowii	3	3																		3																											
Fontinalis squamosa var. dixonii	3																			3																											
Fontinalis squamosa var. squamosa	3												3						3														3														
Fossombronia angulosa		3	3		2	3			1									3		3	3												3		2					3	3	3				
Fossombronia caespitiformis					3													1								3									2					1	3	3				
Fossombronia crozalsii					3															3																3							3				
Fossombronia fimbriata		2	3	3			3													3														2						3	3	3		1		
Fossombronia foveolata		2	3	3			3													3			2			2					2			2	2				3	3	3		1		
Fossombronia husnotii	3	3	3	3			3						3					3					2								3			2	2				3	3	3		2		
Fossombronia incurva					3		3								3			3			3									1	3									3	3	3		3		
Fossombronia maritima					3		2								2			3			3									3				3						3	1	3		3		
Fossombronia pusilla	2	2			3													1			2						3			1				1	3		3			3	3	3	1			
Fossombronia pusilla s.l.	2	2			2		2								2			2			2						3					2		1	3		3			3	3	3	1			
Fossombronia wondraczekii					3		3											3			3						3			3	3			3	3		3			3	3	3				
Frullania dilatata	3	1					2					3	3	1				2												3	3	3	3	3	3		1			3	3		3	2		
Frullania fragilifolia	3											3	3					3														3		3	3					3							
Frullania microphylla	3	1										1						3																2	2		1			3			1	1			
Frullania microphylla var. deciduifolia	3																																						3							
Frullania microphylla var. microphylla	3	1										1						3																2			1			3			1				
Frullania tamarisci	3	3	3		3		3					3	3			3	3	3						3	3	3	3	3	3	3	3			3	3				3	3	3	3	3	3	3	3
Frullania teneriffae	3	2										3			1		3							2		2				3	3	3		3			2		3	3						
Funaria hygrometrica		3	3	2	3	1									1		2				2						3									2		2		3	3	3	3	3	3	3	3
Funaria muhlenbergii		3	3																						3														3						2		
Funaria pulchella		3	3																						3														3								
Geocalyx graveolens	3		1	3	2													3												3																	
Glyphomitrium daviesii		3	3	3	1													3						3																							
Gongylanthus ericetorum	3																								3						3									3	3						
Grimmia alpestris	3	3																																					3				3				
Grimmia anodon	3	3																																					3				3				
Grimmia arenaria	3	2																																					3								
Grimmia atrata	3																																					3	3								
Grimmia crinita		3																																													
Grimmia curvata	3																																						3	3			3				
Grimmia decipiens	3																																					3	3			2				
Grimmia dissimulata	3	3																																					3	3			3				

53

Taxon name	ML	Ord	Stat	Len	Per	LF1	LF2	Tub	Gem	Bul	Bra	Lvs	Sex	Fr	Sp1	Sp2	E	W	Sc	IR	NI	CI	Elem	GBno	IRno	CIno	TJan	TJul	Prec	Alt	L	F	R	N	S	HM
Grimmia donniana	M	Grim	N	15	P	Cu							M	A	10	12	E	W	S	IR	NI		23	44	2		2.4	13.2	1738	1020	7	1	2	1	0	2
Grimmia donniana s.l.	M	Grim	N	15	P	Cu							M	A	10	12	E	W	S	IR	NI		23	214	15		2.2	13.1	1567	1020	7	1	2	1	0	2
Grimmia elatior	M	Grim	N	70	P	Cu	Tf						D	X	10	15			(S)				46	1			2.5	12.4	902	500	6	3	2	2	2	0
Grimmia elongata	M	Grim	N	20	P	Cu	Tf						D	X	12	15	E	W	S				16	9			1.6	12.5	2099	1085	7	3	2	2	2	0
Grimmia funalis	M	Grim	N	40	P	Cu					F		D	O	16	18	E	W	S		NI		43	142	11		1.8	12.2	1897	1205	7	3	5	2	2	0
Grimmia hartmanii	M	Grim	N	40	P	Tf			F				D	X	16	16	E	W	S	IR	NI		43	191	11		2.6	13.0	1742	915	3	5	3	2	2	0
Grimmia incurva	M	Grim	N	25	P	Cu							D	R	15	15	E	W	S				23	22			2.0	13.1	1414	950	8	1	3	2	0	0
Grimmia laevigata	M	Grim	N	15	P	Cu	Tf						D	R	10	15	E	W	S	IR	(NI)	CI	86	40	1	6	4.5	15.6	915	350	7	3	4	1	0	0
Grimmia lisae	M	Grim	N	35	P	Tf	Tuft						D	X	14	17	E	W					83	31			5.5	15.3	1105	600	7	3	6	3	0	0
Grimmia longirostris	M	Grim	N	15	P	Cu							M	F	10	12	E	W	S	IR	(NI)		56	40	1		2.7	12.8	1665	1150	7	1	4	1	0	0
Grimmia montana	M	Grim	N	10	P	Cu	Tf						D	R	12	14	E	W	S			(CI)	76	23			2.8	14.0	1240	500	8	1	4	1	0	0
Grimmia orbicularis	M	Grim	N	40	P	Cu							M	A	10	14	E	W	S	IR			92	52	1		4.2	15.0	1081	390	9	1	9	1	0	1
Grimmia ovalis	M	Grim	N	40	P	Cu							D	R	9	12	E	W	S				56	37			2.8	14.3	1201	500	7	1	4	1	0	0
Grimmia pulvinata	M	Grim	N	30	P	Cu							M	A	8	12	E	W	S	IR	NI	CI	86	1911	261	6	3.5	14.9	1026	950	8	1	8	4	0	0
Grimmia sessitana	M	Grim	N	10	P	Cu	Tf						M	A	8	10			S				13	2			0.7	11.9	1010	410	8	1	5	1	0	0
Grimmia tergestina	M	Grim	N	10	P	Cu	Tf		F				D	O	8	10	E	W	S				85	6			4.1	14.3	1574	230	8	1	7	1	0	0
Grimmia torquata	M	Grim	N	50	P	Cu	Tf		F				D	X	9	9	E	W	S	IR	(NI)		23	152	11		1.6	12.3	1953	1050	7	4	5	2	0	0
Grimmia trichophylla	M	Grim	N	35	P	Cu	Tf		F				D	R	10	14	E	W	S	IR	NI	CI	66	796	77	6	3.4	14.1	1279	990	7	1	2	2	0	0
Grimmia unicolor	M	Grim	N	50	P	Cu							D	O	10	12			S				43	2			1.3	11.9	1377	650	6	7	6	2	0	0
Gymnocolea acutiloba	L	Jung	N	10	P	We							D	Nil				W	S				43	3			1.2	12.2	1790	600	6	5	1	1	0	0
Gymnocolea inflata	L	Jung	N	15	P	Ms	We						D	R	12	18	E	W	S	IR	NI	CI	56	804	79	1	3.1	14.1	1266	1220	7	7	1	1	0	3
Gymnomitrion apiculatum	L	Jung	N	6	P	Cu							D	X	10	10			S				16	3			-1.1	10.5	1825	1340	7	4	2	1	0	0
Gymnomitrion concinnatum	L	Jung	N	12	P	Cu							D	F	12	15	E	W	S	IR	NI		16	147	6		1.3	11.9	2036	1340	7	5	2	1	0	0
Gymnomitrion corallioides	L	Jung	N	15	P	Cu							D	O	12	16	E	W	S	IR			16	12	1		0.6	11.2	2069	1205	8	5	2	1	0	0
Gymnomitrion crenulatum	L	Jung	N	8	P	Cu							D	F	12	16	E	W	S	IR	NI		41	137	46		2.5	12.6	1987	950	7	4	2	1	0	0
Gymnomitrion obtusum	L	Jung	N	20	P	Cu							D	F	12	14	E	W	S	IR	NI		43	179	12		1.5	12.2	2005	1200	7	5	3	1	0	0
Gymnostomum aeruginosum	M	Pott	N	80	P	Tf							D	O	8	14	E	W	S	IR	NI		56	531	64		2.6	13.2	1542	1175	5	8	6	2	0	0
Gymnostomum calcareum	M	Pott	N	20	P	Tf							D	R	8	12	E	W	S	IR	NI		84	73	24		3.4	13.8	1498	560	3	5	9	2	0	0
Gymnostomum viridulum	M	Pott	N	5	P	Tf	Tp		F				D	R	10	12	E	W	S	IR		CI	91	66	15	1	5.1	15.6	1057	230	6	3	9	2	0	1
Gyroweisia reflexa	M	Pott	N	2	P	Tf							D				E		S				91							100	1	5	7	3	0	0
Gyroweisia tenuis	M	Pott	N	2.5	P	Tp	Tf		F				D	O	8	10	E	W	S	IR	NI		73	468	30		3.5	15.3	913	500	6	7	4	3	0	0
Habrodon perpusillus	M	Hypn	N	5	P	Mr			F				D	R	16	24	E	W	S		NI		91	16			2.7	13.8	1584	60	6	4	6	4	0	0
Hamatocaulis vernicosus	M	Hypn	N	120	P	Tf							D	R	14	18	E	W	S	IR	(NI)		46	85	13		3.1	14.0	1445	510	8	9	5	2	0	0
Haplomitrium hookeri	L	Hapl	N	10	PA	Ts							D	F	24	36	E	W	S	IR	NI	CI	43	102	29	3	2.4	12.6	1615	1100	6	8	4	3	0	0
Harpalejeunea molleri	L	Pore	N	12	P	Ms	Sc				O		D	Nil	10	14	E	(W)	S	IR	NI	CI	80	184	57	3	3.2	13.1	1954	600	4	6	4	2	0	0
Harpanthus flotovianus	L	Jung	N	50	P	Mr							D	R	9	12	E	W	S	IR	NI		26	40			0.1	11.0	2012	1130	6	8	5	3	0	0
Harpanthus scutatus	L	Jung	N	16	P	Ms							D	R	19	35	E	W	S	IR	NI		43	108	30		3.2	13.3	1823	490	4	6	3	2	0	0
Hedwigia ciliata	M	Hedw	N	100	P	Ms							D	X	19	35	E	W	S	IR	NI		56	15			3.2	14.7	1216	715	8	1	3	1	0	0
Hedwigia ciliata s.l.	M	Hedw	N	100	P	Mr							D	F	25	35	E	W	S	IR	NI	CI	56	596	101		3.0	13.4	1487	760	8	1	3	1	0	0
Hedwigia ciliata var. ciliata	M	Hedw	N	100	P	Mr							D	X	19	28	E	W	S	IR	NI		56	12			3.2	12.6	1283	530	8	1	3	1	0	0
Hedwigia ciliata var. leucophaea	M	Hedw	N	30	P	Mr							D	X	21	27	E		(S)				52	2			3.5	15.5	920	80	6	8	3	1	0	0
Hedwigia integrifolia	M	Hedw	N	30	P	Mr	Tf		F		O		M	R	23	30	E	W	S	IR	NI		71	65	8		3.0	13.1	1982	720	7	2	4	1	0	0
Hedwigia stellata	M	Hedw	N	50	P	Mr	Tf						M	F	16	20	E	W	S	IR	NI	CI	73	129	6		3.4	13.7	1520	700	8	1	3	1	0	0
Helodium blandowii	M	Hypn	N	150	P	Tf							M	A	29	34	(E)	W	S				46							400	7	8	6	3	0	0
Hennediella heimii	M	Pott	N	10	P	Tf	Tf						M	A	20	22	E	W	S	IR	NI	CI	56	272	17	4	4.4	15.0	969	30	9	7	7	6	5	0
Hennediella macrophylla	M	Pott	AN	25	AP	Tf		F					M	F	20	22	E		S				72	43			3.4	15.6	708	168	5	5	6	6	0	0

Taxon name	RH	RS	RW	SR	SO	PT	GS	DW	DV	DA	BR	EN	EW	AQ	A2	B1	B2	B3	C1	C2	C3	D1	D2	D4	E1	E2	E3	E4	E7	F3	F4	F9	FA	G1	G1R	G3	G3R	H2	H3	H5	I1	I2	J1	J2	J3	J4
Grimmia donniana	3																																					3	3				3	3	3	
Grimmia donniana s.l.	3	3																																				3	3				3	3	3	
Grimmia elatior	3																																						3					3		
Grimmia elongata	3																																					3	3							
Grimmia funalis	3																	1																				3	3							
Grimmia hartmanii	3	1											1							2	2													2				3	3				1			
Grimmia incurva	3																																					3	3							
Grimmia laevigata	3		3															3																					3				3	3		
Grimmia lisae	3		3															3	3																				3				3	3		
Grimmia longirostris	3																	1																				3	3							
Grimmia montana	3																																						3					3		
Grimmia orbicularis	3	3																3																				3	3				3			
Grimmia ovalis	3	3																																					3	1				3	1		
Grimmia pulvinata	3	3		3				1					1					3												2			2	1				3	3				3	3		
Grimmia sessitana	3																																						3							
Grimmia tergestina	3	3																3																				3	3				3			
Grimmia torquata	3																	1																				3	3							
Grimmia trichophylla	3	1																3																				3	3		1		3			
Grimmia unicolor	3																																						3							
Gymnocolea acutiloba	3																																					3	3							
Gymnocolea inflata	3	2	3	3	3	3	3	2	2	2					2		3		3		3	3				3	3	3			3			2		3		3	3	2	1		2	3		
Gymnomitrion apiculatum	2	2	3	3																						3												3	3							
Gymnomitrion concinnatum	2	3	3	3																						3												3	3							
Gymnomitrion corallioides	3	3	2																							3												3	3							
Gymnomitrion crenulatum	3																					1																	3							
Gymnomitrion obtusum	3																									3												3	3							
Gymnostomum aeruginosum	3	2																3																2				3	3				2	2		1
Gymnostomum calcareum		1																																2				3	3				1	1		
Gymnostomum viridulum	3	3	3				3									3		3																				3	3				3	3	2	
Gyroweisia reflexa	3																																						3					3	3	
Gyroweisia tenuis	3	2						1								3		3														3						3					3	3		1
Habrodon perpusillus				3									3															3																		1
Hamatocaulis vernicosus				3																			3		3															3						
Haplomitrium hookeri	3			3			2				3				3								1	3	3			3		3								3	3				3	3	3	
Harpalejeunea molleri											3		2										2	3			3											3	2				3			
Harpanthus flotovianus	3	3		3	3	3				2	2		1					3		2													2					3	3				3	3		
Harpanthus scutatus	3	1		3	3	3	3			2	2		1					3															3						2				1			
Hedwigia ciliata	3	3					1						1					3											1									3	1		3		3	3		1
Hedwigia ciliata s.l.	3	2					1						1																1									3	1		2		2	2		
Hedwigia ciliata var. ciliata	3	3					1						1																1									3	1		3		3	3		1
Hedwigia ciliata var. leucophaea	3	3																																				3					3			
Hedwigia integrifolia	3																																					3					3	1		
Hedwigia stellata	3	2											1																					1				3	3		3		2	2	2	
Helodium blandowii				3		3										3	3					3	3																							
Hennediella heimii			3	3																																				3	3						
Hennediella macrophylla				3																																				3						1

Taxon name	ML	Ord	Stat	Len	Per	LF1	LF2	Tub	Gem	Bul	Bra	Lvs	Sex	Fr	Sp1	Sp2	E	W	Sc	IR	NI	CI	Elem	GBno	IRno	Clno	TJan	TJul	Prec	Alt	L	F	R	N	S	HM
Hennediella stanfordensis	M	Pott	AN	7	AP	Tf			F				D	R			E	W	S				83	75	1		3.9	15.8	775	97	6	5	6	5	0	0
Herbertus aduncus	L	Jung	N	200	P	Tuft	Tf						D	X	25	25	E	W	S		NI		41	171	66		2.9	12.8	2007	1040	6	6	2	2	0	0
Herbertus borealis	L	Jung	N	200	P	Tuft	Tf						D	Nil					S				41	2			1.5	11.6	2599	550	7	6	2	2	0	0
Herbertus stramineus	L	Jung	N	100	P	Tuft	Tf						D	Nil			E	W	S				41	113			1.7	11.8	2259	1180	6	6	4	2	0	0
Herzogiella seligeri	M	Hypn	N	25	P	Mr							M	A	9	12	E	W					53	71			3.6	16.1	734	270	4	6	3	3	0	0
Herzogiella striatella	M	Hypn	N	50	P	Mr							M	A	10	12	(E)		S				43	35			0.2	11.1	2124	950	5	5	3	2	0	0
Heterocladium dimorphum	M	Hypn	N	40	P	Mr							D	X	13	15			S				43	6			-1.3	10.5	1770	1150	6	5	6	2	0	0
Heterocladium heteropterum	M	Hypn	N	30	P	Mr	We						D	R	14	16	E	W	S	IR	NI	CI	72	850	144	1	3.2	13.8	1460	1150	3	6	4	3	0	0
Heterocladium heteropterum var. flaccidum	M	Hypn	N	15	P	Mr							D	Nil			E	W	S	IR	NI	CI	72	300	34	1	3.7	14.5	1361	480	3	6	7	4	0	0
Heterocladium heteropterum var. heteropterum	M	Hypn	N	30	P	Mr	We						D	R	14	16	E	W	S	IR	NI	CI	72	726	120		3.1	13.7	1525	1150	3	6	4	3	0	0
Heterocladium wulfsbergii	M	Hypn	N	30	P	Mr							D	R	14	16	E	W	S	IR	NI		71	32	10		4.2	14.2	1553	165	3	6	4	3	0	0
Heteroscyphus fissistipus	L	Jung	AN	40	P	Ms							D	F						IR			70		1		5.3	14.7	1355	20	5	6	3	3	0	0
Homalia trichomanoides	M	Hypn	N	60	P	Fa							M	F	14	16	E	W	S	IR	NI	(CI)	56	972	70		3.5	15.0	1056	480	5	6	6	5	0	0
Homalothecium lutescens	M	Hypn	N	100	P	We	Mr						D	R	16	20	E	W	S	IR	NI	CI	83	878	156	6	3.7	15.0	969	800	8	3	8	2	0	1
Homalothecium sericeum	M	Hypn	N	100	P	Mr							D	O	11	22	E	W	S	IR	NI	CI	84	2079	342	7	3.5	14.7	1085	610	7	3	7	4	0	0
Homomallium incurvatum	M	Hypn	N	30	P	Mr			O				M	A	8	14	E		S				45	4	1		2.1	13.6	1277	80	4	5	8	4	0	0
Hookeria lucens	M	Hook	N	60	P	Ms							M	F	12	16	E	W	S	IR	NI	CI	72	957	184	2	3.4	13.9	1375	1000	3	7	5	4	0	0
Hygrobiella laxifolia	L	Jung	N	20	P	Ms							D	O	20	26	E	W	S	IR	NI		42	201	38		2.3	12.6	1819	1070	5	8	5	2	0	0
Hygrohypnum duriusculum	M	Hypn	N	60	P	Ms							D	R	20	20	E	W	S	IR			26	20	1		1.6	12.4	1871	860	5	10	5	4	0	0
Hygrohypnum eugyrium	M	Hypn	N	30	P	Ms							M	A	20	22	E	W	S	IR	NI		42	163	25		2.6	12.9	1831	800	5	9	6	3	0	0
Hygrohypnum luridum	M	Hypn	N	70	P	Mr							M	A	16	21	E	W	S	IR	NI		56	766	60		2.7	13.9	1277	1030	6	9	7	4	0	0
Hygrohypnum molle	M	Hypn	N	80	P	Ms							M	X	16	20	E	W	S	IR			42	5			-1.2	10.3	1954	1260	5	10	5	4	0	0
Hygrohypnum ochraceum	M	Hypn	N	80	P	Ms							D	R	16	23	E	W	S	IR	NI		26	615	39		2.6	13.4	1509	1200	5	10	4	3	0	0
Hygrohypnum polare	M	Hypn	N	35	P	Mr							D	Nil					S				16	1			0.2	10.4	2045	670	7	9	6	3	0	0
Hygrohypnum smithii	M	Hypn	N	120	P	Ms							M	R	14	20	E		S				43	9			-0.9	10.8	1796	1075	6	10	6	3	0	0
Hygrohypnum styriacum	M	Hypn	N	20	P	Ms							M	F	14	17	E		S				13	1			-1.5	10.4	1465	760	5	9	5	3	0	0
Hylocomium brevirostre	M	Hypn	N	120	P	We							D	R	22	26	E	W	S	IR	NI	(CI)	73	431	126		3.3	13.7	1620	1180	4	6	5	3	0	0
Hylocomium pyrenaicum	M	Hypn	N	85	P	We							D	X	18	20	E		S				46	21			0.0	11.0	2235	1220	6	5	4	2	0	0
Hylocomium splendens	M	Hypn	N	175	P	We							D	R	14	17	E	W	S	IR	NI	CI	36	1541	332	1	3.2	13.9	1271	1170	6	5	4	2	0	2
Hylocomium umbratum	M	Hypn	N	150	P	We							D	R	14	18	E	W	S	IR	NI		43	226	28		2.2	12.4	2080	860	4	6	3	2	0	0
Hymenostylium insigne	M	Pott	N	120	P	Tf							D	R					S	IR			41	17	5		2.0	12.3	2210	730	6	8	7	2	0	0
Hymenostylium recurvirostrum	M	Pott	N	63	P	Tf	Tuft						D	O	20	20	E	W	S	IR	NI		56	77	8		3.0	13.4	1589	1070	5	8	7	2	0	2
Hymenostylium recurvirostrum s.l.	M	Pott	N	120	P	Tf	Tuft						D	O	18	20	E	W	S	IR	NI		56	232	24		2.5	13.0	1656	770	6	8	7	2	0	2
Hyocomium armoricum	M	Hypn	N	150	P	Mr							M	R	16	16	E	W	S	IR	NI		71	699	135		3.0	13.5	1562	700	3	8	2	1	0	0
Hypnum andoi	M	Hypn	N	80	P	Ms							D	A	18	24	E		S	IR	NI	CI	72	839	53	1	3.5	14.7	1249	1180	3	5	4	3	0	0
Hypnum bambergeri	M	Hypn	N	60	P	Mr							D	X			E	W	S				16	15			-0.4	11.1	2002	1225	5	6	7	3	0	0
Hypnum callichroum	M	Hypn	N	80	P	Ms							D	R	12	16	E	W	S	IR			26	229	19		2.2	12.4	2045	679	8	7	1	1	0	0
Hypnum cupressiforme	M	Hypn	N	60	P	Ms							D	F	13	19	E	W	S	IR	NI	CI	66	2250	354	3	3.4	14.6	1098	1220	6	5	2	2	0	1
Hypnum cupressiforme var. cupressiforme	M	Hypn	N	60	P	Ms							D	F	13	19	E	W	S	IR	NI	CI	66	2250	354	3	3.4	14.6	1098	679	6	5	2	2	0	1
Hypnum cupressiforme var. heseleri	M	Hypn	N	20	P	Ms							D	X	14	18	E						71	2			3.2	16.0	623	65	4	6	3	2	0	0
Hypnum hamulosum	M	Pott	N	50	P	Ms							M	O	12	14	E	W	S		NI		16	74			1.1	11.8	2084	1000	6	8	7	3	0	1
Hypnum imponens	M	Hypn	N	65	P	Ms							D	R	15	20	E	W	S				73	56			2.8	14.4	1170	600	8	7	1	1	0	0
Hypnum jutlandicum	M	Hypn	N	75	P	Ms							D	O	13	15	E	W	S	IR	NI	CI	72	1748	329	11	3.4	14.2	1206	1220	6	5	2	2	0	1
Hypnum lacunosum	M	Hypn	N	100	P	Mr	Ms						D	F	18	20	E	W	S	IR	NI	CI	66	1395	197	4	3.5	14.6	1118	760	7	4	6	4	0	2
Hypnum lindbergii	M	Hypn	N	60	P	Ms							D	X	14	16	E	W	S	IR	NI		36	448	76		3.5	14.6	1218	900	7	7	5	3	0	1
Hypnum resupinatum	M	Hypn	N	50	P	Mr	Ms						D	F	18	24	E	W	S	IR	NI	CI	83	1769	255	8	3.6	14.8	1070	580	4	4	4	4	0	0

56

Taxon name	RH	RS	RW	SR	SO	PT	GS	DW	DV	DA	BR	EN	EW	AQ	A2	B1	B2	B3	C1	C2	C3	D1	D2	D4	E1	E2	E3	E4	E7	F3	F4	F9	FA	G1	G1R	G3	G3R	H2	H3	H5	I1	I2	J1	J2	J3	J4
Hennediella stanfordensis			1	3																																			1	3	2	2				
Herbertus aduncus	3			3	3																										3							3	3							
Herbertus borealis					3																										3							3	3							
Herbertus stramineus	3			3	3										2										3	3					3							3	3							
Herzogiella seligeri					1			3				2	2																				3	1	2											
Herzogiella striatella					3							2															3											3								
Heterocladium dimorphum	3																																					3	3							
Heterocladium heteropterum	3			3	2							1						2															2	3				3	3					2		
Heterocladium heteropterum var. flaccidum	3			2	2							1																						3					3				1			
Heterocladium heteropterum var. heteropterum	3			3	2							1			2			2															2	3				3	3					2		
Heterocladium wulfsbergii	3																				3												3	3					3							
Heteroscyphus fissistipus	3																																									3				
Homalia trichomanoides		3		3	2							3									3				3							1	3	3				3	3				3	3		
Homalothecium lutescens		1	3	3	3		3								1	3	3																					2	2		3	3	3	3		
Homalothecium sericeum	3	3		2	3		1					3			1		3										3					3	3	3				3	3				3	3		
Homomallium incurvatum	3	3		2								3																					2					3	3				3			
Hookeria lucens	2	2	2	3			2	2				1						3			3					2				3		3	3		1			3	3				1			
Hygrobiella laxifolia	3	3																		3	3																									
Hygrohypnum duriusculum	3																			3																										
Hygrohypnum eugyrium	3																			3																										
Hygrohypnum luridum	3	3																	2	3													1	1					3				3			
Hygrohypnum molle	3																			3	3																									
Hygrohypnum ochraceum	3	2			2							2								3	3												1													
Hygrohypnum polare	3																				3																									
Hygrohypnum smithii	3																			3	3																									
Hygrohypnum styriacum	3											3								3																										
Hylocomium brevirostre	3	2					2					3						2						2						2		2	2		2			3	3				1	2		
Hylocomium pyrenaicum	2				3																							3					1					1	2							
Hylocomium splendens				3	3										1	3	3	3				3		3			3			3		3	3	3		3		3	3				1	3		
Hylocomium umbratum	3																													3	3		3	3					3							
Hymenostylium insigne	3																																						3							
Hymenostylium recurvirostrum	3	2		2	2		3								2									3				3											3	2			2	2		
Hymenostylium recurvirostrum s.l.	3	2		2	2										2									3															3	2			2	2		
Hyocomium armoricum	3	2										3									3												2						3				2			
Hypnum andoi	2	2					1					3						2												3		3	3	3		3		2	2							
Hypnum bambergeri	3	3			3																																	3	3							
Hypnum callichroum	3	3			3		1																										3						3							
Hypnum cupressiforme	3	3		3	3		3					3			3	3	3								3	3				3	3	3	3	3		3		3	3				3	3		
Hypnum cupressiforme var. cupressiforme	3	3		3	3		3					3			3	3	3								3					3	3	3	3	3		2			3				3	3		
Hypnum cupressiforme var. heseleri	3											3																3			3		3	3					3							
Hypnum hamulosum	3	3			3																								3										3							
Hypnum imponens	3			3	3	3																3	3																							
Hypnum jutlandicum	3	3		3	3		3					3			3		3								3					3	3	3	3	3				3	3				3	3		
Hypnum lacunosum	2	3		3	3		3					3			3		3								3						3	3	3				3	3	3	2				3	3	
Hypnum lindbergii	3	3		3	3										1	3	3										3								3				3		1	1	3	3		
Hypnum resupinatum	3	3		3	3		3					1	3		3		3								3		3			3		3	3	3	3			3	3				3	3		

57

Taxon name	ML	Ord	Stat	Len	Per	LF1	LF2	Tub	Gem	Bul	Bra	Lvs	Sex	Fr	Sp1	Sp2	E	W	Sc	IR	NI	CI	Elem	GBno	IRno	Clno	TJan	TJul	Prec	Alt	L	F	R	N	S	HM
Hypnum revolutum	M	Hypn	N	55	P	Mr							D	X	12	17			S				16	1			0.5	12.0	2027	1050	6	5	7	2	0	0
Hypnum revolutum var. *dolomiticum*	M	Hypn	N	30	P	Mr							D	X	13	17			S				16							1000	6	5	7	2	0	0
Hypnum revolutum var. *revolutum*	M	Hypn	N	80	P	Mr							D	X	12	15			S				16							1050	6	5	7	2	0	0
Hypnum uncinulatum	M	Hypn	N	30	P	Mr							D	O	12	18				IR			80		1		4.8	14.4	1278	100	3	5	4	3	0	0
Hypnum vaucheri	M	Hypn	N	60	P	Mr							D	X	12	20			S				26	1			-0.2	11.4	2093	732	6	5	7	2	0	0
Isopterygiopsis muelleriana	M	Hypn	N	50	P	Ms			O				D	X	10	12	W		S	IR			42	38	1		1.1	11.6	2331	1070	5	8	6	2	0	0
Isopterygiopsis pulchella	M	Hypn	N	12.5	P	Mr	Thread		O				M	A	8	10	E W		S	IR	NI		26	263	23		2.1	12.7	1809	1170	3	6	6	2	0	0
Isothecium alopecuroides	M	Hypn	N	50	P	De							D	O	12	16	E W		S	IR	NI	CI	53	1415	198	2	3.4	14.5	1159	930	4	6	6	5	0	0
Isothecium holtii	M	Hypn	N	100	P	De							D	R	16	21	E W		S	IR	NI		71	139	18		2.9	13.5	1776	470	4	8	4	3	0	0
Isothecium myosuroides	M	Hypn	N	30	P	De	Mr						D	F	16	24	E W		S	IR	NI	CI	52	1848	303	8	3.4	14.4	1178	980	4	6	4	3	0	0
Isothecium myosuroides var. *brachythecioides*	M	Hypn	N	100	P	Mr							D	Nil			W		S	IR	NI		70	135	26		2.7	12.4	1868	980	4	6	5	4	0	0
Isothecium myosuroides var. *myosuroides*	M	Hypn	N	30	P	De							D	F	16	24	E W		S	IR	NI	CI	52	556	16		3.7	14.8	1249	950	4	6	4	3	0	0
Jamesoniella autumnalis	L	Jung	N	30	P	Ms							D	R	11	15	E		S				56	72			2.3	13.1	2184	360	4	6	2	2	0	0
Jamesoniella undulifolia	L	Jung	N	50	P	Ms							D	R	14	15	E		S				23	8			3.9	14.4	1454	400	7	8	4	2	0	0
Jubula hutchinsiae	L	Pore	N	40	P	Fa	Ms						M(D)	F		28	E W		S	IR	NI		80	130	64		3.8	13.9	1612	610	2	9	6	4	0	0
Jungermannia atrovirens	L	Jung	N	20	P	Ms							D	F	10	19	E W		S	IR	NI	CI	33	756	104		2.7	13.5	1419	1070	5	8	6	3	0	0
Jungermannia borealis	L	Jung	N	15	P	Ms							D	O	18	28	W		S				16	33			1.2	11.9	2087	1205	5	8	5	2	0	0
Jungermannia caespiticia	L	Jung	N	5	P	Ms			F				D	R	12	16	E W						43	13			2.5	14.1	1302	380	6	6	4	3	0	0
Jungermannia confertissima	L	Jung	N	15	P	Ms							M	F	15	22	E W		S				16	27			0.6	11.7	1901	980	6	7	3	3	0	0
Jungermannia exsertifolia	L	Jung	N	80	P	Ms	At						D	O	19	26	E W		S	IR	NI		43	273	15		1.9	12.6	1776	1100	7	9	5	3	0	0
Jungermannia gracillima	L	Jung	N	15	P	Ms							D	F	14	22	E W		S	IR	NI	CI	53	1046	131	2	3.2	14.0	1311	800	6	6	4	3	0	3
Jungermannia hyalina	L	Jung	N	20	P	Ms							D	O	14	24	E W		S	IR	NI		56	305	42		3.0	13.6	1533	400	5	8	5	3	0	0
Jungermannia leiantha	L	Jung	N	30	P	Ms					R			M	F	12	15	E		S				43	4			2.0	13.5	1561	215	5	7	6	3	0	0
Jungermannia obovata	L	Jung	N	50	P	Ms							M	F	18	26	E W		S	IR	NI		43	280	38		2.2	12.9	1662	1100	5	9	5	3	0	0
Jungermannia paroica	L	Jung	N	30	P	Ms							M(D)	F	16	28	E W		S	IR	NI		71	214	17		2.2	12.8	1698	750	5	8	5	3	0	0
Jungermannia polaris	L	Jung	N	6	P	Ms							M	F	15	18			S				26	6			-0.8	11.0	1497	950	6	8	6	2	0	0
Jungermannia pumila	L	Jung	N	15	P	Ms							M	F	16	24	E W		S	IR	NI		36	484	63		2.7	13.4	1503	920	4	8	5	2	0	0
Jungermannia sphaerocarpa	L	Jung	N	30	P	Ms							M	A	15	24	E W		S	IR	NI	CI	26	209	20	1	2.4	13.4	1510	1000	7	8	3	3	0	0
Jungermannia subelliptica	L	Jung	N	10	P	Ms							M	F	16	19	E W		S	IR	NI		43	83	13		1.8	12.2	1712	1070	5	7	5	3	0	0
Kiaeria blyttii	M	Dicr	N	30	P	Tuft	Tf						M	F	14	19	E W		S	IR	NI		23	122	8		1.3	12.0	2034	1344	6	4	2	1	0	0
Kiaeria falcata	M	Dicr	N	20	P	Tuft	Tf						M	A	11	15	E W		S				13	48			0.0	11.0	2181	1340	6	6	2	1	0	0
Kiaeria glacialis	M	Dicr	N	120	P	Tf							M	F	16	20			S				16	19			-0.4	10.8	2081	1330	6	6	2	1	0	0
Kiaeria starkei	M	Dicr	N	40	P	Tuft	Tf						M	F	14	16	E		S				16	51			0.0	11.1	2236	1340	6	5	2	1	0	0
Kurzia pauciflora	L	Jung	N	30	P	Ms	Thread						D	F	12	20	E W		S	IR	NI	CI	52	403	141	1	3.3	13.8	1404	700	7	9	1	1	0	0
Kurzia sylvatica	L	Jung	N	15	P	Ms	Ms						D	R	12	16	E W		S	IR	NI	CI	72	110	21	1	3.5	14.0	1366	600	4	7	2	2	0	0
Kurzia trichoclados	M	Dicr	N	40	P	We	Ms				F			D	F	12	15	E W		S	IR	NI		42	216	67		2.6	12.7	1683	1000	6	8	7	2	0	0
Leiocolea alpestris	L	Jung	N	25	P	Ms							D	O	12	15	E W		S	IR	NI		26	234	24		2.3	12.9	1642	1175	6	8	7	2	0	0
Leiocolea badensis	L	Jung	N	12	P	Ms							D	F	12	15	E W		S	IR	NI		26	195	27		3.0	14.2	1133	520	6	7	8	2	0	0
Leiocolea bantriensis	L	Jung	N	50	P	Ms							D	R	12	16	E W		S	IR	NI		46	248	26		2.1	12.7	1686	900	7	8	6	2	0	0
Leiocolea fitzgeraldiae	L	Jung	N	50	P	We	Ms						D	R			W		S	IR	NI		41	18	4		2.2	12.4	2098	900	5	8	6	2	0	0
Leiocolea gillmanii	L	Jung	N	20	P	Ms					F			M	F	12	15	E		S	IR			26	18	2		1.7	12.4	1545	900	6	8	6	2	0	0
Leiocolea heterocolpos	L	Jung	N	20	P	Ms	We						D	X	11	13	E W		S				26	53	1		1.3	12.5	1742	915	4	8	6	2	0	0
Leiocolea rutheana	L	Jung	N	60	P	Ms							M	F	16	20	E		S	IR			26	6			3.3	15.4	786	380	7	9	7	2	0	0
Leiocolea rutheana var. *laxa*	M	Jung	N	70	P	Ms							M	F			E						23	1			3.1	15.8	687	65	7	9	7	2	0	0
Leiocolea rutheana var. *rutheana*	M	Jung	N	80	P	Ms							M	F	16	20	E W		S	IR			26	2			2.5	14.6	807	380	7	9	6	2	0	0
Leiocolea turbinata	L	Jung	N	10	P	Ms							D	F	15	18	E W		S	IR	NI		91	559	63		3.7	15.1	968	460	6	7	8	2	0	0

Taxon name	RH	RS	RW	SR	SO	PT	GS	DW	DV	DA	BR	EN	EW	AQ	A2	B1	B2	B3	C1	C2	C3	D1	D2	D4	E1	E2	E3	E4	E7	F3	F4	F9	FA	G1	G1R	G3	G3R	H2	H3	H5	I1	I2	J1	J2	J3	J4
Hypnum revolutum	3																																						3							
Hypnum revolutum var. dolomiticum	3																																						3							
Hypnum revolutum var. revolutum	3																																						3							
Hypnum uncinulatum	3																																						3							
Hypnum vaucheri			3																																				3							
Isopterygiopsis muelleriana	3																										3											3								
Isopterygiopsis pulchella		3																																					3							
Isothecium alopecuroides	3		2		1			1																									3	3					3				3			
Isothecium holtii	3												3																																	
Isothecium myosuroides	3				2			3													3									3	3		3	3			2		3	2						
Isothecium myosuroides var. brachythecioides	3												3																										3				3			
Isothecium myosuroides var. myosuroides	3				2			3																						3	3		3	3			2		3				3			
Jamesoniella autumnalis	3	3						3					3																										3	2						
Jamesoniella undulifolia																						3	3			3																				
Jubula hutchinsiae	3											2					3		3														1						3							
Jungermannia atrovirens	3	3	2	3	3			1									3		2				3			3								3				2	3				2			
Jungermannia borealis		3	3																																				3							
Jungermannia caespiticia			1		3														3																				2	3					3	
Jungermannia confertissima					3			2											3					3															3						2	
Jungermannia exsertifolia	3				3		3												3		3		3	3						3					3				2							
Jungermannia gracillima		2			2		3										1		3				3			3				3				3					3				3			
Jungermannia hyalina	2	3		3	3	1	3		1										3				3			3							1	2					3					1		
Jungermannia leiantha			3																														3													
Jungermannia obovata	3				3														3																				3							
Jungermannia paroica	3				3														3														2						3							
Jungermannia polaris				3																																			3							
Jungermannia pumila	3				3												3		3																				3		1		1		1	
Jungermannia sphaerocarpa	3			1			1												3				3																3	1						
Jungermannia subelliptica	3				3		3																																3							
Kiaeria blyttii	3						2																		2													3								
Kiaeria falcata	3				3		3																		3														3							
Kiaeria glacialis	3						3																		3														3							
Kiaeria starkei	3			3			3																		3														3							
Kurzia pauciflora	3				2		3			3												3	3	2						3			3						3							
Kurzia sylvatica		3			3		2			2												3	3							3			3					3								
Kurzia trichoclados	3	3			3		2									1						3								3			3	3					3				1		1	
Leiocolea alpestris	3	3	1		3		1		3															3	3								1	1					3					1	3	
Leiocolea badensis	2	1	2		3		2									3							2	3	2								1	1					3				2		3	
Leiocolea bantriensis	3	3			3											1			3					3															3							
Leiocolea fitzgeraldiae	3				3																			3				3											3							
Leiocolea gillmanii	2				2											2					2			3									1						3							
Leiocolea heterocolpos	3	3			2						3							3						3															3							
Leiocolea rutheana					3																			3																						
Leiocolea rutheana var. laxa					3																			3																						
Leiocolea rutheana var. rutheana					3																			3																						
Leiocolea turbinata	3	3			3		3									3								3									2						3				3		3	

Taxon name	ML	Ord	Stat	Len	Per	LF1	LF2	Tub	Gem	Bul	Bra	Lvs	Sex	Fr	Sp1	Sp2	E	W	Sc	IR	NI	CI	Elem	GBno	IRno	Cino	TJan	TJul	Prec	Alt	L	F	R	N	S	HM
Lejeunea cavifolia	L	Pore	N	20	P	Ms							M	F	24	30	E	W	S	IR	NI		53	805	72		3.1	14.1	1348	1020	4	5	6	4	0	0
Lejeunea flava	L	Pore	N	20	P	Ms							M	R						IR			80		17		4.7	14.3	1355	300	4	6	3	3	0	0
Lejeunea hibernica	L	Pore	N	15	P	Ms							MD	R						IR			80		10		4.6	14.2	1387	370	4	6	5	3	0	0
Lejeunea holtii	L	Pore	N	20	P	Ms							M	R					S	IR			80	2	18		4.8	14.4	1238	330	3	8	6	4	0	0
Lejeunea lamacerina	L	Pore	N	20	P	Ms							M	F			E	W	S	IR	NI	CI	80	558	124	4	3.9	14.3	1425	650	4	6	5	3	0	0
Lejeunea mandonii	L	Pore	N	12	P	Ms							M	R			E		S	IR			80	7	3		4.8	14.3	1558	360	3	6	5	2	0	0
Lejeunea paters	L	Pore	N	15	P	Ms							M	F	16	28	E	W	S	IR	NI		80	437	137		3.2	13.2	1677	800	4	5	4	2	0	0
Lepidozia cupressina	L	Jung	N	40	P	We							D	Nil			E	W	S	IR	NI		80	171	74		3.5	13.4	1617	700	4	6	2	2	0	0
Lepidozia pearsonii	L	Jung	N	50	P	We				R			D	Nil			E	W	S	IR	NI		70	197	26		2.4	12.8	1983	800	5	6	2	2	0	0
Lepidozia reptans	L	Jung	N	20	P	We	Ms						M	F	11	16	E	W	S	IR	NI	CI	56	1306	124	1	3.2	14.2	1262	1000	3	6	2	2	0	0
Leptobarbula berica	M	Pott	N	2	P	Tf	Tp						D	R	7	10	E	W		IR			91	75			3.9	16.1	778	270	1	5	8	4	0	0
Leptobryum pyriforme	M	Spla	N	20	PA	Tuft	Tf	F					M	F	14	16	E	W	S	IR	NI	CI	66	565	22	2	3.6	15.4	834	610	7	6	6	7	0	0
Leptodictyum riparium	M	Hypn	N	133	P	Mr	At						M	F	12	16	E	W	S	IR	NI	CI	76	1196	54	3	3.7	15.5	854	300	6	9	7	7	0	0
Leptodon smithii	M	Hypn	N	25	P	Fa							D	O	16	16	E	W	S	IR	NI	(CI)	91	132	3		4.6	16.1	912	190	6	4	7	4	0	0
Leptodontium flexifolium	M	Pott	N	15	P	Tf			R			O	D	O	12	14	E	W	S	IR	NI		71	297	15		2.7	13.7	1375	750	7	4	2	2	0	0
Leptodontium gemmascens	M	Pott	NA	10	P	Tf			F				Nil	Nil			E						71	15			3.7	16.1	772	200	6	5	3	2	0	0
Leptoscyphus cuneifolius	L	Jung	N	5	P	Ms	Mr				F		D	X				W	S	IR	NI		80	86	23		2.9	12.7	2169	760	5	6	3	2	0	0
Leptotheca gaudichaudii	M	Rhiz	AN	10	P	Ts							D	X						IR			70		1		5.0	14.4	1403	20	4	8	5	5	0	0
Lescuraea saxicola	M	Hypn	N	30	P	Ms							D	X	10	15			(S)				46							950	6	5	7	2	0	0
Leskea polycarpa	M	Hypn	N	30	P	Mr	Ms						M	A	12	16	E	W	S	IR	NI	(CI)	76	665	39		3.6	15.4	890	365	6	5	7	6	0	0
Leucobryum glaucum	M	Dicr	N	200	P	Cu					F		D	R	16	20	E	W	S	IR	NI	CI	73	1018	179	1	3.2	14.0	1333	1030	5	6	2	2	0	0
Leucobryum juniperoideum	M	Dicr	N	105	P	Cu					F		D	F	18	20	E	W	S	IR	NI	CI	73	129	10		3.9	15.2	1263	400	4	5	3	2	0	0
Leucodon sciuroides	M	Hypn	N	50	P	Mr	Fa				F		D	R	20	26	E	W	S	IR	NI	CI	64	432	15	1	3.5	15.2	996	730	6	4	7	4	0	0
Leucodon sciuroides var. morensis	M	Hypn	N	100	P	Mr					F		D	O			E	W	S	IR	NI		83	8	2		4.7	15.1	1110	730	6	4	7	4	0	0
Leucodon sciuroides var. sciuroides	M	Hypn	N	50	P	Mr	Fa				F		D	R			E	W	S	IR	NI	CI	64	98	2		3.8	15.4	1001	270	6	4	7	4	0	0
Lophocolea bidentata	L	Jung	N	60	P	We	Ms						M	F	15	20	E	W	S	IR	NI	CI	73	2265	320	9	3.4	14.6	1094	850	5	6	4	3	0	1
Lophocolea bispinosa	L	Jung	AN	15	P	We	Ms						D	O	12	14	E	W	S	IR			72	22	1		5.2	15.5	1132	160	6	6	4	2	0	0
Lophocolea brookwoodiana	L	Jung	AN	30	P	Ms							D	Nil			E						71	1			3.8	16.6	672	45	6	5	4	3	0	0
Lophocolea fragrans	L	Jung	N	15	P	Ms							M	F	10	16	E	W	S	IR	NI	CI	81	152	49	3	4.1	14.3	1405	360	3	7	5	3	0	0
Lophocolea heterophylla	L	Jung	N	20	P	Ms				R			M	A	10	16	E	W	S	IR	NI	CI	76	1499	41	7	3.6	15.4	907	360	4	5	4	5	0	0
Lophocolea semiteres	L	Jung	AN	30	P	We	Ms		O				D	A	16	19	E	W	S		NI		72	51	1		4.0	15.9	806	250	5	5	2	2	0	0
Lophozia bicrenata	L	Jung	N	10	P	Ms			F				M	F	12	16	E	W	S			CI	56	347	19		3.3	14.6	1182	800	6	6	3	1	0	2
Lophozia capitata	L	Jung	N	20	P	Ms			F				D	R	14	17	E	W					73	18			3.8	16.3	724	210	7	7	3	2	0	0
Lophozia excisa	L	Jung	N	10	P	Ms			F				M	F	15	20	E	W	S			CI	26	370	25	6	3.3	14.4	1203	700	7	5	5	2	0	2
Lophozia herzogiana	L	Jung	NA	10	P	Ms			F				D	X	14	14	E		S				72	2			3.1	14.6	822	150	6	6	3	2	0	0
Lophozia incisa	L	Jung	N	10	P	Ms			F				D	O	10	16	E	W	S	IR	NI		46	535	129		2.7	13.1	1560	850	6	6	2	1	0	0
Lophozia longidens	L	Jung	N	15	P	Ms			F				D	R	13	16	E	W	S				46	50			0.8	11.8	1631	640	5	6	2	2	0	0
Lophozia longiflora	L	Jung	N	8	P	Ms			F				D	F	8	10	E		S				46	1			-1.5	10.4	1465	320	3	7	2	2	0	0
Lophozia obtusa	L	Jung	N	40	P	Ms			R				D	X	11	14	E						23	36			0.9	11.7	1895	1040	5	6	5	2	0	0
Lophozia opacifolia	L	Jung	N	20	P	Ms			F				D	O	16	21	E		S	IR			16	48			0.4	11.3	2116	1330	5	6	3	2	0	0
Lophozia perssonii	L	Jung	N	5	P	Ms			F				D	R	10	16	E						43	19			3.4	15.8	665	230	6	5	9	2	0	0
Lophozia sudetica	L	Jung	N	25	P	Ms	We		F				D	R	10	14	E	W	S	IR	NI		26	243	16		1.8	12.7	1745	1340	6	5	3	1	0	0
Lophozia ventricosa	L	Jung	N	20	P	Ms	Tf		F				D	O	10	18	E	W	S	IR	NI	CI	33	1252	192	3	3.0	13.8	1334	1280	5	6	2	2	0	1
Lophozia wenzelii	L	Jung	N	20	P	Ms			F				D	X	10	10	E		S	IR	NI		16	4			0.6	11.4	2104	1100	5	7	3	1	0	0
Lunularia cruciata	L	Marc	N	40	P	Mt			F				D	R	15	21	E	W	S	IR	NI	CI	92	1392	111	8	3.7	15.3	931	390	4	7	7	7	0	1
Marchantia polymorpha	L	Marc	N	100	P	Mt			F				D	O	10	16	E	W	S	IR	NI	CI	56	1200	78	1	3.2	14.7	998	1100	7	8	6	5	0	1

Taxon name	RH	RS	RW	SR	SO	PT	GS	DW	DV	DA	BR	EN	EW	AQ	A2	B1	B2	B3	C1	C2	C3	D1	D2	D4	E1	E2	E3	E4	E7	F3	F4	F9	FA	G1	G1R	G3	G3R	H2	H3	H5	I1	I2	J1	J2	J3	J4
Lejeunea cavifolia	3	2	3		3		1				3	3	3					3										3	3			3		3				3	3					2		
Lejeunea flava	3		1								3	3																						3				3	3					1		
Lejeunea hibernica	3										3	3																										3	3							
Lejeunea holtii	3		3				1				1	3						3			3												3			1		3		1						
Lejeunea lamacerina	3	3	3		3		3	3			3	3						3		3												3	3	3	1	3		3	3				2			
Lejeunea mandonii	3	3	3		3		2				3	2						3		3													3	3		3		3	3				3			
Lejeunea patens	3	3	3	1	3					3	3	3			1			3	1					3							2		3	3	1		3	3				3	1		
Lepidozia cupressina	3		3		3		2				3	2																			3		3	3	1			3	3							
Lepidozia pearsonii	2				3	3				3											3										3	3	3	3	1			3	3							
Lepidozia reptans	3	3	3		3	3	3	3		2	3	3				3		3			2			1			3	3		3	3	3	3	3		3		3	1				1		1	
Leptobarbula berica	3	3			3		3	3										2		3		3	3			2					3	2	3	3				2	2	1	3		3	3		
Leptobryum pyriforme	1	3			3	3	1				3			1			2					3		3			3						2	2				3	3	3	3	3		3	3	
Leptodictyum riparium	3	3	3		3	3	3	2			3	3		3	3	3			3	3	3								3			3	3				3	3	1	1			1			
Leptodon smithii	1	1			3	3	3	3			3	3																3					3	3		3	3		1								
Leptodontium flexifolium	2		3		3	3	3	3						3							3			3					3		3	2	2		2				2			3				
Leptodontium gemmascens					3	3	3	3													3			3																		3					
Leptoscyphus cuneifolius	3		3		3		3	3	1		3													3						3	3	3	3	3				2									
Leptotheca gaudichaudii											3																															3					
Lescuraea saxicola	3										3																												3								
Leskea polycarpa	2		3		1		3	3			3						2		3											2	2	2	2	2													
Leucobryum glaucum					3	3	3	3		2	2			1							3	3			2						3		3		2		2						1			
Leucobryum juniperoideum	2				3	2	3	3			2			1							3	3									2	3	3		2		2	3									
Leucodon sciuroides	3	3					3	3			3					2											3	3		3		3				3										
Leucodon sciuroides var. morensis	3	3					3	3			3																					3	3		3		3			3		3	3				
Leucodon sciuroides var. sciuroides	3	3					3	3			3					2					3						3		3		3	3	2	2						3		3	3			
Lophocolea bidentata	3	3	3		3	3	3	3		2	3	3		2	3	2	3		3		3	3		3	3	3		3	3	3	3	3	3	3		3		3	3		3		3	3		3
Lophocolea bispinosa	3	1	3		3	3	3					2		3		3						3		3	3	3				3	3	3	3	3				3	3		3		3	3		3
Lophocolea brookwoodiana																								3			3							3												
Lophocolea fragrans	3		3		2		2	3		3	3	3				3		3												3	3		3	3	1		1		3	1				2		
Lophocolea heterophylla	2	3	3	1	3	3	3	3		3	3			3	3			3					3					3		3	3	3	3	3		3		2	2		3		2			
Lophocolea semiteres			3		3	3	3	3		3	3				3	3		3							3		3			3	3	3	3			3	3		3	3		3		3	3	
Lophozia bicrenata		2			3	3	1									3									3							3			2							3		3	3		3
Lophozia capitata			3		3	3	3																3													2		2			3				3	3	
Lophozia excisa	3		3		3	3	2	3		3	3	2			3		3							1		3					3	3		1			3		3	3		3		3	3		3
Lophozia herzogiana							3	3	3		3											3																								3	
Lophozia incisa	3	2	2		3	3	3	3		3	3					3	3					3	3		1					3	3		3	3		1		2	3							
Lophozia longidens	3	2	3		3	3	3	3		3	3																			3	3		3	3	1		1	3	3	3		2			2		
Lophozia longiflora	3						3	3																													3	3									
Lophozia obtusa	3		3		3						1							3		3		2	2	3								2						2	3	3							
Lophozia opacifolia			3		3	3				1									3								3												3	3							
Lophozia perssonii	1	3	1		3																				3																			1	3		
Lophozia sudetica	2	2	3	2	3													3				3					3				2		3	3				3	3				2	3		3
Lophozia ventricosa	3		3		3	3	3	3	3	3	3				3			3				3	3		3		3				3		3	3	2		3	3	3				3	3		3
Lophozia wenzelii	3		3		3																	3					3													3			3	3		
Lunularia cruciata	3	3	3		3	1	2				2	2		1				3	3			2	2	1			3			2	2	2	2	2		2		3	3	3	3	3	3	3	2	2
Marchantia polymorpha	2	3	3		3	3	3				2	3		2			3		3	3		3	3	2	2		3				2	2	2	2				3	3	3	3	3	3	3		3

61

Taxon name	ML	Ord	Stat	Len	Per	LF1	LF2	Tub	Gem	Bul	Bra	Lvs	Sex	Fr	Sp1	Sp2	E	W	Sc	IR	NI	CI	Elem	GBno	IRno	Clno	TJan	TJul	Prec	Alt	L	F	R	N	S	HM
Marchantia polymorpha subsp. montivagans	L	Marc	N	100	P	Mt							D	R	12	14	E		S	IR			26	17	1		1.8	13.3	1126	1100	7	8	6	4	0	0
Marchantia polymorpha subsp. polymorpha	L	Marc	N	150	P	Mt			O				D	R	10	15	E	W	S	IR	NI		53	154	8		3.1	14.7	1031	630	7	9	6	4	0	1
Marchantia polymorpha subsp. ruderalis	L	Marc	N	50	P	Mt			F				D	O	10	15	E	W	S	IR	NI	CI	56	223	9		3.6	15.4	849	500	6	7	6	7	0	0
Marchesinia mackaii	L	Pore	N	50	P	Ms							M	F	7	12	E	W	S	IR	NI		81	185	77		4.1	14.2	1440	500	3	5	7	3	0	0
Marsupella adusta	L	Jung	N	6	P	Tf							M	F	7	12	E	W	S	IR	NI		22	43	6		1.1	11.8	2145	1220	7	3	3	1	0	0
Marsupella alpina	L	Jung	N	15	P	Ms	Tf						D	O	10	11	E	W	S				12	35			0.5	11.4	2127	1340	7	7	2	1	0	0
Marsupella arctica	L	Jung	N	30	P	We							D	Nil					S				16	2			-1.6	10.3	1355	1120	6	9	3	1	0	0
Marsupella boeckii	L	Jung	N	10	P	We							D	R	10	18			S				16	4			-0.4	10.9	2049	1100	6	7	3	1	0	0
Marsupella brevissima	L	Jung	N	8	P	Tf	Ms						M	F	8	15	E	W	S				13	31			-0.2	10.9	2156	1335	8	7	2	1	0	0
Marsupella condensata	L	Jung	N	20	P	Tf	Ms						D	O	10	13	E	W	S				13	10			-1.2	10.4	1794	1240	8	7	2	1	0	0
Marsupella emarginata	L	Jung	N	50	P	Tf	At						D	F	9	20	E	W	S	IR	NI	CI	53	834	126	2	2.8	13.3	1538	1220	6	8	3	1	0	2
Marsupella emarginata var. aquatica	L	Jung	N	80	P	At	Tf						D	F		20	E	W	S	IR	NI		53	56	16		3.0	13.5	1841	1070	7	10	3	1	0	0
Marsupella emarginata var. emarginata	L	Jung	N	20	P	Tf	Ms						D	F	9	13	E	W	S	IR	NI	CI	53	782	120	2	2.8	13.3	1552	1220	6	8	3	1	0	2
Marsupella emarginata var. pearsonii	L	Jung	N	60	P	Ms							D	R			E	W	S	IR	NI		53	16	5		1.9	12.4	1940	860	8	10	3	1	0	0
Marsupella funckii	L	Jung	N	10	P	Tf	Ms						D	R	7	10	E	W	S	IR	NI	CI	52	149	13	3	2.5	12.9	1815	670	7	6	3	1	0	2
Marsupella profunda	L	Jung	N	8	P	Tf							M	A			E		S				81	5			6.2	15.5	1191	280	7	3	3	1	0	0
Marsupella sparsifolia	L	Jung	N	10	P	Tf							M	F	10	12			S				16	3			-2.0	9.9	1386	1150	7	9	3	1	0	0
Marsupella sphacelata	L	Jung	N	20	P	We	Mr						D	O	9	12	E	W	S	IR	NI		23	65	6		1.3	11.9	2020	1225	7	9	3	1	0	0
Marsupella sprucei	L	Jung	N	5	P	Tf							M	A	8	13	E	W	S	IR	NI		26	119	8		1.8	12.5	1900	1335	6	8	3	1	0	0
Marsupella stableri	L	Jung	N	10	P	Ms							D	R	10	15	E	W	S				12	35			0.4	11.3	2295	1200	6	6	3	1	0	0
Mastigophora woodsii	L	Lepi	N	120	P	We							Nil	Nil						IR			41	63	13		2.3	12.1	2175	1000	5	6	3	2	0	0
Meesia triquetra	M	Spla	N	50	P	Tf							D	X	33	38	E	W		IR			26	5	1		3.9	13.6	1450	90	7	9	6	2	0	0
Meesia uliginosa	M	Spla	N	35	P	Tf							M	A	40	50	E	W	S				26	58	1		1.0	11.9	1717	990	8	8	6	2	0	0
Metzgeria conjugata	L	Metz	N	20	P	We	Mt						M	F	18	26	E	W	S	IR	NI		53	453	77	1	3.0	13.5	1633	800	4	5	5	3	0	0
Metzgeria fruticulosa	L	Metz	N	10	P	Tf					F		D	R	19	28	E	W	S	IR	NI	CI	72	658	90		3.9	15.2	1006	450	5	5	6	4	0	0
Metzgeria fruticulosa s.l.	L	Metz	N	25	P	Mt				F			D	R	19	28	E	W	S	IR	NI	CI	72	841	120	1	3.8	15.0	1105	480	5	5	5	4	0	0
Metzgeria furcata	L	Metz	N	25	P	Mt				F			D	F	21	32	E	W	S	IR	NI	CI	53	1772	303	9	3.5	14.7	1122	600	5	4	5	3	0	0
Metzgeria leptoneura	L	Metz	N	100	P	We				O			D	X	15	24	E	W	S	IR	NI		80	131	25		2.8	12.8	2113	930	5	7	5	2	0	0
Metzgeria temperata	L	Metz	N	25	P	Mt				F			D	X	18	21	E	W	S	IR	NI	CI	72	473	44	1	3.9	15.0	1257	480	5	5	5	3	0	0
Microbryum curvicolle	M	Pott	N	2	A	Ts	Tf						M	A	20	30	E	W	S	IR	NI	CI	92	142	19	1	4.0	15.9	794	365	8	3	8	5	0	0
Microbryum davallianum	M	Pott	N	1.3	A	Ts	Tf						M	A	31	40	E	W	S	IR	NI	CI	92	488	15		3.5	16.1	707	220	8	3	8	5	0	0
Microbryum floerkeanum	M	Pott	N	1.2	A	Ts	Ts						M	A	15	25	E	W	S	IR	NI	CI	73	118			4.2	15.9	851	290	8	5	8	4	0	0
Microbryum rectum	M	Pott	N	0.9	A	Ts	Ts						M	A	23	30	E	W	S	IR	NI	(CI)	91	276	15		5.0	15.7	954	360	8	3	7	3	0	0
Microbryum starckeanum	M	Pott	N	2	A	Ts	Ts						M	A	19	42	E	W	S	IR	(NI)	CI	92	83	2	2	4.0	15.9	803	365	8	3	7	3	1	2
Microbryum starckeanum s.l.	M	Pott	N	2	A	Ts	Ts						M	A	19	42	E	W	(S)	IR	NI	CI	72	519	21	3	3.9	14.7	1336	460	5	3	5	4	0	2
Microlejeunea ulicina	L	Pore	N	6	P	Ms	Sc				F		D	Nil			E	W	S	IR	NI	CI	72	725	11	8	3.9	14.7	1336	460	5	3	5	2	0	0
Micromitrium tenerum	M	Pott	N	1.5	A	Tp							M	A	17	20	E	W	S				72	4			4.5	15.9	949	125	8	6	5	5	0	0
Mielichhoferia elongata	M	Brya	NA	15	P	Tf							D	R	12	15	E		S				42	4			1.4	12.4	1246	820	4	6	2	1	0	0
Mielichhoferia mielichhoferiana	M	Brya	NA	15	P	Tf							D	X			E	W		IR			43	2			-0.6	11.0	2184	830	4	6	2	1	0	0
Mnium ambiguum	M	Brya	N	70	P	Tf							D	R	22	34	E	W	S				46	6			-0.4	11.2	2198	1205	4	6	7	3	0	0
Mnium hornum	M	Brya	N	70	P	Tf	Tuft						D	F	26	35	E	W	S	IR	NI	CI	73	2304	301	8	3.4	14.5	1129	976	4	5	4	4	0	1
Mnium marginatum	M	Brya	N	40	P	Tf	Tuft						M(D)	F	24	34	E	W	S	IR	NI		56	192	11		2.3	13.3	1554	1170	3	6	6	4	0	0
Mnium marginatum var. dioicum	M	Brya	N	40	P	Tf	Tuft						D	Nil	24	34	E	W	S	IR	NI		53	2			2.2	13.1	1600	230	3	6	6	4	0	0
Mnium marginatum var. marginatum	M	Brya	N	40	P	Tf	Tuft						M	F	24	34	E	W	(S)	IR	NI	CI	56	174	11		-0.6	11.0	2023	480	3	6	6	4	0	2
Mnium spinosum	M	Brya	N	80	P	Tf							D	R	20	28	E		S				46	9			-0.6	11.0	2023	1100	4	6	4	3	0	0
Mnium stellare	M	Brya	N	60	P	Tf							D	R	20	30	E	W	S	IR	NI		56	520	20		2.9	14.2	1264	580	2	6	7	4	0	0

Taxon name	RH	RS	RW	SR	SO	PT	GS	DW	DV	DA	BR	EN	EW	AQ	A2	B1	B2	B3	C1	C2	C3	D1	D2	D4	E1	E2	E3	E4	E7	F3	F4	F9	FA	G1	G1R	G3	G3R	H2	H3	H5	I1	I2	J1	J2	J3	J4
Marchantia polymorpha subsp. *montivagans*	2														3										3														3							
Marchantia polymorpha subsp. *polymorpha*		2	2	3	3	2	3													3	3	3	3																		1			2		
Marchantia polymorpha subsp. *ruderalis*			3	3	3	3	1	1		2										2		3	3	2						2			2	2						3	3	3	3	3		
Marchesinia mackaii	3		1	3			1	1					3				3																3					3						1		
Marsupella adusta	2	3			2															3					3													3	3	3						
Marsupella alpina	3	2			1															3					3													3	3							
Marsupella arctica					3																				3													3								
Marsupella boeckii	3			3																																		3								
Marsupella brevissima				2	3																			3																						
Marsupella condensata					3																			3																						
Marsupella emarginata	3	1		3	3		3									3	3		3	3		3		3									3	3	3	3	2		3	3				3	3	
Marsupella emarginata var. *aquatica*	3				3														3	3																			3								
Marsupella emarginata var. *emarginata*	3	1	3		3		3									3			3	3		3		3								3	3	3	3	2		3	3	3				3	3	
Marsupella emarginata var. *pearsonii*	3																													3										3						
Marsupella funckii	1		3	3	3		3										3	3	3	3		3	3	3											2			3	3	3				3	3	
Marsupella profunda		3			3																																									
Marsupella sparsifolia	3				3		3													3																		3	3							
Marsupella sphacelata	3		3	3	3		3													3	3		3														3	3						3		
Marsupella sprucei	3	3			3																	3										2					3	3	3							
Marsupella stableri	3	3			3		3													3		3		3													3	3	3							
Mastigophora woodsii					3																		3							3							3									
Meesia triquetra	3														3																															
Meesia uliginosa	3	3		2	2		3						3				3			3					3					3	3	3	3	3		1		3	3	3				1		
Metzgeria conjugata	1	3	1						1		1		3						1											3	3	3	3	1			1		1							
Metzgeria fruticulosa	2	1							1		1		3						1										3	3	3	3	3			1									
Metzgeria fruticulosa s.l.	3	3	2	3	2	2	2		1				3	2		3			3														2			1		3						3		
Metzgeria furcata	3				2	2	2		1					2					3											3	3	3	3					3	3	3				2		
Metzgeria leptoneura	3			3									3				2			3					3					3	3	3	3	1			1	3	3	3	3	3		2		
Metzgeria temperata	3			3			1								3									3									3					3		3						
Microbryum curvicolle				3	3								3			3	2							3						3	3	3	3		2		2	3	3	2	3	3	3			
Microbryum davallianum				3	3	3	2						3			3								3										2		2		3	3	3	3	3		3		
Microbryum floerkeanum				3																				3										2		2				3	2			3		
Microbryum rectum				3	3												2							3														3	3	3	3	3		3		
Microbryum starckeanum		1	1	3	3		3						3				3			1			1						1	1				1	1				3	3	3	3	3		
Microbryum starckeanum s.l.		3	1	3			2						2			3	3			2					3					1			2		2				3	3	3	3	3		
Microlejeunea ulicina	2				1								3	1			2							3						3	3	3	3	3		2		3	2	3	3	3		3		
Micromitrium tenerum					3								3						3																				2							
Mielichhoferia elongata		3																	3																				3							
Mielichhoferia mielichhoferiana	3				3																																		3							
Mnium ambiguum	3																																						3							
Mnium hornum	3	3			3	3	3						3			3			1			3		3					3	3	3	3	3	3		3		3	3	3	3	3		2		
Mnium marginatum	3	3			3								2			3			2			3		3						3	3	3	1	1				3	3	3	3	3				
Mnium marginatum var. *dioicum*	3	3		3	3												3																					3	3	3	3	3		3		
Mnium marginatum var. *marginatum*	3	3		3	3		2						2						2											1				1	2				3	3	3	3	3		3		
Mnium spinosum	3				3																																	3	3	3						
Mnium stellare	3	3	3	3	3		3									3						3								3	3	3	3	3		3		3	3	3	3	3		3		

63

Taxon name	ML	Ord	Stat	Len	Per	LF1	LF2	Tub	Gem	Bul	Bra	Lvs	Sex	Fr	Sp1	Sp2	E	W	Sc	IR	NI	Cl	Elem	GBno	IRno	Cino	TJan	TJul	Prec	Alt	L	F	R	N	S	HM
Mnium thomsonii	M	Brya	N	60	P	Tf							D	R	25	36	E	W	S	IR	NI		26	57	8		1.1	12.1	1973	1180	4	6	7	3	0	0
Moerckia blyttii	L	Metz	N	25	P	Mt							D	F	30	46			S				14	44			-0.2	10.8	2159	1220	7	7	3	1	0	0
Moerckia hibernica	L	Metz	N	35	P	Mt							D	F	32	52	E	W	S	IR	NI		43	81	20		3.1	13.9	1179	800	7	8	7	2	0	0
Molendoa warburgii	M	Pott	N	10	P	Tf			F				D	R				W	S	IR			41	128	1		1.7	12.0	2179	1070	5	8	7	2	0	0
Mylia anomala	L	Jung	N	30	P	Ms	Sc		F				D	R	15	20	E	W	S	IR	NI		46	487	98		2.9	13.6	1364	1070	7	9	1	1	0	0
Mylia taylorii	L	Jung	N	60	P	Tuft	Ms		F				D	O	17	21	E	W	S	IR	NI		42	501	94		2.5	12.8	1704	1226	6	7	2	2	0	0
Myrinia pulvinata	M	Hypn	N	30	P	Mr							M	A	12	20	E	W	S				46	29			3.3	15.1	918	150	6	5	7	6	0	0
Myurella julacea	M	Hypn	N	10	P	Mr							D	R	9	11	E	(W)	S	IR	NI		26	35	4		0.7	11.7	1837	1205	6	5	7	2	0	0
Myurella tenerrima	M	Hypn	N	10	P	Mr							D	X	10	10			S				16	3			-0.1	11.5	1992	1180	6	4	7	2	0	0
Myurium hochstetteri	M	Hypn	N	60	P	Mr						O	D	X					S	IR			80	43	1		4.0	12.8	1693	110	6	6	3	2	2	0
Nardia breidleri	L	Jung	N	5	P	Sc	Ms						D	F	10	14			S				16	15			-0.5	10.8	2162	1340	8	7	2	1	0	0
Nardia compressa	L	Jung	N	120	P	At	Ms						D	O	10	13	E	W	S	IR	NI		42	283	43		2.5	13.1	1680	1150	7	10	2	1	0	0
Nardia geoscyphus	L	Jung	N	10	P	Ms							M	F	14	16	E	W	S	IR			26	105	12		1.9	12.9	1522	1070	6	7	3	2	0	0
Nardia insecta	L	Jung	N	10	P	Ms							M	F	18	22	E						43	1			1.9	13.7	1107	300	5	7	3	1	0	0
Nardia scalaris	L	Jung	N	20	P	Ms	Tf						D	F	15	18	E	W	S	IR	NI	Cl	53	1231	163	5	3.1	13.8	1354	1340	6	6	3	1	0	3
Neckera complanata	M	Hypn	N	50	P	Fa	Ms				F		D	O	14	26	E	W	S	IR	NI	Cl	53	1392	304	3	3.6	14.7	1104	600	5	4	7	4	0	0
Neckera crispa	M	Hypn	N	200	P	We	Fa				O		D	O	24	30	E	W	S	IR	NI		73	580	94		3.0	14.1	1395	700	6	4	8	3	0	0
Neckera pennata	M	Hypn	N	83	P	Fa					O		M	A	18	32	(S)		S				46							100	5	5	4	3	0	0
Neckera pumila	M	Hypn	N	40	P	Ms	Fa		F		F		D	O	15	20	E	W	S	IR	NI		72	459	96	1	4.0	14.9	1280	410	5	5	5	4	0	0
Nowellia curvifolia	L	Jung	N	20	P	Ms							D	F	11	16	E	W	S	IR	NI		53	669	74		3.0	13.8	1443	800	4	7	2	2	0	0
Octodiceras fontanum	M	Dicr	N	30	P	At					X		M	X	18	21	E	W		IR		Cl	73	50	2		3.8	15.9	777	245	5	12	7	6	0	0
Odontoschisma denudatum	L	Jung	N	20	P	Ms			F				D	R	12	16	E	W	S	IR	NI		53	273	99		3.3	13.8	1444	490	7	6	1	1	0	0
Odontoschisma elongatum	L	Jung	N	30	P	Ms	Sc		R				D	R	12	18	E	W	S	IR			26	46	3		1.7	11.9	1970	910	7	9	5	2	0	0
Odontoschisma macounii	L	Jung	N	15	P	Ms			X				D	X	14	17			S				16	4			0.3	11.2	2461	1159	5	8	6	2	0	0
Odontoschisma sphagni	L	Jung	N	80	P	Ms	Sc						D	R	10	15	E	W	S	IR	NI		72	615	215		3.3	13.6	1436	880	8	8	1	1	0	0
Oedipodium griffithianum	M	Oedi	N	10	P	Ts	Tf		F				M	O	24	30	E	W	S	IR			41	52	1		1.3	12.3	2115	1200	6	6	3	1	0	0
Oligotrichum hercynicum	M	Poly	N	40	P	Tf	Ts						D	O	12	15	E	W	S	IR	NI		26	501	54		2.2	12.8	1688	1330	7	5	2	1	0	0
Oncophorus virens	M	Dicr	N	57	P	Tf							M	F	20	28	E		S				26	25			0.3	11.4	2016	970	7	8	5	2	0	0
Oncophorus wahlenbergii	M	Dicr	N	30	P	Tf							M	F	20	28	E	W	S				26	16			0.3	11.4	2353	1005	7	8	6	2	0	0
Orthodontium gracile	M	Brya	AN	10	P	Tf	Tp		O				M	A			E	(W)			NI		81	9	1		3.2	14.9	998	580	3	6	4	2	0	0
Orthodontium lineare	M	Brya	N	10	P	Tf							M	A	16	20	E	W	S	IR	NI	Cl	73	1137	19	1	3.4	15.4	873	700	4	5	3	4	0	0
Orthothecium intricatum	M	Hypn	N	28	P	Ms							D	R	10	15	E	W	S	IR	NI		23	218	26		2.0	12.9	1733	1175	5	6	6	2	0	0
Orthothecium rufescens	M	Hypn	N	80	P	Ms							D	R	10	14	E	W	S	IR	NI		26	83	9		1.5	12.2	2001	1250	6	7	7	3	0	0
Orthotrichum affine	M	Orth	N	25	P	Cu			O				M	A	16	24	E	W	S	IR	NI	Cl	53	1494	134	4	3.5	15.0	991	530	6	4	6	5	0	0
Orthotrichum anomalum	M	Orth	N	32	P	Cu	Tuft						M	A	14	14	E	W	S	IR	NI	Cl	63	1357	187	6	3.5	14.9	1036	634	8	2	8	4	0	0
Orthotrichum consimile	M	Orth	N	10	P	Cu			F				M	A	16	22	(E)						71							40	6	5	6	4	0	0
Orthotrichum cupulatum	M	Orth	N	20	P	Cu	Tuft						M	A	14	16	E	W	S	IR	NI		74	556	62		3.3	14.7	1020	620	7	4	8	4	0	0
Orthotrichum diaphanum	M	Orth	N	10	P	Cu	Tf		O				M	A	14	18	E	W	S	IR	NI	Cl	83	1528	81	9	3.7	15.3	929	380	7	3	7	5	0	0
Orthotrichum gymnostomum	M	Orth	N	30	P	Cu			F			X	D	X	18	21	E		S				43	2			0.9	12.4	999	250	6	4	5	3	0	0
Orthotrichum lyellii	M	Orth	N	40	P	Tuft			F				D	R	26	40	E	W	S	IR	NI	Cl	72	747	64	1	3.5	15.0	1042	450	6	4	6	4	0	0
Orthotrichum obtusifolium	M	Orth	N	5	P	Cu	Tf		F				D	X	16	20	E		S				46	7			1.8	13.2	905	290	6	4	4	4	0	0
Orthotrichum pallens	M	Orth	N	10	P	Cu							M	A	10	16	E			IR			53	5	1		2.0	13.4	1256	140	6	4	5	4	0	0
Orthotrichum pulchellum	M	Orth	N	10	P	Cu							M	A	16	22	E	W	S	IR	NI		71	591	54		3.7	15.0	1025	405	6	5	6	4	0	0
Orthotrichum pumilum	M	Orth	N	5	P	Cu							M	A	12	16	E						73	3			2.1	13.4	923	120	6	4	6	4	0	0
Orthotrichum rivulare	M	Orth	N	30	P	Cu							M	A	14	20	E	W	S	IR	NI		72	222	16		3.2	14.4	1099	400	6	6	4	5	0	0
Orthotrichum rupestre	M	Orth	N	40	P	Cu							M	A	14	20	E	W	S	IR	NI		53	199	17		2.9	13.0	1369	700	8	2	5	3	0	0

Taxon name	RH	RS	RW	SR	SO	PT	GS	DW	DV	DA	BR	EN	EW	AQ	A2	B1	B2	B3	C1	C2	C3	D1	D2	D4	E1	E2	E3	E4	E7	F3	F4	F9	FA	G1	G1R	G3	G3R	H2	H3	H5	I1	I2	J1	J2	J3	J4
Mnium thomsonii	3																			3								3										3	3							
Moerckia blyttii				3	3														3	2					3													3	3						3	
Moerckia hibernica		3		3	3	3				3					3				3	2				3														2						2		
Molendoa warburgii	2	3																		3										3				2				3								
Mylia anomala				2		3		2		3		2										3	3										3					3								
Mylia taylorii	2			3	3	3		2		2		3		3					3		3	3				3		3		3		3	3					3	3							
Myrinia pulvinata	3	3		3																																		3								
Myurella julacea	3			3																																		3								
Myurella tenerrima	3																	3																												
Myurium hochstetteri	3				3																							3																			
Nardia breidleri	3			3	3	3										2	3		3																											
Nardia compressa	3	2		3	3	3													2							3				3				2				3	3	3				3	
Nardia geoscyphus				3	3	3																				3													3	3					
Nardia insecta				3	3																																			3					
Nardia scalaris	3	3		3	3	3		3	2		2		1			3			3		3				3			3		3		3	2	2		3		3	2	3				3	
Neckera complanata	3	3		3	3								3									3			3	2		3		3		3	3	3				3	3				3		
Neckera crispa	3	3		3																		3			3							3						3						3	
Neckera pennata													3														3					3													
Neckera pumila	1			1	3		3	2		2		3							2		3				3			3	2	3	3	3					1			2			1		
Nowellia curvifolia	1	1		1	3		3	3		2		3										3			3			3		2	2	3	3	3				1							
Octodiceras fontanum	3	3						3											3	3																										
Odontoschisma denudatum	3			3	3	3		3		2		2							3		3				3					3		2		2				3	3						
Odontoschisma elongatum	1			1	3	3	3												3	3						2		3		3										3						
Odontoschisma macounii	1			3	3					3									3		3				3							3		2											
Odontoschisma sphagni								2				1				1																														
Oedipodium griffithianum				3	3																																	3	3							
Oligotrichum hercynicum	1			3	3	3													3					3		2									2	2		2	3					3	
Oncophorus virens	2			3	3																			3			3											2								
Oncophorus wahlenbergii				3																				3			3									3										
Orthodontium gracile	3	3		3	3	3	3						3																																	
Orthodontium lineare	3	3		3	3	3	3		1				3																	3				3				3			1		1			
Orthothecium intricatum	3	3																																3				3			1		1			
Orthothecium rufescens	3	3			2														2															3				3					2			
Orthotrichum affine	2	2						1				3																		3	3	3					1				2					
Orthotrichum anomalum	3	3										1						1												3							3			3	3	3	1
Orthotrichum consimile																																3												
Orthotrichum cupulatum	3	3						1											3										3	3	3					3			3	3	3
Orthotrichum diaphanum	3	3			3			3											3										3	3	3					3			3	3	3
Orthotrichum gymnostomum												3																			3	3											
Orthotrichum lyellii								1				3																	3	3	3					3			1			
Orthotrichum obtusifolium												3																		3	3											
Orthotrichum pallens	1	1					1				1								1										3	3	2					1			1	1		
Orthotrichum pulchellum											3																		3	3												
Orthotrichum pumilum	3	2									3								3																								
Orthotrichum rivulare	3	3				3					2															3												3	3				3

Taxon name	ML	Ord	Stat	Len	Per	LF1	LF2	Tub	Gem	Bul	Bra	Lvs	Sex	Fr	Sp1	Sp2	E	W	Sc	IR	NI	CI	Elem	GBno	IRno	Cino	TJan	TJul	Prec	Alt	L	F	R	N	S	HM
Orthotrichum shawii	M	Orth	N	30	P	Cu							M	A	14	17			(S)				91							50	6	4	6	4	4	0
Orthotrichum speciosum	M	Orth	N	40	P	Cu							M	A	34	36	(E)		S				26	14			0.4	12.1	1133	350	6	4	6	4	4	0
Orthotrichum sprucei	M	Orth	N	10	P	Tuft	Tf		O				M	F	14	16	E	W	S	IR	NI		71	115	5		3.6	15.2	978	110	6	5	7	5	5	0
Orthotrichum stramineum	M	Orth	N	10	P	Cu							M	A	12	14	E	W	S	IR	(NI)		73	413			3.0	14.4	1168	440	6	5	6	4	4	0
Orthotrichum striatum	M	Orth	N	30	P	Cu							M	A	24	28	E	W	S	IR	NI	CI	53	317	34	2	3.5	14.4	1343	450	6	4	6	4	4	0
Orthotrichum tenellum	M	Orth	N	5	P	Cu			O				M	A	10	18	E	W	S	IR	NI	CI	92	319	26	5	4.2	15.3	1123	300	6	4	6	5	5	0
Pallavicinia lyellii	L	Metz	N	40	P	Mt	Sc						D	R	20	26	E	W	S	IR			82	22	7		4.1	15.5	999	460	4	8	4	3	3	0
Paludella squarrosa	M	Spla	N	150	P	Tf	Sc						D	X	15	20	(E)		S	IR			26		1		4.1	13.9	1370	70	7	9	6	3	3	0
Palustriella commutata	M	Hypn	N	100	P	We	Mr						D	R	16	20	E	W	S	IR	NI	(CI)	56	1063	134		2.9	13.7	1318	1070	7	9	7	2	2	0
Palustriella commutata var. commutata	M	Hypn	N	100	P	We							D	R			E	W	S	IR	NI	(CI)	54	858	88		2.8	13.7	1361	900	6	9	8	2	2	0
Palustriella commutata var. falcata	M	Hypn	N	100	P	We							D	R			E	W	S	IR	NI		56	505	66		2.8	13.5	1389	1070	8	9	6	2	2	0
Palustriella decipiens	M	Hypn	N	80	P	We							D	X	18	20			S				23	15			-0.3	11.1	1883	1000	9	9	6	2	2	0
Paraleptodontium recurvifolium	M	Pott	N	100	P	Tuft	Ts						D	Nil			(E)		S	IR			41	47	12		2.1	12.2	2150	920	7	9	6	2	2	0
Paraleucobryum longifolium	M	Dicr	N	40	P	Tf							D	X	27	34			S				46	6			-0.9	10.4	1689	1000	6	7	6	2	2	0
Pedinophyllum interruptum	L	Jung	N	40	P	We	Tf						M	R	12	16	E		S	IR	NI		73	23	8		2.1	13.4	1583	500	4	7	9	2	2	0
Pellia endiviifolia	L	Foss	N	50	P	Mt					F		D	F	70	80	E	W	S	IR	NI	CI	86	1690	221	6	3.5	14.7	1097	915	4	8	7	4	4	0
Pellia epiphylla	L	Foss	N	50	P	Mt							M	F	70	116	E	W	S	IR	NI	CI	56	1879	245	5	3.3	14.3	1188	1230	4	8	4	4	4	0
Pellia neesiana	L	Foss	N	50	P	Mt					F		D	F	76	96	E	W	S	IR	NI	CI	56	666	93	1	3.1	13.8	1374	1000	6	8	5	3	3	0
Petalophyllum ralfsii	L	Foss	N	15	PA	St							D	F	40	56	E	W	S	IR	NI		91	25	11		5.0	15.2	1108	60	9	8	8	2	1	1
Phaeoceros carolinianus	H	Anth	NA	20	AP	St							M	F	38	56	E	W	S	IR	NI		73	15			3.7	15.2	1051	226	8	7	5	4	4	0
Phaeoceros laevis	H	Anth	N	40	AP	Mt	St	O					D	F	30	46	E	W	S	IR	NI	(CI)	91	112	40		5.0	15.2	1120	275	7	7	5	4	4	0
Phaeoceros laevis s.l.	H	Anth	N	40	AP	Mt	St	O					MD	F	30	56	E	W	S	IR	NI	(CI)	83	193	77	1	4.7	15.1	1133	275	7	7	5	4	4	0
Philonotis arnellii	M	Brya	N	10	P	Tf	Sc				F		D	R	22	24	E	W	S	IR	NI	CI	73	87	2	7	3.1	13.9	1458	640	6	6	5	4	4	0
Philonotis caespitosa	M	Brya	N	50	P	Tf							D	R	24	24	E	W	S	IR	NI		56	75	10	1	3.5	14.4	1237	950	8	9	4	3	3	0
Philonotis calcarea	M	Brya	N	100	P	Tf							D	R	20	28	E	W	S	IR	NI		53	325	58		2.7	13.6	1294	640	9	8	9	2	2	0
Philonotis cernua	M	Brya	N	5	P	Tf					R		M(D)	A	28	40	(W)	W	S	IR			70	2	3		3.0	13.0	1985	530	7	7	7	0	0	0
Philonotis fontana	M	Brya	N	100	P	Tf							D	O	26	30	E	W	S	IR	NI	CI	66	1245	193	1	3.0	13.7	1362	1335	7	9	4	3	3	0
Philonotis marchica	M	Brya	N	50	P	Tf				F			D	R	20	25	E		S	IR			83	1			5.0	16.5	789	170	6	7	6	5	5	0
Philonotis rigida	M	Brya	N	10	P	Tf			F				M	F	28	32	E	W	S	IR	NI	CI	91	17	9	2	4.5	14.5	1387	60	8	5	4	4	4	0
Philonotis seriata	M	Brya	N	97	P	Tf							D	R	18	22	E	W	S	IR			24	32			-0.1	11.0	1858	1220	9	8	4	2	2	0
Philonotis tomentella	M	Brya	N	50	P	Tuft							D	R	18	24	E	W	S	IR	NI		16	15	3		1.3	11.7	1886	1125	9	6	7	2	2	0
Physcomitrium eurystomum	M	Funa	N	3	A	Tf	Ts						M	A	30	40	E	W			NI		75	5			3.2	16.0	657	40	8	7	7	7	0	0
Physcomitrium pyriforme	M	Funa	N	5	A	Tuft	Ts						M	A	28	36	E	W	S	IR	NI	CI	76	652	35	4	4.0	15.6	882	275	7	8	7	6	6	0
Physcomitrium sphaericum	M	Funa	N	4	A	Tf	Ts						M	A	24	32	E	W	S		NI		75	17	1		2.7	14.3	1193	330	8	8	8	5	5	0
Plagiobryum demissum	M	Brya	N	5	P	Tuft							D	F	25	30			S				16	6			0.0	11.4	2216	1150	8	6	7	2	2	0
Plagiobryum zieri	M	Brya	N	20	P	Tuft	Tf						D	F	34	40	E	W	S	IR	NI		26	218	14		1.7	12.5	1855	1205	6	6	6	2	2	0
Plagiochila asplenioides	L	Jung	N	100	P	We	Tf						D	R	12	12	E	W	S	IR	NI	CI	73	1161	123	1	3.4	14.6	1182	610	5	6	6	4	4	0
Plagiochila asplenioides s.l.	L	Jung	N	100	P	We	Tf						D	R	12	20	E	W	S	IR	NI	CI	56	1628	258	2	3.3	14.3	1206	1220	5	6	4	3	3	2
Plagiochila atlantica	L	Jung	N	100	P	Tf	We						D	Nil			E	W	S	IR			70	54	3	2	2.6	12.7	2344	250	5	6	4	4	4	0
Plagiochila britannica	L	Jung	N	70	P	Tf	We						D	R	16	18	E	W	S	IR	NI		52	135	15		3.0	13.8	1490	450	8	6	3	3	3	0
Plagiochila carringtonii	L	Jung	N	100	P	We						O	D	Nil					S	IR			41	86	2		1.7	11.6	2254	1070	4	6	7	3	3	0
Plagiochila exigua	L	Jung	N	20	P	We							D	Nil			E	W	S	IR	NI		80	120	32		3.0	13.0	2045	610	5	6	3	2	2	0
Plagiochila killarniensis	L	Jung	N	30	P	Tf							D	X			E	W	S	IR	NI	CI	80	207	43	2	3.8	13.6	1727	430	4	6	4	2	2	0
Plagiochila norvegica	L	Jung	N	25	P	Tf							Nil	Nil			E		S	IR			52	1			4.0	15.7	968	200	5	5	6	5	5	0
Plagiochila porelloides	L	Jung	N	60	P	Tf	We						D	R	14	20	E	W	S	IR	NI	CI	56	1447	235	2	3.2	14.1	1252	1220	3	5	7	4	4	0
Plagiochila punctata	L	Jung	N	30	P	We	Tf					F	D	Nil			E	W	S	IR	NI		80	293	86		3.3	13.2	1841	650	4	6	6	4	4	2

Taxon name	RH	RS	RW	SR	SO	PT	GS	DW	DV	DA	BR	EN	EW	AQ	A2	B1	B2	B3	C1	C2	C3	D1	D2	D4	E1	E2	E3	E4	E7	F3	F4	F9	FA	G1	G1R	G3	G3R	H2	H3	H5	I1	I2	J1	J2	J3	J4
Orthotrichum shawii													3																3																	
Orthotrichum speciosum			1										3																3					3									1			
Orthotrichum sprucei													3								3																									
Orthotrichum stramineum							1						3																3	3	2			3								1	1			
Orthotrichum striatum	1						2						3																3	3	3			3					1			1	1			
Orthotrichum tenellum	1		1										3						1										3	3	3			2					1				1			
Pallavicinia lyellii		3		3	3	3		3	3				2									3	3				3				3			3					3							
Paludella squarrosa				3																																										
Palustriella commutata		3		3	3														3			3		3										3					1							
Palustriella commutata var. commutata		3		3															3			3		3										3												
Palustriella commutata var. falcata					3																	3		3																						
Palustriella decipiens				3	3																			3																						
Paraleptodontium recurvifolium		3		3															3																				3							
Paraleucobryum longifolium		3																																					3							
Pedinophyllum interruptum			3																3																				3							
Pellia endiviifolia	2	3		3	3		3								3	3		3	3			3		3		2				3				1	2			3	3	3	3				3	
Pellia epiphylla	3	3	2	3	2	2			1						1				3			3	3			2				3				1	2	3		3	3	3	3		1	3		
Pellia neesiana	2			3	2	2	3									3	2		3			3	3			3								1	3	3		2		2		1	1			
Petalophyllum ralfsii		2			3		3									3	2																					2		2	3					
Phaeoceros carolinianus				3															3																				3	3	3	2				
Phaeoceros laevis		2		3	3														3															2					3	3	3	2	1			
Phaeoceros laevis s.l.		2		3	3														3															2					3	3	3	2	1			
Philonotis arnellii		3		3	3														3			3					3							2	3			3	3	3						
Philonotis caespitosa		3		3	3		3												3			3	3												3			3	3							
Philonotis calcarea			1	2	3											3			2				3	3						3								2								1
Philonotis cernua				3	3														3				3			2				3				2		3		2	3	3	1				3	1
Philonotis fontana	3	1		3	3		3						3						3			3																	3							
Philonotis marchica		3		3									3				3		3							3						1						2	3	3						
Philonotis rigida	3												3				3		3																			2	3	3						
Philonotis seriata				3									2											2																						
Philonotis tomentella	3			2	3		2						1						1																			3	3							
Physcomitrium eurystomum				3									3						3																											
Physcomitrium pyriforme		3		3			3						3						3								3					1								3	2					
Physcomitrium sphaericum		3		3									2						3																					3						
Plagiobryum demissum																								2	3														3							
Plagiobryum zieri	3	3		2																		3				3								3				3	3				2			
Plagiochila asplenioides	3	3		3		3	2						3									3			3	3							3	3	3			3	1				3			
Plagiochila asplenioides s.l.	3	3		3		3	3						3									3			3		3						3	3		3		3	3				3			
Plagiochila atlantica	3			1									3																					3					3	3						
Plagiochila britannica	3		2	2									2												3									3					3				2			
Plagiochila carringtonii		3																						2							3			2				3	3							
Plagiochila exigua	3	2		3									1														3							3				3	1							
Plagiochila killarniensis	3	3		3							3		3					3	3															3					3					3		
Plagiochila norvegica	3	3		3		3	3						3		3										3								3	3				3	3				3		3	
Plagiochila porelloides	3	3		3		3	3						3		3			3	3														3	3				3	3						3	
Plagiochila punctata	3	1	1	3			3						3		3			3	3						3								3	3				3	3				3		3	

67

Taxon name	ML	Ord	Stat	Len	Per	LF1	LF2	Tub	Gem	Bul	Bra	Lvs	Sex	Fr	Sp1	Sp2	E	W	Sc	IR	Ni	Cl	Elem	GBno	IRno	Clno	TJan	TJul	Prec	Alt	L	F	R	N	S	HM
Plagiochila spinulosa	L	Jung	N	100	P	We	Tf					O	D	Nil			E	W	S	IR	NI		80	305	50		3.0	13.2	1815	730	4	6	4	2	0	0
Plagiochila spinulosa s.l.	L	Jung	N	100	P	We	Tf					O	D	X			E	W	S	IR	NI		80	531	151	2	3.3	13.4	1653	760	4	6	4	2	0	0
Plagiomnium affine	M	Brya	N	100	P	Ms							D	R	18	24	E	W	S	IR	NI	Cl	73	876	14	2	3.6	15.3	975	660	6	6	6	4	0	1
Plagiomnium cuspidatum	M	Brya	N	40	P	Ms							M	F	18	36	E	W	S	IR	NI		56	349	19		3.3	14.5	1116	650	6	6	6	5	0	1
Plagiomnium elatum	M	Brya	N	100	P	Tf							D	X	17	25	E	W	S	IR	NI		53	385	45		2.9	14.1	1198	850	6	9	6	4	0	0
Plagiomnium ellipticum	M	Brya	N	90	P	Tf	Ms						D	R	24	40	E	W	S	IR	NI		26	250	26		3.0	13.9	1262	700	7	8	5	3	0	0
Plagiomnium medium	M	Brya	N	60	P	Ms							M	X	19	27	E	W	S				46	7			-0.2	11.1	2261	1070	6	7	5	3	0	0
Plagiomnium rostratum	M	Brya	N	50	P	Ms							M	A	18	30	E	W	S	IR	NI	Cl	53	1124	104	1	3.3	14.8	1039	580	5	7	6	4	0	0
Plagiomnium undulatum	M	Brya	N	150	P	Tf	De						D	R	24	32	E	W	S	IR	NI	Cl	73	2182	324	3	3.4	14.6	1099	850	5	6	6	5	0	1
Plagiopus oederianus	M	Brya	N	60	P	Tuft	Tf						M	A	18	25	E	W	S	IR	(NI)		26	76	1		1.3	12.6	1867	950	6	5	7	2	0	0
Plagiothecium cavifolium	M	Hypn	N	50	P	Ms		O					D	R	9	14	E	W	S	IR			46	40	2		2.1	12.6	1820	1205	5	6	6	2	0	0
Plagiothecium curvifolium	M	Hypn	N	33	P	Ms		F					M	F	10	14	E	W	S	IR		Cl	73	634	2	3	3.3	15.6	801	490	3	5	3	5	0	0
Plagiothecium denticulatum	M	Hypn	N	50	P	Ms	Mr	F					M	A	8	12	E	W	S	IR	NI	Cl	56	1385	38	3	3.3	14.8	1086	1205	4	6	4	5	0	0
Plagiothecium denticulatum var. denticulatum	M	Hypn	N	50	P	Ms							M	A	8	12	E	W	S	IR	NI	Cl	56	1054	24	1	3.3	14.8	1091	1085	4	6	4	5	0	0
Plagiothecium denticulatum var. obtusifolium	M	Hypn	N	50	P	Ms	Mr						M	A			E	W	S	IR	NI		56	90	8		1.2	11.9	1983	1205	5	6	5	2	0	0
Plagiothecium laetum	M	Hypn	N	23	P	Ms		F					M	F	10	10	E	W	S	IR	NI		46	86	3		2.4	13.9	1185	490	3	5	3	4	0	0
Plagiothecium latebricola	M	Hypn	N	20	P	Mr	We	F					M	R	9	13	E	W	(S)	IR			76	193	1		3.9	16.0	828	490	2	8	5	5	0	0
Plagiothecium nemorale	M	Hypn	N	60	P	Ms		F					D	O	11	14	E	W	S	IR	NI		73	1099	43	9	3.7	15.3	1015	425	3	6	5	5	0	0
Plagiothecium piliferum	M	Hypn	N	25	P	Ms							M	A	13	15			(S)				46							740	6	6	6	2	0	0
Plagiothecium platyphyllum	M	Hypn	N	100	P	Ms		O					M	F	10	16	E	W	S	IR			43	24	1		1.0	11.5	2081	860	5	8	5	5	0	0
Plagiothecium ruthei	M	Hypn	N	60	P	Ms		F					MD	O	10	15	E	W	S	IR	NI	Cl	53	103			3.9	15.5	963	380	4	6	4	5	0	0
Plagiothecium succulentum	M	Hypn	N	60	P	Ms							MD	O	12	14	E	W	S	IR	NI	Cl	54	1425	77	4	3.3	14.6	1156	1165	3	5	5	4	0	1
Plagiothecium undulatum	M	Hypn	N	100	P	Ms							D	F	10	15	E	W	S	IR	NI	Cl	52	1512	162	1	3.0	14.0	1272	1100	4	2	5	2	0	2
Platydictya jungermannioides	M	Hypn	N	10	P	Thread		O					D	R	14	14	E	W	S	IR	NI		26	57	6		2.0	13.2	1511	1175	3	5	7	4	0	0
Platygyrium repens	M	Hypn	N	50	P	Ms	Mr			F			D	R	16	20	E	W	S				76	88			3.5	16.0	707	200	4	4	5	4	0	0
Pleuridium acuminatum	M	Dicr	N	10	PA	Tf		X					M	A	22	30	E	W	S	IR	NI	Cl	73	814	27	7	3.7	15.2	1018	580	6	5	4	4	0	2
Pleuridium subulatum	M	Dicr	N	10	PA	Tf							M	A	28	30	E	W	S	IR	NI	Cl	76	357	23	2	3.9	15.2	991	360	7	6	5	4	0	0
Pleurochaete squarrosa	M	Pott	N	70	P	Tf							D	X			E	W		IR		Cl	92	95	5	7	5.0	15.9	933	300	8	2	9	2	0	0
Pleurocladula albescens	L	Jung	N	30	P	Ms			R				D	R	10	16			S		NI		16	18			-0.4	10.8	2160	1335	5	5	2	1	0	0
Pleurozia purpurea	L	Pleu	N	150	P	Tf	We					R	D	Nil			E	W	S	IR	NI		41	295	137		3.0	12.7	1738	915	7	7	2	1	0	0
Pleurozium schreberi	M	Hypn	N	120	P	We		O					D	O	12	18	E	W	S	IR	NI	Cl	56	1646	257	1	3.2	14.0	1253	1210	6	5	2	2	0	1
Pogonatum aloides	M	Poly	N	20	P	Tp	Tf	F					D	A	8	13	E	W	S	IR	NI	Cl	53	1359	206	9	3.3	14.1	1287	700	4	6	3	3	0	2
Pogonatum nanum	M	Poly	N	5	P	Tp	Tf						D	A	14	17	E	W	S	IR	NI	Cl	73	231	13	3	3.5	14.5	1234	750	5	6	3	2	0	0
Pogonatum urnigerum	M	Poly	N	60	P	Tf		A			R		D	A	10	14	E	W	S	IR	NI	Cl	26	988	151		2.9	13.5	1432	1330	7	5	3	1	0	1
Pohlia andalusica	M	Brya	N	30	P	Tf	Ts			F			D	R	14	24	E	W	S	IR	NI		42	16	2		5.5	15.3	1212	600	6	6	4	2	0	4
Pohlia annotina	M	Brya	N	40	PA	Tf	Ts	O		F			D	R	14	22	E	W	S	IR	NI	Cl	53	952	100	4	3.1	14.0	1289	700	6	6	4	3	0	3
Pohlia bulbifera	M	Brya	N	20	PA	Tuft	Ts	A		F			D	R	14	24	E	W	S	IR	NI		56	153	24		2.4	13.1	1512	735	7	7	4	3	0	0
Pohlia camptotrachela	M	Brya	N	20	PA	Tuft	Ts	A		F			D	X	14	24	E	W	S	IR	NI		42	225	21		3.2	13.9	1394	390	7	7	4	3	0	0
Pohlia cruda	M	Brya	N	40	P	Tuft	Tf	A					MD	A	20	24	E	W	S	IR	NI		26	26	2		1.1	11.7	2122	1050	4	7	4	2	0	0
Pohlia crudoides	M	Brya	N	35	P	Tuft							D	X					S				16	1			1.8	12.8	1631	1180	5	6	5	2	0	0
Pohlia drummondii	M	Brya	N	40	PA	Tf	Ts	O		F			D	O	12	20	E	W	S	IR	NI		26	198	12		2.1	12.8	1697	1220	7	6	3	2	0	1
Pohlia elongata	M	Brya	N	35	P	Tuft	Tf	A					M	A	16	24	E	W	S	IR	NI		46	197	14		2.0	12.6	1994	1050	4	6	4	3	0	0
Pohlia elongata subsp. elongata	M	Brya	N	50	P	Tuft	Tf	A					M	A	20	24	E	W	S	IR	NI		46	179	13		2.0	12.6	2026	1050	4	6	4	3	0	0
Pohlia elongata subsp. polymorpha	M	Brya	N	10	P	Tuft	Tf	A					MD	A	20	24	E	W	S	IR	NI		46	26	2		1.1	11.7	2122	1050	4	7	4	2	0	0
Pohlia filum	M	Brya	N	40	PA	Ts	Tf	R		F			D	R	12	22	E	W	S	IR	NI		26	58	6		1.6	12.5	1553	330	5	6	5	2	0	0
Pohlia flexuosa	M	Brya	N	20	PA	Tf	Ts	X		F			D	X			E	W	S	IR	NI		42	93	18		2.7	13.1	1835	800	5	7	4	2	0	1

Taxon name	RH	RS	RW	SR	SO	PT	GS	DW	DV	DA	BR	EN	EW	AQ	A2	B1	B2	B3	C1	C2	C3	D1	D2	D4	E1	E2	E3	E4	E7	F3	F4	F9	FA	G1	G1R	G3	G3R	H2	H3	H5	I1	I2	J1	J2	J3	J4
Plagiochila spinulosa	3				3					2		3						3															3					3	3					3	3	
Plagiochila spinulosa s.l.	3		3	3	3							3						3															3					3	3					3	3	
Plagiomnium affine			1	3	3		3	3				3			1										3	3		3			2	3		3			3			2	3	1	1		1		
Plagiomnium cuspidatum	3	3	3		3			3				3													2	1	3			3	3	3	3	3					3			1		3		
Plagiomnium elatum					3														3				3	3			3			3	3	3	3													
Plagiomnium ellipticum	3				3														3				3	3			3				3		3						3							
Plagiomnium medium					3																													3					3							
Plagiomnium rostratum	3	3	3	3	3		3					3							3				2		3						3	3	3	3		1		3	3	1		3				
Plagiomnium undulatum	3	2	2	3	3		2	3				3													3	3		3			3	3	3	3		2	2	3	3	3	3					
Plagiopus oederianus	3				1																												2					3								
Plagiothecium cavifolium	3			1	1							3																		1		3	1		3			3								
Plagiothecium curvifolium			3	3	3		3	3	3			3							3						3	3		2		3	3	3	3			3	3		3	3	3		3			3
Plagiothecium denticulatum	3	3	3	3	3		3	3	3			3							3						3	3				3	3	3	3			3	3		3	3	3		3			3
Plagiothecium denticulatum var. denticulatum	3	3			3			3	3			3							3							3		3											3	3							3
Plagiothecium denticulatum var. obtusifolium																																														
Plagiothecium laetum	1		3	3	3			3				3																					3		1				3								
Plagiothecium latebricola			2	2	2			3	3			3																					3		1												
Plagiothecium nemorale	2	2	3		3			3				3																					3		3			2	3							2	
Plagiothecium piliferum	3				3																														2			3								
Plagiothecium platyphyllum	3				3			3	3										3				3	3														3								
Plagiothecium ruthei	3	2			3			3	3			3						2														3	3	3		1		3	3	3			2				
Plagiothecium succulentum	2	2	3	3	3			2	1			3										2				3				3	3	3	3	3		2		3	3	3						
Plagiothecium undulatum	2	3	3	3	3			3	3			2										3			2		3			3	1	3	3			3		3	3							
Platydictya jungermannioides	3	3	3		3																												3						3							
Platygyrium repens												3							3			3			3			3					2	2	3	3		3	3							
Pleuridium acuminatum	1				3		3					3							1						3	3	3				3			2	2		3	3	3					3	3	
Pleuridium subulatum					3		3					3					3								3									2	2				3	3					3	
Pleurochaete squarrosa			1	3	3			3							3			3	1						3		3			2						3			1							
Pleurocladula albescens					3																							3												2							
Pleurozia purpurea	3				3	3		1				1					3			3						3	3	3			3			2	2		3		3	3					3	3	
Pleurozium schreberi	1		2	3	3	3	3								1								3		3	2				3	3	3	3	3		3							3	1	3	
Pogonatum aloides				1	3		3											3															3		3	3		3	3					3	3	
Pogonatum nanum				3	3																						3			3			1	3	3		3		2	2				3	3	
Pogonatum urnigerum		3	3	1	3	3													3									3		1			2	2		3		3	3		2	2		3	3	
Pohlia andalusica			3		3							3						3										3						3						3					3	
Pohlia annotina	1		3	3	3	3	3					3						3	3						3		3			3	3		1	1		3		3	3	3				3	3	
Pohlia bulbifera			3	3	3	3	3					3							3						3									3		3		3	3					3	3	
Pohlia camptotrachela	1				3														3						3		3									3			3		3			3	3	
Pohlia cruda	3	2													3		2																			3		2	2	3			2			
Pohlia crudoides	3																																						3							
Pohlia drummondii	3				3												3											3		3							2		3	3				3	3	
Pohlia elongata	3		3	3	3																							2						3					3	3				3	3	
Pohlia elongata subsp. elongata	3		3	3	3																																		3	3				3	3	
Pohlia elongata subsp. polymorpha			3	3	3																						2												3					3	3	
Pohlia filum	3		2	3	3		3					3							3																	2		3	3						3	
Pohlia flexuosa	3		2	3	3		3					3							3							2											2	3	3						3	

69

Taxon name	ML	Ord	Stat	Len	Per	LF1	LF2	Tub	Gem	Bul	Bra	Lvs	Sex	Fr	Sp1	Sp2	E	W	Sc	IR	NI	CI	Elem	GBno	IRno	CIno	TJan	TJul	Prec	Alt	L	F	R	N	S	HM
Pohlia lescuriana	M	Brya	N	5	PA	Tf	Ts	F						D	O	12	15	E	W	S	IR			74	105	3		3.6	15.0	1040	400	6	6	5	4	0	0
Pohlia ludwigii	M	Brya	N	60	P	Tf								D	R	14	18	E	W	S				16	50			0.0	11.1	2065	1340	6	8	3	2	0	0
Pohlia lutescens	M	Brya	N	8	PA	Ts	Tf							D	X	12	18	E	W	S	IR	NI	CI	73	376	8	2	3.8	15.1	1099	500	5	5	5	4	0	0
Pohlia melanodon	M	Brya	N	10	PA	Tf	Ts	F						D	O	14	22	E	W	S	IR	NI	CI	86	1429	103	3	3.6	15.1	949	580	6	7	7	6	0	0
Pohlia nutans	M	Brya	N	68	P	Tuft	Tf			O				M	A	18	28	E	W	S	IR	NI	CI	36	1737	153	1	3.2	14.4	1151	1340	5	5	2	2	0	3
Pohlia obtusifolia	M	Brya	N	25	P	Tuft								M	F	30	36			S				16	4			-0.6	10.5	2174	1100	8	9	4	2	0	0
Pohlia proligera	M	Brya	N	15	PA	Tf	Ts		F					D	X	15	20	E	W	S	IR	NI		43	19	1		0.8	12.1	1374	800	7	6	4	3	0	0
Pohlia scotica	M	Brya	N	60	P	Tf								Nil	Nil					S				42	9			1.0	11.6	2510	650	7	6	4	2	0	0
Pohlia wahlenbergii	M	Brya	N	75	PA	Tf								D	R	16	20	E	W	S	IR	NI	CI	36	1283	241		3.2	14.2	1223	1200	6	8	6	4	0	1
Pohlia wahlenbergii var. calcarea	M	Brya	N	15	P	Tf								D	X			E		S	IR			73	5	3		3.4	14.2	1436	250	6	7	7	4	0	0
Pohlia wahlenbergii var. glacialis	M	Brya	N	118	P	Tf								D	R			E	W	S	IR			16	39	1		0.3	11.3	2131	1100	7	9	4	4	0	0
Pohlia wahlenbergii var. wahlenbergii	M	Brya	N	60	PA	Tf								D	R	16	20	E	W	S	IR	NI		36	203	2		4.0	15.1	1185	1170	7	6	4	4	0	1
Polytrichum alpinum	M	Poly	N	100	P	Tf								D	A	18	20	E	W	S	IR	NI		26	387	45		2.1	12.5	1733	1335	6	5	2	2	0	0
Polytrichum commune	M	Poly	N	250	P	Tf								D	F	8	12	E	W	S	IR	NI	CI	36	1580	241	1	3.1	14.0	1255	1220	6	7	2	2	0	1
Polytrichum commune var. commune	M	Poly	N	250	P	Tf								D	F	8	12	E	W	S	IR	NI	CI	36	349	14		3.4	14.5	1349	270	6	7	2	2	0	1
Polytrichum commune var. perigoniale	M	Poly	N	60	P	Tf								D	F			E	W	S				56	22			3.1	14.3	1167	355	6	7	2	2	0	0
Polytrichum formosum	M	Poly	N	100	P	Tf								D	F	12	16	E	W	S	IR	NI	CI	56	1755	253	6	3.4	14.5	1164	700	4	6	3	3	0	1
Polytrichum juniperinum	M	Poly	N	70	P	Tf								D	A	8	10	E	W	S	IR	NI	CI	36	1806	241	9	3.4	14.4	1146	910	8	5	3	2	0	2
Polytrichum longisetum	M	Poly	N	87	P	Tf								D	A	20	26	E	W	S	IR	NI		56	319	28		3.2	15.0	960	1030	5	6	3	3	0	0
Polytrichum piliferum	M	Poly	N	45	P	Tf								D	A	12	15	E	W	S	IR	NI	CI	36	1479	155	7	3.2	14.1	1238	1170	9	3	3	1	0	2
Polytrichum sexangulare	M	Poly	N	50	P	Tf								D	O	18	20	E	W	S				13	21			-0.7	10.5	2047	1335	6	5	2	1	0	0
Polytrichum strictum	M	Poly	N	200	P	Tf								D	O	14	18	E	W	S	IR	NI		26	461	73		2.5	13.3	1533	980	8	7	2	1	0	0
Porella arboris-vitae	L	Pore	N	80	P	Ms	Fa							D	Nil	30	49	E	W	S	IR	NI	CI	92	293	30	1	3.1	13.9	1545	670	6	5	7	2	0	0
Porella cordaeana	L	Pore	N	80	P	Ms	Fa							D	R	30	49	E	W	S	IR	NI		53	218	15		2.4	13.6	1236	1000	6	6	6	3	0	0
Porella obtusata	L	Pore	N	80	P	Ms								D	X	45	50	E	W	S	IR	NI	CI	81	115	30	4	4.3	14.0	1384	400	7	5	5	2	1	0
Porella pinnata	L	Pore	N	60	P	At	Fa							D	X	30	42	E	W	S	IR	NI		81	66	19		4.3	14.8	1301	300	5	9	5	4	0	0
Porella platyphylla	L	Pore	N	50	P	Fa	Ms							D	R		55	E	W	S	IR	NI	CI	56	838	56	2	3.5	15.2	968	700	6	4	8	3	0	0
Pottiopsis caespitosa	M	Pott	N	2	P	Ts								M	A	15	19	E	W		IR	NI		73	23			4.0	16.1	786	220	8	2	8	2	0	0
Preissia quadrata	L	Marc	N	30	P	Mt								MD	F	48	70	E	W	S	IR	NI	CI	26	496	85		2.6	13.2	1565	1175	6	7	7	2	0	0
Pseudephemerum nitidum	M	Dicr	N	5	A	Ts					R			M	A	20	32	E	W	S	IR	NI	CI	73	821	89	4	3.8	15.0	1048	400	7	7	5	5	0	0
Pseudobryum cinclidioides	M	Brya	N	90	P	Tf								D	R	24	36	E	W	S				46	48			2.0	12.4	1587	1000	6	9	5	4	0	0
Pseudocrossidium hornschuchianum	M	Pott	N	15	P	Tf								D	R	8	10	E	W	S	IR	NI	CI	84	1027	57	2	3.8	15.3	927	510	8	3	7	5	0	2
Pseudocrossidium revolutum	M	Pott	N	15	P	Tf								D	R	10	14	E	W	S	IR	NI	CI	92	788	134	3	3.8	15.1	1004	600	6	3	8	3	0	0
Pseudoleskea incurvata	M	Hypn	N	40	P	Ms								D	R	12	14	E	W			NI		43	8			-0.7	11.0	1506	1165	6	5	7	2	0	0
Pseudoleskea patens	M	Hypn	N	60	P	Ms								D	R	12	14	E	W	S				43	19			-0.4	10.4	1983	1200	6	5	7	3	0	0
Pseudoleskeella catenulata	M	Hypn	N	15	P	Mr				F				D	X	16	18	E	W	S		NI		43	26			0.3	11.7	1569	1100	7	5	7	2	0	0
Pseudoleskeella catenulata s.l.	M	Hypn	N	20	P	Mr	De							D	X	9	18	E	W	S	IR	(NI)	CI	46	36		5	0.5	11.6	1763	1100	7	5	7	2	0	0
Pseudoleskeella nervosa	M	Hypn	N	20	P	Mr								D	X	15	17			S	(IR)	(NI)		46	1			-1.5	10.4	1435	820	7	5	7	2	0	0
Pseudoleskeella rupestris	M	Hypn	N	20	P	Mr								D	X	9	12	(E)		S	(IR)			46	17			0.7	11.3	1896	1100	7	5	7	2	0	0
Pseudotaxiphyllum elegans	M	Hypn	N	30	P	Ms						F		D	R	10	14	E	W	S	IR	NI	CI	52	1620	154	3	3.3	14.5	1178	950	3	6	3	4	0	1
Pterigynandrum filiforme	M	Hypn	N	50	P	Ms		F			X		D	R	12	12	E	(W)	(NI)				46	68			0.6	11.6	1773	1100	6	5	6	2	0	0
Pterogonium gracile	M	Hypn	N	40	P	Mr	De							D	R	30	30	E	W	S	IR	(NI)	CI	92	325	32	5	3.5	14.0	1510	700	7	4	5	2	0	0
Pterygoneurum lamellatum	M	Pott	N	2	A	Ts								M	A	10	30	E		S	IR			86	2			3.3	16.3	590	80	8	3	9	2	0	0
Pterygoneurum ovatum	M	Pott	N	2	A	Ts								M	A	20	40	E	W	S	IR	NI		86	65			2.4	15.8	688	305	8	3	8	2	0	0
Ptilidium ciliare	M	Lepi	N	60	P	We								D	R	24	36	E	W	S	IR	NI		26	664	10		2.4	13.5	1402	1340	6	5	3	2	0	0
Ptilidium pulcherrimum	L	Lepi	N	30	P	We	Mr							D	R	24	34	E	W	S	IR			46	235	1		2.8	14.7	1036	600	6	4	4	3	0	0

Taxon name	RH	RS	RW	SR	SO	PT	GS	DW	DV	DA	BR	EN	EW	AQ	A2	B1	B2	B3	C1	C2	C3	D1	D2	D4	E1	E2	E3	E4	E7	F3	F4	F9	FA	G1	G1R	G3	G3R	H2	H3	H5	I1	I2	J1	J2	J3	J4
Pohlia lescuriana																					3					1									2				3	3	3					
Pohlia ludwigii																							3					3										3	3	3				3	3	
Pohlia lutescens			1		3													1								1													1	3	1					
Pohlia melanodon		2	1	2	3	3		2								2		3								3				3	2	2	3	2	3				3	3	3	2	2	3		
Pohlia nutans	3	3	3	3	3	3	3	3	3	1	3		3			3	3				3	3	3		3			3		3	3	3	3	3		3		3	3	3			3	3	3	
Pohlia obtusifolia	3				3																		3															3	3							
Pohlia proligera	3	3	3	3	3			3																															3	3						
Pohlia scotica			3	3	3																																			3						
Pohlia wahlenbergii	3	3	1	1	3	3		3								1					3		3		2					1	3		3		3		3		3	3	1			3		
Pohlia wahlenbergii var. calcarea					3																		3		3																					
Pohlia wahlenbergii var. glacialis	3				3																		3																							
Pohlia wahlenbergii var. wahlenbergii	3	3	1	1	3	3		3								1					3		3		3						3		3		3		3		3	3	1	1				3
Polytrichum alpinum					3																	3	3				3			3	3			3				3	3	3		1				3
Polytrichum commune					3	3		3							1						3	3	3				3			3	3	3		3		3			3	3						3
Polytrichum commune var. commune					3	3		3							1						3	3	3								3	3		3		3			3	3						3
Polytrichum commune var. perigoniale	3				3	3																								3	3						3		3							
Polytrichum formosum	3	3			3	3		3	2							3		3							3					1	3	3	3	3	3	3		3	3	3	3		3	1	1	
Polytrichum juniperinum					3	3	3	3	1							3		3							3					3	3			2	3	3		3	3	3		2	3	3	3	3
Polytrichum longisetum					3	3		3								3		3							3						3			3		3		3	3	2	3		3	1	3	3
Polytrichum piliferum		3			3	3										1		2			3	3	3		3						3				2	3			3	3	3	1	3	3	3	
Polytrichum sexangulare					3										1													2						1			3	3								
Polytrichum strictum						3																3						2						1	3	1										
Porella arboris-vitae	3	3			3								3					3							3					3	3			1	3				3	3	1		3			
Porella cordaeana	3	3	1	3	3								3								3									3				3	1				3	3	2		2			
Porella obtusata			2		2								1					3			3										3			1					3	3	2					
Porella pinnata	3	3			3								3							3	3																									
Porella platyphylla	3	3			3				1				3			2					3											3		3					3	3	3		3	3		3
Pottiopsis caespitosa					3	2										1								3	3														3							
Preissia quadrata		2			3	3		3								3					3			3			3	3									1		3	3					3	
Pseudephemerum nitidum					3	2		3							1						3						3								3						3	3					
Pseudobryum cinclidioides					3																3		3								3	3					1			3	3					
Pseudocrossidium hornschuchianum	3	2		3	3			3								3					3				2							2		3					3	3	2		2	3		
Pseudocrossidium revolutum	3	3		2	1													1							1														3				3	3		
Pseudoleskea incurvata	3												3								3																		3		1					
Pseudoleskea patens	3				3								3																									3	3							
Pseudoleskeella catenulata	3																																						3							
Pseudoleskeella catenulata s.l.	3																																						3							
Pseudoleskeella nervosa	3										1																												3							
Pseudoleskeella rupestris	3																																						3							
Pseudotaxiphyllum elegans	3	3			3				3	3		3									3	3			3					3	3		3	3		3			3	3			3	3		2
Pterigynandrum filiforme	3	1		3	3	1							1								2				1									1					3							
Pterogonium gracile				3	3								3					3										3						3					3				2	3	3	
Pterygoneurum lamellatum																																						3	3							
Pterygoneurum ovatum			3		3								1																					2	2			3	3	3		2	3	3	3	
Ptilidium ciliare	1	3		3	3	1							1								1	3					3		3					3	1				3	3	1		2	3	3	3
Ptilidium pulcherrimum	2				3	3		3					3					3							3				3		3			3	1				3				3	3	1	

71

Taxon name	ML	Ord	Stat	Len	Per	LF1	LF2	Tub	Gem	Bul	Bra	Lvs	Sex	Fr	Sp1	Sp2	E	W	Sc	IR	NI	CI	Elem	GBno	IRno	CIno	TJan	TJul	Prec	Alt	L	F	R	N	S	HM
Ptilium crista-castrensis	M	Hypn	N	80	P	We							D	R	11	13	E	W	S	IR			46	254	1		1.6	12.3	1957	915	5	6	3	2	0	0
Ptychodium plicatum	M	Hypn	N	100	P	Ms							D	R	15	24	E	W					23	6			-0.9	10.8	1690	1190	6	5	7	2	0	0
Ptychomitrium polyphyllum	M	Grim	N	40	P	Cu							M	A	10	14	E	W	S	IR	NI	CI	81	689	208	1	3.5	13.8	1457	760	7	3	4	2	0	1
Pylaisia polyantha	M	Hypn	N	45	P	Mr	Ms						M	A	13	16	E	W	S	IR	NI	(CI)	76	47	5		3.2	15.0	876	240	6	4	5	4	0	0
Racomitrium aciculare	M	Grim	N	60	P	Tf	Cu						D	F	16	20	E	W	S	IR	NI		52	1131	202		2.9	13.5	1414	1220	6	8	2	2	0	1
Racomitrium affine	M	Grim	N	50	P	Mr							D	O	12	20	E	W	S	IR	NI	CI	73	100	8		2.8	14.0	1426	425	7	2	2	1	0	0
Racomitrium aquaticum	M	Grim	N	120	P	Mr							D	O	14	20	E	W	S	IR	NI	CI	72	615	94		2.8	13.2	1651	1200	5	6	3	1	0	0
Racomitrium canescens	M	Grim	N	80	P	Tf							D	R	8	10	E	W	S	IR	NI	CI	26	40	3	1	3.2	14.4	1105	1000	8	3	6	2	0	0
Racomitrium canescens s.l.	M	Grim	N	80	P	Tf							D	O	8	12	E	W	S	IR	NI	CI	36	842	111	2	2.8	13.3	1447	1340	7	5	4	2	0	0
Racomitrium ellipticum	M	Grim	N	30	P	Cu	Tf						D	F	18	20	E	W	S	IR	NI	CI	41	164	31	2	2.6	12.4	1985	800	6	6	3	1	0	0
Racomitrium elongatum	M	Grim	N	60	P	Tf							D	X	9	11	E	W	S	IR	(NI)		52	92	1		2.4	13.4	1635	1175	8	4	4	2	0	2
Racomitrium ericoides	M	Grim	N	60	P	Tf							D	O	9	12	E	W	S	IR	NI		32	283	33		2.9	13.5	1572	1340	7	5	4	2	0	2
Racomitrium fasciculare	M	Grim	N	100	P	Mr							D	F	13	15	E	W	S	IR	NI		53	962	145		2.8	13.3	1478	1330	7	2	2	1	0	0
Racomitrium heterostichum	M	Grim	N	50	P	Mr							D	O	10	18	E	W	S	IR	NI		52	383	33		3.0	13.8	1505	730	7	2	2	1	0	0
Racomitrium himalayanum	M	Grim	N	40	P	Tf							D	F	12	16	E	W	S				41	2			-0.2	11.3	2316	1100	7	5	6	1	0	0
Racomitrium lanuginosum	M	Grim	N	150	P	Tf	We						D	O	8	12	E	W	S	IR	NI		26	1051	218		3.0	13.4	1450	1340	6	4	4	2	0	2
Racomitrium macounii	M	Grim	N	55	P	Cu	Tf						D	R	12	14	E	W	S	IR			43	18	3		1.1	11.9	1839	1180	6	6	4	1	0	0
Racomitrium sudeticum	M	Grim	N	50	P	Cu	Tf						D	F	12	16	E	W	S	IR	NI		26	109	17		2.1	12.6	1892	1344	7	2	2	1	0	0
Radula aquilegia	L	Radu	N	50	P	Ms							D	R	30	56	E	W	S	IR	NI		80	139	51		3.1	12.9	1999	920	5	6	4	2	0	0
Radula carringtonii	L	Radu	N	40	P	Ms							D	R	30	40			S	IR			80	4	12		4.5	14.0	1555	360	3	6	6	3	0	0
Radula complanata	L	Radu	N	30	P	Ms	Ms		F				M	A	28	42	E	W	S	IR	NI	CI	56	1238	232	4	3.4	14.5	1165	760	5	4	6	3	0	0
Radula holtii	L	Radu	N	20	P	Ms	Tf		R				M	F	20	25			S	IR			80		13		4.6	14.1	1399	330	2	8	5	3	0	0
Radula lindenbergiana	L	Radu	N	30	P	Ms	Tf		F				D	R	28	38	E	W	S	IR	NI	CI	43	165	15	2	2.5	12.8	1899	1200	6	5	6	3	1	0
Radula voluta	L	Radu	N	50	P	Ms			X				D	Nil	28		E	W	S	IR	NI		70	28	19		3.3	13.4	1926	760	4	7	5	2	0	0
Reboulia hemisphaerica	L	Marc	N	40	P	Mt							D	F	56	86	E	W	S	IR	NI	CI	86	295	15	5	3.5	14.5	1259	590	6	4	6	4	0	0
Rhabdoweisia crenulata	M	Dicr	N	30	P	Cu	Tuft						M	A	18	24	E	W	S	IR	NI	CI	41	108	21		2.5	12.9	2076	800	3	6	3	2	0	0
Rhabdoweisia crispata	M	Dicr	N	15	P	Cu	Tuft						M	A	18	20	E	W	S	IR	NI	CI	42	200	21		2.5	13.1	1896	950	4	5	3	2	0	0
Rhabdoweisia fugax	M	Dicr	N	10	P	Cu	Tuft						M	A	14	20	E	W	S	IR	NI		43	145	6		2.4	13.1	1791	800	4	5	3	2	0	0
Rhizomnium magnifolium	M	Brya	N	70	P	Tf							M	X	30	40	E		S		NI		43	22			-0.2	11.0	1967	1070	6	9	5	3	0	0
Rhizomnium pseudopunctatum	M	Brya	N	93	P	Tf							M	F	30	50	E	W	S	IR	NI	CI	46	225	16		2.5	13.5	1438	970	7	9	6	2	0	0
Rhizomnium punctatum	M	Brya	N	70	P	Tf	Tp						D	F	25	50	E	W	S	IR	NI	CI	56	1909	206	5	3.2	14.4	1170	1165	5	8	5	4	0	1
Rhodobryum roseum	M	Brya	N	35	P	Tuft	Ts						D	R	16	24	E	W	S	IR	NI	CI	56	217	16		3.2	14.5	1123	820	6	5	6	2	0	0
Rhynchostegiella curviseta	M	Hypn	N	30	P	Ms							M	F	13	16	E	W	S	IR	NI	(CI)	91	90	1		3.9	16.1	802	200	7	9	7	6	0	0
Rhynchostegiella litorea	M	Hypn	N	30	P	Mr							M	A	10	15	E		S	(IR)	NI		91	19			3.8	16.4	703	150	3	4	8	5	0	0
Rhynchostegiella tenella	M	Hypn	N	40	P	Mr	Ms						M	A	10	15	E	W	S	IR	NI	CI	92	903	123	8	4.0	15.4	984	350	3	4	8	5	0	0
Rhynchostegiella tenella s.l.	M	Hypn	N	40	P	Mr	Ms						M	A	10	15	E	W	S	IR	NI	CI	92	1057	177	6	3.9	15.4	980	350	3	4	8	5	0	0
Rhynchostegiella teneriffae	M	Hypn	N	30	P	Ms							M	F	13	16	E	W	S	IR	NI	CI	92	233	20		3.4	14.9	1086	390	2	9	7	4	0	0
Rhynchostegium alopecuroides	M	Hypn	N	40	P	Ms	At						M	R	16	20	E	W	S	IR	NI	CI	71	70	14		3.6	14.0	1569	450	5	11	4	3	0	0
Rhynchostegium confertum	M	Hypn	N	30	P	Mr	Ms						M	A	10	14	E	W	S	IR	NI	CI	73	1570	93	8	3.7	15.4	932	500	4	5	7	6	0	0
Rhynchostegium megapolitanum	M	Hypn	N	60	P	Mr	We						M	F	12	16	E	W	S	IR	NI	CI	92	222	6		4.5	16.1	812	150	5	4	7	5	0	0
Rhynchostegium murale	M	Hypn	N	40	P	Mr							M	A	12	16	E	W	S	IR	NI	CI	73	784	28		3.5	15.4	907	730	4	5	7	5	0	0
Rhynchostegium riparioides	M	Hypn	N	112	P	Ms							M	F	16	22	E	W	S	IR	NI	CI	86	1770	180	7	3.4	14.6	1113	1100	4	10	6	6	0	0
Rhynchostegium rotundifolium	M	Hypn	NA	40	P	Mr							M	A	14	16	E						73	2			3.9	16.2	829	230	5	5	8	5	0	0
Rhytidiadelphus loreus	M	Hypn	N	217	P	We							D	R	14	18	E	W	S	IR	NI	CI	52	1191	190	2	3.0	13.6	1389	1225	5	6	2	2	0	2
Rhytidiadelphus squarrosus	M	Hypn	N	138	P	We							D	R	12	17	E	W	S	IR	NI	CI	53	2321	386	7	3.4	14.5	1121	1225	7	5	5	4	0	2
Rhytidiadelphus subpinnatus	M	Hypn	N	120	P	We							D	X	20	20	E	W		IR			46	5	1		3.7	14.6	1610	120	5	6	4	3	0	0

Taxon name	RH	RS	RW	SR	SO	PT	GS	DW	DV	DA	BR	EN	EW	AQ	A2	B1	B2	B3	C1	C2	C3	D1	D2	D4	E1	E2	E3	E4	E7	F3	F4	F9	FA	G1	G1R	G3	G3R	H2	H3	H5	I1	I2	J1	J2	J3	J4
Ptilium crista-castrensis	3																														3							2								
Ptychodium plicatum	3			3	3																						3											3	3							
Ptychomitrium polyphyllum	3		3	3													2																		3				3				3	2		1
Pylaisia polyantha							1						3																			3	3													
Racomitrium aciculare	3	2															2				3												2	2					3				2			1
Racomitrium affine	3	3				1	1									1	2						1										1					3	3			3	3			
Racomitrium aquaticum	3			1												3	2						1		3			1						3					3							
Racomitrium canescens				3	3	3	3									3									3															3							
Racomitrium canescens s.l.			3	3	3	3										3									3						3				2		2		2	3						
Racomitrium ellipticum	3																																					3							
Racomitrium elongatum	2	3	3	3	3	3	3									1								3							3				2		2		2	2						
Racomitrium ericoides	2	3	3	3	2	3	3									2								3							3				2		2		2	3			2			
Racomitrium fasciculare	3	3	3	2								1					3																	3		2			3				3	3	3	1
Racomitrium heterostichum	3	3	1			2										2																							3				3	3	3	1
Racomitrium himalayanum	3																																					3							
Racomitrium lanuginosum	3	3	3	3									3							3		3	3	3	3			3			3							3	3	3			3	3	3	1
Racomitrium macounii	3																																					3	3							
Racomitrium sudeticum	3			2	2	1							1			3									3		2						3					3	3			1			
Radula aquilegia	3	3	3	3	1				3							3																	3	3				3							
Radula carringtonii	3	3	2	1	2		1						3			3													3	3	2	3	3	3				3				2			
Radula complanata	3						1										2			3																										
Radula holtii	3	1		3									1		1				3												2	2	1	1		1			3	3			1			
Radula lindenbergiana	2		3	3			1						1		1		2		3														2	2					3	3						
Radula voluta	2		3	3													3																3						3	3			3			
Reboulia hemisphaerica	3																																					3	3							
Rhabdoweisia crenulata	3			3	2								2																					2				3	3						2	
Rhabdoweisia crispata	3		2	3									3							3														2				3	3				2			
Rhabdoweisia fugax	3																					3																									
Rhizomnium magnifolium																							3					3			3															
Rhizomnium pseudopunctatum				3	3		3	2															3									3			1											1	
Rhizomnium punctatum	3			3	3		3						3			3	2		3		3				3				3		3	3	3	3		3			3				2			
Rhodobryum roseum	3	3			3								3						3														2	2										3			
Rhynchostegiella curviseta	3												3																			3	2	2												
Rhynchostegiella litorea	3												3																			3	3													
Rhynchostegiella tenella	3	3					3						1				3															3		3		3			3				3	3		
Rhynchostegiella tenella s.l.	3	3	3	3			1						2				3														3	3		3		3			3				3	3		
Rhynchostegiella teneriffae	3	3											3								3																	3								
Rhynchostegium alopecuroides	3				3															3																											
Rhynchostegium confertum	3			3	3		3						3			3									3		3			3	3	3	3	3		1			3				3	3	3	
Rhynchostegium megapolitanum	3	3		3	3		3						3			3									3		3					3	3	3		3									3	
Rhynchostegium murale	3	3		3	1		1						3		3				3	3					3	3						2	3	2	3			3				3	3		
Rhynchostegium riparioides	3	3		3	1								3		3				3	3			2			3			3				3	2					3				3	3		
Rhynchostegium rotundifolium	3	3					3						3																			3	3	3									3	3		
Rhytidiadelphus loreus	3			3	3		3						1				2						3		3	3	3	3	3		3	3	3	3		3		3	3				3	3	3	3
Rhytidiadelphus squarrosus		1		3	3	3	1						1		3										3	3	3	3		3	3			3		3		2	2	1	2	1	3	2	3	1
Rhytidiadelphus subpinnatus		3		3																					3	3	3	3													3					

Taxon name	ML	Ord	Stat	Len	Per	LF1	LF2	Tub	Gem	Bul	Bra	Lvs	Sex	Fr	Sp1	Sp2	E	W	Sc	IR	NI	CI	Elem	GBno	IRno	Clno	TJan	TJul	Prec	Alt	L	F	R	N	S	HM
Rhytidiadelphus triquetrus	M	Hypn	N	200	P	We							D	R	14	21	E	W	S		NI		56	1591	286	4	3.3	14.2	1194	980	6	6	6	3	0	1
Rhytidium rugosum	M	Hypn	N	100	P	We	Mr						D	X	16	16	E	W	S		NI		26	55	2		2.0	13.3	1552	915	8	4	7	2	0	0
Riccardia chamedryfolia	L	Metz	N	40	P	Mt	Sc		O				M	F	15	22	E	W	S	IR	NI	CI	53	1128	177	4	3.5	14.4	1203	950	6	9	6	3	0	1
Riccardia incurvata	L	Metz	N	15	P	Sc			F				D	R	20	25	E	W	S	IR	NI		43	102	19		3.0	13.4	1418	670	8	8	5	2	0	0
Riccardia latifrons	L	Metz	N	15	P	Mt			R				M	F	16	24	E	W	S	IR	NI	CI	56	265	100	1	3.5	13.6	1419	880	7	8	1	1	0	0
Riccardia multifida	L	Metz	N	25	P	Mt			R				M	F	14	19	E	W	S	IR	NI	CI	56	791	106	3	3.1	13.8	1379	975	7	9	5	2	0	0
Riccardia palmata	L	Metz	N	15	P	Mt			F				D(M)	F	12	16	E	W	S	IR	NI	CI	46	321	76		2.8	12.9	1679	600	4	7	2	2	0	0
Riccia beyrichiana	L	Ricc	N	25	P	St	Mt						M	A	90	130	E	W	S	IR	NI	CI	52	74	20	3	4.1	14.2	1402	800	8	5	5	3	0	0
Riccia bifurca	L	Ricc	N	10	P	St							M	F	70	100	E	W	S				83	3			6.7	15.9	951	75	8	5	5	3	0	0
Riccia canaliculata	L	Ricc	N	20	A	St							M	F	75	95	E	W	S				73	9			3.1	14.6	1015	245	7	9	5	5	0	0
Riccia cavernosa	L	Ricc	N	30	A	St							M	A	60	94	E	W	S	IR	NI		76	91	10		3.8	15.4	848	250	7	9	7	6	0	0
Riccia crozalsii	L	Ricc	N	14	AP	St							M	A	64	90	E	W		IR		CI	91	26		6	6.5	16.0	1019	90	8	5	5	3	0	0
Riccia crystallina	L	Ricc	AN	25	A	St							M	A	60	86	E		S				91	8			6.4	15.6	1093	75	8	7	5	6	0	0
Riccia fluitans	L	Ricc	N	20	P	Le	St						D	R	56	75	E	W		IR	NI		86	215	13		3.8	16.0	757	214	7	10	7	6	0	0
Riccia glauca	L	Ricc	N	20	AP	St							M	A	70	100	E	W	S	IR	NI	CI	86	574	57	4	3.9	15.5	934	300	7	6	6	6	1	0
Riccia huebeneriana	L	Ricc	N	10	A	St							M	A	54	70	E	W	S				73	21	1		3.3	14.8	1140	450	7	9	5	5	0	0
Riccia nigrella	L	Ricc	N	15	PA	St							M	A	56	80	E	W				CI	91	5		5	5.5	15.8	1004	230	8	4	4	3	0	0
Riccia rhenana	L	Ricc	AN	20	P	Le	St						Nil	Nil			E			IR			73	11	1		3.9	16.3	734	100	7	10	7	6	0	0
Riccia sorocarpa	L	Ricc	N	20	AP	St	Mt						M	A	64	95	E	W	S	IR	NI	CI	64	761	73	6	3.7	15.0	1002	830	7	5	5	4	0	1
Riccia subbifurca	L	Ricc	N	10	AP	St	Mt						M	A	75	94	E	W	S	IR	NI		92	111	31		4.2	14.9	1170	800	7	5	5	4	0	0
Ricciocarpos natans	L	Ricc	N	15	P	Le	St						M	X	42	56	E	W		IR	NI		86	71	11		3.7	15.9	700	150	7	11	7	6	0	0
Saccogyna viticulosa	L	Jung	N	50	P	Ms	We						D	R	11	16	E	W	S	IR	NI	CI	81	645	158	4	3.7	13.8	1545	800	3	6	3	2	0	0
Saelania glaucescens	M	Dicr	N	35	P	Tf							M	O	14	16	E		S				26	3			-1.4	10.5	1379	760	7	5	8	2	3	0
Sanionia orthothecioides	M	Hypn	N	80	P	We	Mr						M	R	13	18	E		S				26	11			4.0	12.4	1415	300	6	5	4	2	3	0
Sanionia uncinata	M	Hypn	N	100	P	We	Mr						M	F	12	16	E	W	S	IR	NI		26	654	44		2.5	13.4	1345	1230	6	4	4	2	0	1
Scapania aequiloba	L	Jung	N	40	P	Ms	We		F				D	X	12	10	E	W	S	IR	NI		23	102	9		1.6	12.3	1873	1175	5	7	7	2	0	0
Scapania aspera	L	Jung	N	60	P	We	Ms		F				D	R	14	20	E	W	S	IR	NI		53	352	81		2.8	13.6	1439	1040	7	6	8	2	0	0
Scapania calcicola	L	Jung	N	25	P	Ms	Sc		F				D	Nil			E	W	S				26	22			0.6	11.7	2009	1150	5	6	7	2	0	1
Scapania compacta	L	Jung	N	25	P	Mr	Ms		F				MD	F	16	21	E	W	S	IR	NI	CI	92	503	46	9	3.5	14.1	1404	780	7	4	3	2	0	3
Scapania curta	L	Jung	N	15	P	Ms	Sc		F				D	R	13	15	E		S	IR	NI		46	16	1		3.2	14.9	1030	350	6	6	3	2	0	0
Scapania cuspiduligera	L	Jung	N	15	P	Ms	Sc		F				D	Nil			E	W	S	IR	NI		26	42	2		1.7	12.8	1498	1175	6	7	7	2	0	0
Scapania degenii	L	Jung	N	50	P	Ms			F				D	Nil			E		S				46	37			0.4	11.6	1934	980	6	8	6	2	0	0
Scapania gracilis	L	Jung	N	50	P	We	Mr		F				D	F	12		E	W	S	IR	NI	CI	80	763	187	3	3.2	13.4	1542	850	5	6	2	2	0	1
Scapania gymnostomophila	L	Jung	N	15	P	Ms	Sc		F				D	Nil				W	S				26	12	3		1.0	11.9	1793	950	5	7	7	2	0	0
Scapania irrigua	L	Jung	N	25	P	Ms	Ms		F				D	R	10	12	E	W	S	IR	NI		56	741	111		3.1	13.8	1349	980	7	8	4	3	0	2
Scapania lingulata	L	Jung	N	8	P	Ms	Sc		F				D	Nil			E	W	S				43	20	2		2.1	12.7	1552	1220	6	6	4	2	0	0
Scapania nemorea	L	Jung	N	60	P	We	Ms		F				D	F	10	14	E	W	S	IR	NI	CI	53	755	122	2	3.2	14.0	1402	670	5	7	4	2	0	2
Scapania nimbosa	L	Jung	N	70	P	We			R				Nil	Nil			(W)	S					41	52	5		1.5	11.5	2298	1070	5	7	6	2	0	2
Scapania ornithopodioides	L	Jung	N	100	P	We			R				D	Nil			E	W	S	IR			41	86	14		1.8	11.8	2207	1000	5	6	6	2	0	0
Scapania paludicola	L	Jung	N	60	P	Ms			F				D	Nil			E	W					26	11			2.8	14.1	1552	430	7	8	3	2	0	0
Scapania paludosa	L	Jung	N	80	P	Ms							D	X	17	17	E	W	S				26	18			-0.1	11.1	2092	1150	7	10	5	2	0	0
Scapania parvifolia	L	Jung	N	10	P	Ms	Sc		F				D	R	14	17	E		S				16	3			0.2	11.5	2786	990	4	6	3	2	0	0
Scapania praetervisa	L	Jung	N	8	P	Ms	Sc		F				D	X			E		S				26	5			0.8	12.4	1210	275	5	8	6	2	0	0
Scapania scandica	L	Jung	N	8	P	Ms	Sc		F				D	R	10	14	E	W	S	IR	NI		46	275	18		2.1	12.9	1606	1220	6	6	3	1	0	0
Scapania subalpina	L	Jung	N	30	P	Ms	Sc		F				D	F	14	18	E	W	S	IR	NI		26	228	15		1.8	12.5	1697	1180	7	8	4	2	0	0
Scapania uliginosa	L	Jung	N	100	P	Ms			R				D	R	14	20	E	W	S	IR	NI		16	82			0.8	11.6	2136	1160	7	9	4	2	0	0

Taxon name	RH	RS	RW	SR	SO	PT	GS	DW	DV	DA	BR	EN	EW	AQ	A2	B1	B2	B3	C1	C2	C3	D1	D2	D4	E1	E2	E3	E4	E7	F3	F4	F9	FA	G1	G1R	G3	G3R	H2	H3	H5	I1	I2	J1	J2	J3	J4
Rhytidiadelphus triquetrus																3							1		3	3		3		3									3							
Rhytidium rugosum																2							3		3										1				3						3	
Riccardia chamedryfolia	3	2	3	2	3	3	3	3					3			3	3			3	3	3	3	3			3				2				2				3	3	2			3	3	
Riccardia incurvata	3				3		3	3								3				3	3	3	3	3																3					3	
Riccardia latifrons				1	1	3	1	3	3	3																					1			2		1			1						1	
Riccardia multifida	3			3	3	3	3	3	3		2					3	3				3	3	3	3			3				2			1		1			3	3	3			3		
Riccardia palmata				3	1	3	3	3	3								3					1									3			3				3	3							
Riccia beyrichiana				3	3											3	3	3			3										3			3					2	3	1			3		
Riccia bifurca				3	3												3														3								3							
Riccia canaliculata				3	3																3										3															
Riccia cavernosa				3	3		3									3					3																			3	2					3
Riccia crozalsii			3	3	3												3																							2	2		3			
Riccia crystallina					3																1																			2	3					
Riccia fluitans			3	3	3	3	3							3		2		3			3		2	2								2									2				2	
Riccia glauca			1	1	3		3										2				3						3				3				3				3	3	3	3			2	
Riccia huebeneriana					3									3				3	3		3		2														2									
Riccia nigrella				3	3			1										3			3													3					1	3	1		3			
Riccia rhenana					3								3					3			3														3					3				3		
Riccia sorocarpa			3	3	3												3			2	3														3				3	3	3	3		3		
Riccia subbifurca			3	3	3												3	3	3		3	2													3		2		3	3	3	3				
Ricciocarpos natans	3			2	2			2				3		3					3		2		2														2									
Saccogyna viticulosa	3	3		3	3			1		2		2					3														3		3	3									2			
Saelania glaucescens		3		3																								3																		
Sanionia orthothecioides				3	3												3	3																												
Sanionia uncinata	3			2	2				1		3		3			2									3		2					3		2					1							
Scapania aequiloba	3	3		3	3		1			3					2	2												3											3							
Scapania aspera	3	3	2	3	3		3	3								3	3				3				3		3				3			3					3	3			3	3		
Scapania calcicola	1	3	3	3	3																3				3														3					3	3	
Scapania compacta	3	3	3	3	3	2		3					3								3		3			2					3			1	2				3	3				3	2	
Scapania curta	3	3		3	3		3								2										3		2								2				3					2	2	
Scapania cuspiduligera	3	3		3	2		1																	3	3														3							
Scapania degenii	3			3	3																		3	3				3											3							
Scapania gracilis	3	3	2	2	2	3	3	3	1				3									3	2		3						3			3				3	3	1				3	3	
Scapania gymnostomophila				3	2					3																																					
Scapania irrigua	3			3	3		3	3					1		2	2					3	3	3				3				3				2				3	3				3		3
Scapania lingulata		2		3	3		3	1	1								3																	1					3	3	3			3	3	
Scapania nemorea	3	3		3	3	2	3	3					3				3	3			3	3	3				3				3			3					3	3	3			3	3	
Scapania nimbosa					3																		3					3										3	2							
Scapania ornithopodioides					3																		3				3	3			3							3	3							
Scapania paludicola	3			3	3					3			3		2							3	3		3		3				3								3							
Scapania paludosa	3			2	2															3			2	3		3		3											3					3		
Scapania parvifolia				3	3								3																		3								3							
Scapania praetervisa					3																		3					3			3				2				3					3	3	
Scapania scandica	3		3	3	3		2	2	2	2			2		3							3						3			3				2	3			3	3	3			2	3	
Scapania subalpina	3	3		3	3		3	2					2							3	3					3								3					3	1				3	1	
Scapania uliginosa	3			2	2		3		3	2						3				3	3	3	3	3		3		3		3	3								3							

75

Taxon name	ML	Ord	Stat	Len	Per	LF1	LF2	Tub	Gem	Bul	Bra	Lvs	Sex	Fr	Sp1	Sp2	E	W	Sc	IR	NI	CI	Elem	GBno	IRno	CIno	TJan	TJul	Prec	Alt	L	F	R	N	S	HM
Scapania umbrosa	L	Jung	N	20	P	Ms			F				D	F	10	13	E	W	S	IR	NI		43	443	82		2.6	13.0	1612	1000	2	6	2	2	0	0
Scapania undulata	L	Jung	N	100	P	Ms	At		F				D	F	15	21	E	W	S	IR	NI	CI	53	1229	184	1	3.0	13.6	1382	1220	6	10	4	2	0	1
Schistidium agassizii	M	Grim	N	50	P	Cu	At						M	O	16	20	E	W	S	IR			43	9	1		1.7	12.5	1712	1100	7	9	5	3	0	0
Schistidium apocarpum s.l.	M	Grim	N	50	P	Tuft	Tf						M	A	8	15	E	W	S	IR	NI		66	1870	312	3	3.4	14.5	1123	1205	7	2	7	4	0	0
Schistidium apocarpum s.str.	M	Grim	N	50	P	Tuft	Tf						M	A	11	15	E	W	S	IR	NI		54	112	22	3	3.5	14.1	1353	880	7	2	7	4	0	0
Schistidium atrofuscum	M	Grim	N	30	P	Cu							M	O	8	11	E		S				43	5			-0.8	11.1	1376	700	7	5	7	2	0	0
Schistidium confertum	M	Grim	N	15	P	Cu							M	A	8	10	E	W	S	(IR)	(NI)		73	17			1.9	13.0	1450	550	7	2	7	2	0	0
Schistidium crassipilum	M	Grim	N	30	P	Cu	Tf						M	A	9	11	E	W	S	IR	NI		83	440	23		3.6	15.1	1023	970	7	1	8	4	0	3
Schistidium dupretii	M	Grim	N	15	P	Cu	Tuft						M	A	8	11			S				46	2			-1.0	10.6	1963	1100	7	2	7	2	0	0
Schistidium elegantulum	M	Grim	N	40	P	Cu	Tf						M	A	8	10	E	W	S	IR	NI		75	10	2		3.9	14.5	1394	175	7	2	7	2	0	0
Schistidium elegantulum subsp. elegantulum	M	Grim	N	30	P	Cu	Tf						M	A	8	10	E	W	S	(IR)	NI		75	5	1		3.0	13.5	1701	175	7	2	7	2	0	0
Schistidium elegantulum subsp. wilsonii	M	Grim	N	50	P	Cu							M	A	8	10	E	W	S	IR			72	2	1		4.4	15.8	985	170	7	2	7	2	0	0
Schistidium flaccidum	M	Grim	N	18	P	Cu							M	A	8	10		W					73	1			2.4	12.7	3130	580	7	2	7	2	0	0
Schistidium frigidum	M	Grim	N	32	P	Cu	Tf						M	A	10	13	(E)	W	S				16	14			1.5	12.3	1720	1200	7	2	7	2	0	0
Schistidium frigidum var. frigidum	M	Grim	N	50	P	Cu	Tf						M	A	10	13	(E)	W	S				16	10			1.5	12.4	1549	600	7	2	7	2	0	0
Schistidium frigidum var. havaasii	M	Grim	N	15	P	Cu							M	A	10	13	(E)	W	S				42	5			1.8	12.1	2132	1200	7	2	7	2	0	0
Schistidium maritimum	M	Grim	N	20	P	Cu							M	A	20	26	E	W	S	IR	NI	CI	51	435	64	6	4.2	13.7	1396	90	8	7	5	5	0	0
Schistidium papillosum	M	Grim	N	80	P	Ms							M	A	10	13		W	S				26	8			0.4	11.7	1691	630	7	2	7	2	0	0
Schistidium platyphyllum	M	Grim	N	40	P	At							M	A	16	20	E	W	S	IR	NI		26	99	3		2.1	13.5	1203	480	7	8	5	3	0	0
Schistidium pruinosum	M	Grim	N	30	P	Cu	Tf						M	A	10	14	E		S		(NI)		73	8			1.9	12.7	1475	400	7	6	7	2	0	0
Schistidium rivulare s.l.	M	Grim	N	100	P	At							M	A	16	20	E	W	S	IR	NI		36	574	37		2.7	13.6	1350	1100	7	8	5	3	0	0
Schistidium rivulare s.str.	M	Grim	N	80	P	At							M	A	16	20	E	W	S	IR	NI		36	419	32		2.8	13.6	1382	1100	7	8	5	3	0	0
Schistidium robustum	M	Grim	N	30	P	Cu							M	O	8	12	E		S	IR			43	36	2		2.1	12.3	1855	720	7	2	7	2	0	0
Schistidium strictum	M	Grim	N	95	P	Cu	Tf						M	A	12	15	E	W	S	IR	(NI)		26	132	13		2.0	12.4	1935	1000	6	4	7	2	0	0
Schistidium trichodon	M	Grim	N	80	P	Ms							M	A	10	14	E	(W)	S	IR	NI		43	20	2		0.3	11.6	1709	1190	7	5	7	2	0	0
Schistostega pennata	M	Dicr	N	15	P	Tp							M	O	8	12	E	W	S			CI	52	139		1	4.1	15.1	1142	305	1	7	4	4	0	0
Scleropodium cespitans	M	Hypn	N	50	P	Ms	Mr						D	R	12	24	E	W	S	IR	NI	CI	72	372	14	7	4.0	15.9	864	300	6	5	7	6	0	0
Scleropodium purum	M	Hypn	N	150	P	We							D	R	12	16	E	W	S	IR	NI	CI	73	2164	382	6	3.4	14.5	1116	1000	7	5	6	3	0	2
Scleropodium touretii	M	Hypn	N	80	P	Mr							D	R	12	15	E	W	S	IR	(NI)	CI	91	174	2	10	5.0	15.8	954	490	8	3	6	2	1	0
Scopelophila cataractae	M	Pott	NA	50	P	Tf		X					M	X	11	13	E	W					86	13			5.6	15.4	1194	154	7	6	1	1	0	5
Scorpidium scorpioides	M	Hypn	N	150	P	We							D	R	18	22	E	W	S	IR	NI		26	574	99		3.0	13.2	1519	880	8	10	6	2	0	0
Scorpidium turgescens	M	Hypn	N	218	P	We							D	X	12	18	E		S				16	2			1.5	13.1	1437	990	7	9	6	2	0	0
Scorpiurium circinatum	M	Hypn	N	10	P	Mr							D	X	14	18	E	W	S	IR		CI	91	123	20	6	5.1	15.9	949	305	6	3	7	2	0	0
Seligeria acutifolia	M	Grim	N	2	P	Ts							M	A	12	14	E	W	S	IR	NI		73	38	7		2.5	14.0	1421	560	2	7	8	2	0	2
Seligeria brevifolia	M	Grim	N	1	P	Ts							M	A	11	13	E	W	S				44	3			1.0	12.3	1948	700	2	7	6	2	0	0
Seligeria calcarea	M	Grim	N	2	P	Ts	Tp						M	A	14	18	E		S				73	125	2		3.6	16.1	730	250	3	5	9	3	0	0
Seligeria calycina	M	Grim	N	2	P	Ts	Tp						M	A	9	12	E		S				72	166	1		3.7	16.2	760	305	3	5	9	4	0	0
Seligeria campylopoda	M	Grim	N	1.5	P	Ts							M	A	8	10	E	W					54	6			3.6	15.7	1039	350	2	5	8	4	0	0
Seligeria carniolica	M	Grim	N	3	P	Ts							M	A	20	27	E		(S)				42	1			2.3	13.5	888	230	2	6	6	2	0	0
Seligeria diversifolia	M	Grim	N	2	P	Ts							M	A	10	14	E		S				46	2			2.0	13.4	1534	400	3	5	8	2	0	0
Seligeria donniana	M	Grim	N	2	P	Ts							M	A	10	14	E	W	S	IR	NI		44	114	12		2.2	13.5	1494	730	2	5	8	2	0	0
Seligeria oelandica	M	Grim	N	15	P	Ts							M	A	22	30							23	4			3.4	13.7	1348	305	3	9	9	3	0	0
Seligeria patula	M	Grim	N	4	P	Ts							M	O	16	22		W		IR			43	1	2		2.8	13.7	1393	400	3	9	9	3	0	0
Seligeria pusilla	M	Grim	N	3	P	Ts							M	A	10	12	E	W	S	IR	NI		53	107	8		2.5	14.1	1325	470	2	5	8	2	0	0
Seligeria recurvata	M	Grim	N	3	P	Ts							M	A	8	10	E	W	S	IR	NI		53	223	16		2.5	13.6	1412	700	3	6	6	2	0	0
Seligeria trifaria s.l.	M	Grim	N	7	P	Ts							M	O	16	32	E	W	S	IR	NI		73	20	4		1.5	12.9	1548	500	3	9	9	3	0	0

Taxon name	RH	RS	RW	SR	SO	PT	GS	DW	DV	DA	BR	EN	EW	AQ	A2	B1	B2	B3	C1	C2	C3	D1	D2	D4	E1	E2	E3	E4	E7	F3	F4	F9	FA	G1	G1R	G3	G3R	H2	H3	H5	I1	I2	J1	J2	J3	J4
Scapania umbrosa	3	3	3	3	3		3	3					2						3	3	3	3					1			3	3			3					2							
Scapania undulata	3	3	3	3	3		2	2					2						3	3	3	2								3	3			2					2	3					3	
Schistidium agassizii	3																		3																				3							
Schistidium apocarpum s.l.	3	3	3	3			1						2																										3		3		3	3	3	
Schistidium apocarpum s.str.	3	3	3										2					3			3																		3		3		3	3	3	
Schistidium atrofuscum		3																																				3	3							
Schistidium confertum	3																																					3	3		3	3	3	3	3	3
Schistidium crassipilum	3	3											2					3																					3				3	3	3	3
Schistidium dupretii	3																																						3				3			
Schistidium elegantulum	3		3																																				3				3			
Schistidium elegantulum subsp. elegantulum	3																																						3				3			
Schistidium elegantulum subsp. wilsonii	3		3																																				3				3			
Schistidium flaccidum	3																																						3							
Schistidium frigidum	3		1				1																															2	3		1		1			1
Schistidium frigidum var. frigidum	3		1																																				3		1		1			1
Schistidium frigidum var. havaasii	3																																					3	3							
Schistidium maritimum	3		1	1		2										3																														
Schistidium papillosum	3																																						3							
Schistidium platyphyllum	3		1																3																				3							1
Schistidium pruinosum	3																																						3							
Schistidium rivulare s.l.	3		3										3						3																			2	3							1
Schistidium rivulare s.str.	3		3										3						3																				3							1
Schistidium robustum	3																	2																					3							
Schistidium strictum	3		3																																				3							
Schistidium trichodon	3					3										2					3												3	2				3	3	3				3		
Schistostega pennata	3	3	3	3									3		1		3													3		3	3	2									2	2		
Scleropodium cespitans		3	2	2	3										3		3						3		3	3	3		3	3		3	3	3		3							3	3		
Scleropodium purum	3	3	3	3	3											3		3					3		3								2	2					3	3	1		3	3		
Scleropodium tourettii			2	3	3				1										2												2								2							3
Scopelophila cataractae	2																		3				3							2																
Scorpidium scorpioides	3		3	3	3											3			3				3		3														3							
Scorpidium turgescens	3		3		3																		3																3							
Scorpiurium circinatum	3	3	3	3	3								2			3			2				3										2	2					3				3			
Seligeria acutifolia	3																																						3							
Seligeria brevifolia	3																																						3							
Seligeria calcarea	1	3	1																		3					2							3	3					3				1	3		
Seligeria calycina	3																																3											3	
Seligeria campylopoda	3																																						3							
Seligeria carniolica			3																																				3							
Seligeria diversifolia	3																																						3							
Seligeria donniana	3		3																3														3													
Seligeria oelandica	3																		3																											
Seligeria patula	3																																													
Seligeria pusilla	3	2	3																														2					3					1		
Seligeria recurvata	3	3	1																														3					3							
Seligeria trifaria s.l.	3																		3																											

77

Taxon name	ML	Ord	Stat	Len	Per	LF1	LF2	Tub	Gem	Bul	Bra	Lvs	Sex	Fr	Sp1	Sp2	E	W	Sc	IR	NI	CI	Elem	GBno	IRno	CIno	TJan	TJul	Prec	Alt	L	F	R	N	S	HM
Sematophyllum demissum	M	Hypn	N	50	P	Ms							M	A	12	18		W					71	4	16		4.4	14.2	1540	330	4	7	3	2	0	0
Sematophyllum micans	M	Hypn	N	20	P	Ms							D	X	11	15	E	(W)	S				71	34	16		3.0	12.9	2167	490	4	6	3	2	0	0
Sematophyllum substrumulosum	M	Hypn	N	30	P	Mr							M	A	12	16	E			IR			81	8	1		6.1	15.8	1081	120	4	5	4	3	0	0
Southbya nigrella	L	Jung	N	5	P	Ms	Sc						M	F	16	24	E						91	3			5.2	16.3	798	120	6	6	8	2	0	0
Southbya tophacea	L	Jung	N	6	P	Ms							D	F	16	28	E	W		IR			91	8	2		5.0	15.1	1063	160	6	7	8	2	0	0
Sphaerocarpos michelii	L	Sphae	AR	20	A	St							D	F	80	130	E					CI	91	46		5	4.1	16.3	665	100	8	6	5	5	0	0
Sphaerocarpos texanus	L	Sphae	AR	20	A	St							D	F	84	150	E					CI	91	28		5	4.4	16.3	712	95	8	6	5	5	0	0
Sphagnum affine	M	Sphag	N	150	P	Tf							D	R	24	28	E	W	S	IR	(NI)		42	52	3		2.2	12.7	2041	400	8	9	3	2	0	0
Sphagnum angustifolium	M	Sphag	N	200	P	Tf							D	X	22	24	E	W	S	IR	NI		46	78	14		2.5	13.5	1499	500	7	8	3	2	0	0
Sphagnum austinii	M	Sphag	N	150	P	Tuft	Tf						D	R	24	27	E	W	S	IR	NI		70	84	46		2.8	13.1	1417	520	8	8	1	1	0	0
Sphagnum balticum	M	Sphag	N	150	P	Tf							D	X	26	28	E	W	S				26	6			1.7	13.4	1032	650	8	9	1	1	0	0
Sphagnum capillifolium	M	Sphag	N	150	P	Tf	Tuft						D	O	24	27	E	W	S	IR	NI		56	1131	261		3.0	13.6	1387	1220	7	7	2	1	0	0
Sphagnum capillifolium subsp. capillifolium	M	Sphag	N	150	P	Tuft	Tf						M	F	24	27	E	W	S	IR			56	17	1		3.0	13.8	1497	270	7	7	2	1	0	0
Sphagnum capillifolium subsp. rubellum	M	Sphag	N	150	P	Tf	Tuft						D	R	24	27	E	W	S	IR	NI		56	121	2		3.8	14.9	1217	300	7	7	2	1	0	0
Sphagnum compactum	M	Sphag	N	100	P	Tf	Tuft						M	F	30	35	E	W	S	IR	NI		56	628	106		3.0	13.4	1466	1050	8	8	1	1	0	0
Sphagnum contortum	M	Sphag	N	150	P	Tf							D	X	24	27	E	W	S	IR	NI		46	223	26		3.0	13.4	1601	800	8	9	5	2	0	0
Sphagnum cuspidatum	M	Sphag	N	150	P	Tf	Ac						D	O	32	37	E	W	S	IR	NI		53	902	222		3.1	13.7	1361	1030	8	10	1	2	0	0
Sphagnum denticulatum	M	Sphag	N	200	P	Tf	Ac						D	O	30	33	E	W	S	IR	NI	CI	53	1153	200	3	3.2	13.9	1353	1220	7	9	2	2	0	1
Sphagnum denticulatum s.l.	M	Sphag	N	200	P	Tf	Ac						D	O	30	34	E	W	S	IR	NI	CI	53	1217	220	3	3.2	13.9	1340	1220	7	8	2	2	0	1
Sphagnum fallax	M	Sphag	N	200	P	Tf	Tuft						M	F	30	35	E	W	S	IR	NI		56	554	32		3.1	14.3	1306	1000	7	9	3	3	0	0
Sphagnum fimbriatum	M	Sphag	N	200	P	Tf							M	A	25	28	E	W	S	IR	NI		36	802	38		3.2	14.4	1154	700	6	8	3	3	0	2
Sphagnum flexuosum	M	Sphag	N	200	P	Tf							D	X	23	26	E	W	S	IR			53	129	5		3.3	14.6	1205	500	8	9	3	3	0	0
Sphagnum fuscum	M	Sphag	N	150	P	Tuft	Tf						D	R	24	27	E	W	S	IR	NI		26	201	49		2.0	12.5	1424	1000	8	7	1	1	0	0
Sphagnum girgensohnii	M	Sphag	N	200	P	Tf							D	R	22	25	E	W	S	IR	NI		26	426	12		2.1	12.8	1601	1100	6	8	3	2	0	0
Sphagnum imbricatum s.l.	M	Sphag	N	150	P	Tf	Tuft						D	R	24	28	E	W	S	IR	NI		42	204	81		2.8	12.9	1524	700	8	9	2	1	0	0
Sphagnum inundatum	M	Sphag	N	200	P	Tf							D	O	31	34	E	W	S	IR	NI		53	637	94		3.1	13.7	1426	930	7	9	3	2	0	0
Sphagnum lindbergii	M	Sphag	N	200	P	Tf							M	R	29	32	E		S				26	18			-0.8	10.4	1735	1150	8	9	2	2	0	0
Sphagnum magellanicum	M	Sphag	N	200	P	Tf	Tuft						D	R	26	30	E	W	S	IR	NI		46	420	125		2.9	13.4	1418	1030	8	8	1	1	0	0
Sphagnum majus	M	Sphag	N	250	P	Tf							D	R	27	38	E		S	IR			46	5			1.4	12.1	1786	345	8	10	2	2	0	0
Sphagnum molle	M	Sphag	N	100	P	Tf	Tuft						M	A	28	32	E	W	S	IR	NI		72	150	36		2.8	13.3	1614	820	8	8	2	1	0	0
Sphagnum obtusum	M	Sphag	N	200	P	Tf							D	X	23	27	(E)						26							10	6	9	3	3	0	0
Sphagnum palustre	M	Sphag	N	250	P	Tf	Tuft						D	O	26	32	E	W	S	IR	NI	CI	56	1342	199	1	3.1	13.9	1292	1000	7	8	3	2	0	0
Sphagnum palustre var. centrale	M	Sphag	N	250	P	Tf	Tuft						D	O	25	30	(E)	W					56	1			3.3	16.3	562	300	7	8	3	2	0	0
Sphagnum palustre var. palustre	M	Sphag	N	250	P	Tf	Tuft						D	O	26	32	E	W	S	IR	NI	CI	52	141	3		4.1	15.1	1161	350	7	8	3	2	0	0
Sphagnum papillosum	M	Sphag	N	200	P	Tf	Tuft						D	O	27	30	E	W	S	IR	NI		53	1025	247		3.1	13.6	1393	1050	8	8	1	1	0	0
Sphagnum platyphyllum	M	Sphag	N	150	P	Tf							D	X	32	35	(E)	W	S	IR	(NI)		46	42	4		2.8	13.0	1842	550	8	9	5	2	0	0
Sphagnum pulchrum	M	Sphag	N	150	P	Tf							D	X	27	30	E	W	S	IR	NI		52	30	16		3.8	14.4	1327	400	8	10	1	1	0	0
Sphagnum quinquefarium	M	Sphag	N	200	P	Tf							M	O	22	25	E	W	S	IR	NI		42	373	44		2.7	13.1	1730	760	5	6	2	2	0	0
Sphagnum recurvum s.l.	M	Sphag	N	200	P	Tf							D	O	27	30	E	W	S	IR	NI		56	1206	162		2.9	13.8	1325	1000	7	9	3	3	0	0
Sphagnum riparium	M	Sphag	N	250	P	Tf							D	R	25	27	E	W	S				46	20			1.0	12.3	1395	940	7	9	2	2	0	0
Sphagnum russowii	M	Sphag	N	200	P	Tf							D	R	24	27	E	W	S	IR	NI		26	279	14		2.0	13.1	1473	1200	6	7	2	2	0	0
Sphagnum skyense	M	Sphag	N	110	P	Tf							Nil	Nil				W	S				70	9			3.4	12.6	2128	350	6	8	3	2	0	0
Sphagnum squarrosum	M	Sphag	N	200	P	Tf							M	A	27	30	E	W	S	IR	NI		36	753	55		3.0	14.1	1246	1030	6	9	4	3	0	0
Sphagnum strictum	M	Sphag	N	150	P	Tf							M	F	28	30	(E)	W	S	IR	NI		70	131	22		2.7	12.4	1998	550	7	8	2	1	0	0
Sphagnum subnitens	M	Sphag	N	200	P	Tf	Tuft						M	A	26	30	E	W	S	IR	NI	CI	52	1195	254	1	3.2	13.8	1332	1050	7	8	3	2	0	0
Sphagnum subnitens var. ferrugineum	M	Sphag	N	200	P	Tf	Tuft						M	X	26	30	E	W	S	IR	NI		41	7			4.0	13.9	1329	200	7	8	3	2	0	0

Taxon name	RH	RS	RW	SR	SO	PT	GS	DW	DV	DA	BR	EN	EW	AQ	A2	B1	B2	B3	C1	C2	C3	D1	D2	D4	E1	E2	E3	E4	E7	F3	F4	F9	FA	G1	G1R	G3	G3R	H2	H3	H5	I1	I2	J1	J2	J3	J4
Sematophyllum demissum	3																																													
Sematophyllum micans	3																																													
Sematophyllum substrumulosum					3								3			3	3														3			3	3				2							
Southbya nigrella	3	3	3	3	3																																			3						
Southbya tophacea	3	3		3	3		3									3	3	3						3	3																				3	3	
Sphaerocarpos michelii					3	3																																	2	3	3	3				
Sphaerocarpos texanus					3																																			3	3	3		2		
Sphagnum affine					3	3	3														3																									
Sphagnum angustifolium					3	3	3														2	3	3										3													
Sphagnum austinii					3	3															3																									
Sphagnum balticum					3	3													3		3	3	3								1															
Sphagnum capillifolium					3	3	3												3		3	3	3				3				3			3				3								
Sphagnum capillifolium subsp. capillifolium					3	3	3														3	3	3								3			3												
Sphagnum capillifolium subsp. rubellum					3	3	3														3	3	3				3				3			3				3								
Sphagnum compactum					3	3															3	3	3				3				3			3												
Sphagnum contortum					3	2															3	3	2											2												
Sphagnum cuspidatum					2	3													3	3	3	3	3				3			2	2		2	3					3							
Sphagnum denticulatum	3				3	3													3	3	3	3	3				3			2	3		3	3	1				3	1				1		
Sphagnum denticulatum s.l.	3				3	3													3	3	3	3	3							2	3		3	3	1				3	1				1		
Sphagnum fallax	2				2	3														3	3	3	3				3			3	3		3	3	2				2					1		
Sphagnum fimbriatum					3	3														2	3	2	3				3			3	3		3	3	1									1		
Sphagnum flexuosum	2				2	3														2	2	3	3				3					3	3	3	1				3							
Sphagnum fuscum					2	2															3	3	3								1															
Sphagnum girgensohnii					3	3															3	3	3				3				3		3	3	2				3							
Sphagnum imbricatum s.l.					3	3															3	3	3																							
Sphagnum inundatum					3	3							3								3	3	3				3			2	2		3	3												
Sphagnum lindbergii				1	3	3																3	1					2			1															
Sphagnum magellanicum					3	3															3	3										3	3													
Sphagnum majus					3	3															3	3					3				3															
Sphagnum molle					3	3															3	3	3				3																			
Sphagnum obtusum					3	3															3	3					3				3															
Sphagnum palustre					3	3															3	3	3				3				1	3		3	3											
Sphagnum palustre var. centrale						3																										3														
Sphagnum palustre var. palustre					3	3															3	3	3				3				1	3		3	3											
Sphagnum papillosum	2				2	3														2	3	3	3				2				2		2					2								
Sphagnum platyphyllum	2				2	3															3	3	3								2		2													
Sphagnum pulchrum						3																3																								
Sphagnum quinquefarium	2				3	3															3	3	3				3				3			3			3									
Sphagnum recurvum s.l.	2				3	3															3	3	3				3				3			3	2				3							
Sphagnum riparium					3	3															3	3	3								3			3	2				3					1		
Sphagnum russowii					3	2															2	3	2								3	1		3	2											
Sphagnum skyense					3	3																3	3				3				3	3	3	3	1									1		
Sphagnum squarrosum					3	3															3	3	3				3				3	3		3												
Sphagnum strictum					3	3															3	3	3								3	3		3	2											
Sphagnum subnitens	3				3	3															3	2	3				3				3	3		3	2				3							
Sphagnum subnitens var. ferrugineum	3					3		3													3	2	3				3				3															

79

Taxon name	ML	Ord	Stat	Len	Per	LF1	LF2	Tub	Gem	Bul	Bra	Lvs	Sex	Fr	Sp1	Sp2	E	W	Sc	IR	NI	CI	Elem	GBno	IRno	CIno	TJan	TJul	Prec	Alt	L	F	R	N	S	HM
Sphagnum subnitens var. subnitens	M	Sphag	N	200	P	Tf	Tuft						M	A	26	30	E	W	S	IR	NI	Cl	52	305	11		3.3	14.1	1472	200	7	8	3	2	0	0
Sphagnum subsecundum	M	Sphag	N	150	P	Tf							D	R	27	29	E	W	S	IR	NI		46	69	5		2.8	13.7	1556	740	8	9	4	2	0	0
Sphagnum subsecundum s.l.	M	Sphag	N	200	P	Tf							D	O	27	34	E	W	S	IR	NI	Cl	56	1261	225	3	3.2	13.9	1332	1220	7	9	3	2	0	0
Sphagnum tenellum	M	Sphag	N	100	P	Tf							D	F	35	40	E	W	S	IR	NI		52	652	189	3	3.2	13.6	1428	1100	8	8	1	1	0	0
Sphagnum teres	M	Sphag	N	200	P	Tf							D	R	24	26	E	W	S	IR	NI		26	288	13		2.3	13.1	1542	1050	7	9	4	2	0	0
Sphagnum warnstorfii	M	Sphag	N	150	P	Tf							D	X	20	24	E	W	S	IR	NI		26	158	6		1.8	12.7	1671	950	7	8	4	2	0	0
Sphenolobopsis pearsonii	L	Jung	N	10	P	Ms							D	Nil			E	W	S	IR	NI		42	76	15		2.6	12.7	2154	980	5	6	3	1	0	0
Splachnum ampullaceum	M	Spla	N	30	A	Tuft							M	A	7	10	E	W	S	IR	NI		46	173	53		3.0	13.4	1530	915	8	8	4	6	0	0
Splachnum sphaericum	M	Spla	N	20	A	Tuft							D	A	8	12	E	W	S	IR	NI		26	260	47		2.0	12.5	1725	1220	8	8	2	6	0	0
Splachnum vasculosum	M	Spla	N	70	A	Tuft							D	F	8	10	E		S	IR	NI		16	23			0.2	11.6	1670	930	7	9	5	6	0	0
Stegonia latifolia	M	Pott	N	2	P	Ts							M	A	34	40	E		S				16	6			-1.1	10.9	1246	550	7	5	7	2	0	0
Syntrichia amplexa	M	Pott	AN	6	A	Ts		F					D	X	8	12	E						72	3			3.4	15.9	727	110	7	5	6	4	0	0
Syntrichia intermedia	M	Pott	N	40	P	Tuft	Tf						D	F	14	16	E	W	S	IR	NI	Cl	92	1068	51	6	3.7	15.5	918	625	8	1	8	4	0	0
Syntrichia laevipila	M	Pott	N	15	P	Tf						O	MD	O	14	20	E	W	S	IR	NI	Cl	92	866	54	7	3.8	15.4	962	350	6	4	6	5	0	0
Syntrichia latifolia	M	Pott	N	30	P	Tf		F					D	R	10	12	E	W	S	IR	NI	Cl	73	607	17		3.6	15.6	821	480	6	6	7	6	0	0
Syntrichia norvegica	M	Pott	N	35	P	Tuft	Tf						D	X	10	14	E		S				16	3			-1.2	10.5	1797	1050	8	4	7	2	0	0
Syntrichia papillosa	M	Pott	N	10	P	Tuft	Tf	F					D	X	16	22	E	W	S	IR	NI	Cl	73	291	25	3	3.8	15.3	914	180	4	4	6	5	0	0
Syntrichia princeps	M	Pott	N	40	P	Tf							M	F	12	14	E	W	S	IR	(NI)		73	18	1		2.2	13.3	1329	500	8	4	7	4	0	0
Syntrichia ruraliformis	M	Pott	N	50	P	Tf							D	R	8	14	E	W	S	IR	NI	Cl	83	461	46	8	4.2	15.0	955	250	8	3	7	3	1	0
Syntrichia ruralis	M	Pott	N	50	P	Tf	Tuft						D	O	10	12	E	W	S	IR	NI	Cl	66	1043	58	5	3.6	15.4	879	380	8	3	7	4	0	0
Syntrichia ruralis s.l.	M	Pott	N	50	P	Tf	Tuft						D	O	10	12	E	W	S	IR	NI	Cl	66	1206	94	9	3.7	15.2	922	380	8	3	7	4	0	0
Syntrichia virescens	M	Pott	N	30	P	Tf							D	R	8	12	E	W	S	IR	NI	Cl	73	137		9	3.3	15.9	659	150	6	4	6	6	0	0
Targionia hypophylla	L	Marc	NA	25	P	Mt							M(D)	F	54	76	E	W	S	(IR)	(NI)	Cl	91	44		6	4.1	15.0	1250	300	7	4	6	4	0	0
Taxiphyllum wissgrillii	M	Hypn	N	30	P	Ms							D	R	10	12	E	W	S	IR	NI		73	266	15		3.5	15.2	1011	380	2	5	7	4	0	0
Tayloria lingulata	M	Spla	N	50	P	Tuft							M	F	20	30	E		S				26	5			-0.6	11.2	1514	940	8	9	6	3	0	0
Tayloria tenuis	M	Spla	N	20	P	Tuft							M	F	12	12	E		S		(NI)		46	2			1.8	12.4	1063	600	8	9	6	3	0	0
Telaranea longii	L	Jung	AN	20	P	We	Ms						D	Nil			E						71	1			3.8	16.7	679	40	4	7	3	3	0	0
Telaranea murphyae	L	Jung	AN	20	P	We	Ms						D	Nil			E						71	3			6.8	16.4	880	22	4	6	3	2	0	0
Telaranea nematodes	L	Jung	N	15	P	Ms			O				M	F	13	18	E			IR			80	2			5.0	15.0	1250	180	3	5	7	2	0	0
Tetralophozia setiformis	L	Jung	N	40	P	We	Tf		X				D	X	13	15	E		S		NI		16	43	18		-0.3	11.2	1426	1280	2	6	6	3	0	0
Tetraphis pellucida	M	Tetr	N	15	P	Tf			F				M	O	10	12	E	W	S	IR	NI		56	1191	65		3.1	14.6	1176	700	3	6	3	3	0	0
Tetraplodon angustatus	M	Spla	N	60	A	Tuft							M	A	10	10	E	W	S	IR	NI		46	23	1		0.6	11.5	1714	915	7	8	2	6	0	0
Tetraplodon mnioides	M	Spla	N	60	A	Tuft							M	A	10	12	E	W	S	IR	NI		26	196	29		2.0	12.7	1727	1000	7	7	2	6	0	0
Tetrodontium brownianum	M	Tetr	N	2	P	Tp							M	A	14	16	E	W	S	IR	NI		72	183	15		2.5	13.4	1572	850	7	7	5	3	0	2
Tetrodontium repandum	M	Tetr	N	5	P	Tp					F		M	X	16	16	E						42	2			2.9	14.9	919	300	2	7	5	3	0	0
Thamnobryum alopecurum	M	Hypn	N	80	P	De							D	O	10	12	E	W	S	IR	NI	Cl	73	1596	262	4	3.5	14.7	1128	715	3	6	7	6	0	0
Thamnobryum angustifolium	M	Hypn	N	40	P	Mr							D	Nil			E						71	1			2.4	14.4	1136	244	3	8	9	4	0	0
Thamnobryum cataractarum	M	Hypn	N	50	P	De							Nil	Nil			E			IR			71	1			1.5	13.2	1702	210	3	11	7	5	0	0
Thamnobryum maderense	M	Hypn	NA	80	P	De							D	X	10	15	E						80	1			3.0	15.4	749	100	3	9	6	6	0	0
Thuidium abietinum	M	Hypn	N	120	P	We	Mr						D	R	16	18	E	W	S	IR	NI	(Cl)	26	101	10		3.6	15.8	846	850	8	3	8	2	0	0
Thuidium abietinum subsp. abietinum	M	Hypn	N	120	P	We	Mr						D	R			E	W	S	IR	NI	(Cl)	26	53	6		3.5	15.5	869	850	8	3	8	2	0	0
Thuidium abietinum subsp. hystricosum	M	Hypn	N	120	P	We	Mr						D	X			E	(S)		IR	NI		25	56	5		3.7	16.1	819	230	3	8	8	2	0	0
Thuidium delicatulum	M	Hypn	N	122	P	We	Mr						D	O	16	20	E	W	S	IR	NI		76	420	66		3.0	13.3	1712	800	6	6	6	5	0	0
Thuidium philibertii	M	Hypn	N	100	P	We	Mr						D	X	12	16	E	W	S	IR	NI		76	226	29		3.4	14.5	1090	900	7	4	8	2	0	1
Thuidium recognitum	M	Hypn	N	90	P	We	Mr						D	R	11	16	E	W	S	IR	NI		76	34	9		2.2	13.0	1566	950	6	5	8	2	0	0
Thuidium tamariscinum	M	Hypn	N	140	P	We	Mr						D	O	12	20	E	W	S	IR	NI	Cl	73	2011	395	6	3.4	14.4	1160	880	5	6	5	4	0	1

Taxon name	RH	RS	RW	SR	SO	PT	GS	DW	DV	DA	BR	EN	EW	AQ	A2	B1	B2	B3	C1	C2	C3	D1	D2	D4	E1	E2	E3	E4	E7	F3	F4	F9	FA	G1	G1R	G3	G3R	H2	H3	H5	I1	I2	J1	J2	J3	J4
Sphagnum subnitens var. *subnitens*	3																					2	3		3	3				3	3	3		3		2			3							3
Sphagnum subsecundum																						3	3		3	2				2	2								2							3
Sphagnum subsecundum s.l.					3																	3	3		3	3				3	3								2							3
Sphagnum tenellum					3	3																	3							3	3															
Sphagnum teres					3	2																									3	2														
Sphagnum warnstorfii	3			3	3							1											3							3	3		2	2					3						3	3
Sphenolobopsis pearsonii			3																																											
Splachnum ampullaceum										3												3	3								3					3			3							3
Splachnum sphaericum										3												3	3								3					3										3
Splachnum vasculosum										3												3																	3							
Stegonia latifolia				3	3																																									3
Syntrichia amplexa	3	3	3	1	1	3								2																2									3	1			3	3		3
Syntrichia intermedia	2	2			1									3		1														3	3		3	3				1	1		2		2			3
Syntrichia laevipila	3	3	3						2					3						3									1			1						2	2		2		3			3
Syntrichia latifolia	3	3					2							3						3																			3							
Syntrichia norvegica	3	3	3	3										3																3		3	3						3		3		3			2
Syntrichia papillosa	2	2			2									3		1																3	2													
Syntrichia princeps	3	1	3	3										1		1	3																			3			3		3		3			3
Syntrichia ruraliformis	2	3	2	2	3			3						1	3															2							2	3	3		3		3			3
Syntrichia ruralis	3	3	3	3	3			3						2	3															2	2		2				3	3	3		3		3	3	3	3
Syntrichia ruralis s.l.	3	3	3	3	3			1						3																3		3	3						3	1	3	1		3	3	3
Syntrichia virescens		3		3										3		2														3		3					3					3				3
Targionia hypophylla	3	3			3	3								3								3											1	3												
Taxiphyllum wissgrillii					3	3								3																			3													
Tayloria lingulata					3			3															3								3																
Tayloria tenuis					3																										3								3							
Telaranea longii	2				3	3	3			3				3																												3					
Telaranea murphyae	2				3	3	3		3					3																3	3		3		3						3					
Telaranea nematodes	2				3	2	2		2						2											2					3		3				2				3					
Tetralophozia setiformis	3				1	2	3							1						3													3		3			3		3						
Tetraphis pellucida	3				3	3	3							2																	3	3	3		3		3			3							
Tetraplodon angustatus										3												3	3				3			3	3	3														
Tetraplodon mnioides										3												3	3				3				3								3						3	
Tetrodontium brownianum		3										3																					3						3							
Tetrodontium repandum		3										1				1																							3							
Thamnobryum alopecurum	3	3			3	3	3	1						3				3			3					2				3	3	3		3		2			3				3			2
Thamnobryum angustifolium	3				3	3														3																										
Thamnobryum cataractarum	3				3	3														1																										
Thamnobryum maderense	3													1						3																			3	3							
Thuidium abietinum					3	3	3									3									3			1		3	3		3									1				2
Thuidium abietinum subsp. *abietinum*	3				3	3										3									3			1		3	3		2									1				2
Thuidium abietinum subsp. *hystricosum*	3				3	3										1									3					3	3		3													2
Thuidium delicatulum	3				3	3	3							1		3							3		3	3				3	3	3		3					3							3
Thuidium philibertii	3				3	1										1							2		3	2	3			3	3	2		2					3							2
Thuidium recognitum	3				3	3	1							1		1							3		3	3	3			3	3	3		3					3						3	2
Thuidium tamariscinum	3	3			3	3	3	2						3		3				3			3		3	3	3	3		3	3	3	3	3		2			3				3		3	2

Taxon name	ML	Ord	Stat	Len	Per	LF1	LF2	Tub	Gem	Bul	Bra	Lvs	Sex	Fr	Sp1	Sp2	E	W	Sc	IR	NI	CI	Elem	GBno	Rno	Clno	TJan	TJul	Prec	Alt	L	F	R	N	S	HM
Timmia austriaca	M	Timm	N	90	P	Tf							D	X	14	17			S	IR			26	3	1		-0.3	11.2	1519	915	7	5	7	2	0	0
Timmia megapolitana	M	Timm	N	40	P	Tf							M	O			E						76	1			3.7	16.2	603	0	5	9	7	6	0	0
Timmia norvegica	M	Timm	N	80	P	Tuft	Ts						D	X	17	20			S	IR			26	11	2		0.5	11.6	2165	1200	7	5	7	2	0	0
Tomentypnum nitens	M	Hypn	N	150	P	Tf							D	R	16	20	E	W	S	IR	NI		26	51	11		2.1	13.4	1199	840	7	9	7	2	0	0
Tortella bambergeri	M	Pott	N	20	P	Tuft	Cu						D	R	11	12	E	W	S	IR			73	23	2		1.9	13.2	1646	940	7	4	7	2	0	0
Tortella densa	M	Pott	N	40	P	Tuft							D	Nil			E	W	S	IR	NI		72	24	10		2.8	13.4	1504	580	7	4	9	2	0	2
Tortella flavovirens	M	Pott	N	15	P	Tuft	Tf						D	R	12	14	E	W	S	IR	NI	CI	92	279	44	10	4.7	14.8	1089	130	9	5	7	4	4	0
Tortella fragilis	M	Pott	N	25	P	Tuft						F	D	X	11	14	E		S		NI		26	9	1		2.9	12.9	1091	1060	8	6	8	2	0	0
Tortella inclinata	M	Pott	N	10	P	Tuft	Tf					O	D	R	10	16	E	W	S	IR	NI		76	33	4		3.9	14.8	988	500	8	3	9	4	0	0
Tortella inflexa	M	Pott	N	6	P	Tp						F	D	R	8	10	E				NI		91	84			3.8	16.2	791	250	2	5	9	4	0	0
Tortella limosella	M	Pott	N	8	P	Tuft							Nil	Nil					(S)				51							5	9	5	7	4	0	0
Tortella nitida	M	Pott	N	10	P	Cu	Tuft					F	D	X	10	16	E	W	S	IR	NI	CI	91	172	38	1	4.7	15.2	1209	360	8	2	9	2	0	0
Tortella tortuosa	M	Pott	N	40	P	Tuft	Cu					O	D	R	10	16	E	W	S	IR	NI	CI	56	881	221	1	3.1	13.7	1378	1205	7	4	7	2	0	1
Tortula acaulon	M	Pott	N	5	AP	Ts	Tf						M	A	25	40	E	W	S	IR	NI	CI	86	1222	81	9	3.8	15.6	816	300	8	5	7	6	0	0
Tortula acaulon var. acaulon	M	Pott	N	4.5	AP	Ts	Tf						M	A	25	40	E	W	S	IR	NI	CI	86	403	10		3.8	15.8	772	185	8	5	7	6	0	0
Tortula acaulon var. papillosa	M	Pott	N	6	A	Ts	Tf						D	A			E	(W)			NI		82	22	1		5.7	15.8	996	30	8	5	7	6	0	0
Tortula acaulon var. pilifera	M	Pott	N	4.5	PA	Ts	Tf						M	A	24	26	E	W	S			CI	83	54		1	4.6	15.9	783	45	9	4	7	5	1	0
Tortula acaulon var. schreberiana	M	Pott	N	9	A	Ts	Tf						M	A			E						86	27			3.5	16.1	626	97	8	5	7	6	0	0
Tortula atrovirens	M	Pott	N	4	P	Tf							M	A	24	26	E	W	S	IR	(NI)	CI	86	73	5		5.6	15.5	949	30	8	5	6	4	4	0
Tortula canescens	M	Pott	N	5	P	Tf							M	A	14	16	E	W	S			(CI)	91	18		6	5.8	15.6	1130	270	7	4	6	3	0	0
Tortula cernua	M	Pott	N	7	P	Tf							M	A	36	40	E						46	5			3.5	15.8	691	55	7	5	8	6	0	0
Tortula cuneifolia	M	Pott	N	5	P	Tf							M	A	14	18	E	W		IR	(NI)	CI	91	13	3	2	5.6	15.9	999	225	7	5	5	4	0	0
Tortula freibergii	M	Pott	NA	2	P	Tf							MD	A	8	12	E						82	16			3.8	15.4	816	30	5	3	7	5	0	0
Tortula lanceola	M	Pott	N	5	P	Tf		X					M	A	21	30	E	W	S	IR			86	229	4		3.7	15.7	774	550	8	3	8	3	0	0
Tortula leucostoma	M	Pott	N	3	P	Tf							M	A	20	26	E		S				16	2			-1.2	10.7	1280	550	7	5	8	2	0	0
Tortula marginata	M	Pott	N	3	P	Tf							D	A	8	8	E	W	S	IR	NI	CI	91	308	9		3.8	16.1	757	210	3	4	8	5	0	0
Tortula modica	M	Pott	N	11	PA	Tf	Tf	X					M	A	27	34	E	W	S	IR	(NI)	CI	76	339	11	5	3.9	15.8	827	290	8	5	6	6	2	0
Tortula muralis	M	Pott	N	10	P	Tf	Tuft						M	A	7	12	E	W	S	IR	NI	CI	86	2101	354	3	1.9	13.1	1052	950	6	2	8	5	0	0
Tortula protobryoides	M	Pott	N	5	P	Ts	Tf	X					M	A	25	32	E	W	S	(IR)	(NI)		73	177			3.3	15.1	936	365	7	4	7	3	0	0
Tortula solmsii	M	Pott	N	2.5	P	Tf							D	O	10	15	E		S				91	5			6.7	15.9	1020	85	3	5	8	4	0	1
Tortula subulata	M	Pott	N	10	P	Tuft							M	A	10	28	E	W	S	IR	NI	CI	84	732	26	8	3.0	14.6	1023	700	5	4	8	5	0	0
Tortula subulata var. angustata	M	Pott	N	10	P	Tuft	Tuft						M	A	10	12	E	(W)	S	IR	(NI)		84	16			3.4	15.2	751	300	5	4	7	3	0	0
Tortula subulata var. graeffii	M	Pott	N	10	P	Tuft							M	A	14	20	E	W	S	IR	NI		83	55	2		1.9	13.1	1437	700	5	4	7	3	0	0
Tortula subulata var. subulata	M	Pott	N	10	P	Tuft							M	A	10	20	E	W	S	IR	NI		84	187	2		2.7	12.6	2061	900	5	4	7	3	0	0
Tortula truncata	M	Pott	N	10	AP	Tf	Ts	O					M	A	24	36	E	W	S	IR	NI	CI	76	1508	169	8	3.7	15.1	951	360	8	5	6	6	0	1
Tortula vahliana	M	Pott	N	5	P	Tf							M	O	12	16	E			(IR)			91	15			3.9	16.4	651	61	2	4	9	5	0	0
Tortula viridifolia	M	Pott	N	5	P	Tf							M	A	25	35	E	W	S	IR	NI	CI	91	117	7	8	5.4	15.3	998	30	8	5	6	4	0	0
Tortula wilsonii	M	Pott	N	5	P	Tf							M	A	19	27	E	W		IR		CI	91	23	1	1	5.9	15.9	982	160	8	5	6	4	3	0
Trematodon ambiguus	M	Dicr	N	10	P	Tuft							M	A	30	36	E		(S)				43							350	7	7	4	4	0	0
Trichocolea tomentella	L	Lepi	N	100	P	We							D	R	14	18	E	W	S	IR	NI		73	381	40		3.3	13.9	1517	700	5	9	5	4	0	0
Trichostomum brachydontium	M	Pott	N	40	P	Tf	Tuft						D	R	14	18	E	W	S	IR	NI	CI	92	918	135	10	3.7	14.0	1337	700	8	5	7	3	2	2
Trichostomum crispulum	M	Pott	N	40	P	Tf							D	R	16	18	E	W	S	IR	NI	CI	86	723	136	1	3.7	14.4	1235	1175	7	4	8	3	0	1
Trichostomum hibernicum	M	Pott	N	45	P	Tuft							D	R			E		S	IR			70	47	14		2.7	12.6	2061	900	7	4	8	5	2	0
Trichostomum tenuirostre	M	Pott	N	45	AP	Tf	Ts	X					D	R	16	18	E	W	S	IR	NI	CI	56	493	78		3.0	13.4	1669	820	4	7	3	2	0	1
Tritomaria exsecta	L	Jung	N	20	P	Ms			F				D	X	9	12	E	W	S	IR			46	89	9		2.7	12.9	2155	380	5	3	2	2	0	0
Tritomaria exsectiformis	L	Jung	N	20	P	Ms			F				D	X	9	12	E	W	S	IR	NI		56	285	57		2.8	13.4	1499	640	5	5	2	2	0	0

Taxon name	RH	RS	RW	SR	SO	PT	GS	DW	DV	DA	BR	EN	EW	AQ	A2	B1	B2	B3	C1	C2	C3	D1	D2	D4	E1	E2	E3	E4	E7	F3	F4	F9	FA	G1	G1R	G3	G3R	H2	H3	H5	I1	I2	J1	J2	J3	J4
Timmia austriaca					3																																		3							
Timmia megapolitana																																3							3							
Timmia norvegica	3				3	3																																	3							
Tomentypnum nitens																							3	3															3							
Tortella bambergeri	3																																						3							2
Tortella densa	3	3		2	2											3	3	3									3												3							
Tortella flavovirens	3	3	2	3	3			1							1	3	3	3																					3	2				2		
Tortella fragilis	3				3		3									3																							3							
Tortella inclinata	1			3	3		3									3																							3							
Tortella inflexa		3																									3			3			3							2						
Tortella limosella	3						3									3																							3							
Tortella nitida	3	3	3	3													3	3					3											3										3		
Tortella tortuosa	3	3	3	2	3		3									3	3	3	2				3											3	2			3	3	3	3			2		
Tortula acaulon				3	3		3										3	3	2				3												2			3	3	3	3	3		3	3	
Tortula acaulon var. acaulon			3	3	3		3										3	3					3																3	3	3	3		3		
Tortula acaulon var. papillosa					3		3									3	3	3					3																	3	3			3		
Tortula acaulon var. pilifera					3		3										3	3					3																	3		3				
Tortula acaulon var. schreberiana					3												3																								3					
Tortula atrovirens		3	3	3	3		3										3	3					3																3					3		
Tortula canescens		3	3	3	3		3										3	3																										3		
Tortula cernua					3												3																											3		
Tortula cuneifolia		3	3	3	3		3						2				3	3															1							3				3		
Tortula freibergii		3	3	3	3												3	3																					3	2	2			3		
Tortula lanceola			3	3	3		2										3	3					3																3	1						
Tortula leucostoma	3	3	3																																											
Tortula marginata	3	3	3	3	3		3								2		2	3							2								2	2	2				3	3	2	2	3	3		
Tortula modica		3	3	3	3		3			1							3	3																					3	3	3	3	3	3		
Tortula muralis	3	3	2	2	2		2						2				3	3							3					2			2	2	2				3	3	3	2	3	3		
Tortula protobryoides			3	3	3		3										3	3															3						3	3			3	3		
Tortula solmsii		3	3	3	3												3	3																						3	3			3		
Tortula subulata	3	3	3	3	3		3						3		2	2	3	3							3					1			3	3					3	3	3	3	3	3		2
Tortula subulata var. angustata					3		3										3													1			3	3						3						
Tortula subulata var. graeffii			3	3	3		3										3																													
Tortula subulata var. subulata	3	3	3	3	3								3		2	2	3	3							3								3	3					3	3	3	3	3	3		2
Tortula truncata	1	2	2	2	3		3				3					3	3		2						3		3							2	2		2		3	3	3	3	3	3		2
Tortula vahliana				3	3										1		3								3								3						3				1			
Tortula viridifolia			3	3	3								2				3																						3		3					
Tortula wilsonii				3	3																																		3							
Trematodon ambiguus	3				3												3				3		3																3							
Trichocolea tomentella	3	2	3	3	3		3		1					1	1	3	3	3							3							3	3	3	1				3	2			3	3	3
Trichostomum brachydontium	3	3	3	3	3		3								3	3	3								3							3	3						3				3	3	3
Trichostomum crispulum	3	3	3	3	3		2										1			3															1				3				3	3		3
Trichostomum hibernicum	3																		2			2											2						3					1		
Trichostomum tenuirostre	2	2		3	2	2	3				1	1			1		3		2			1			3								3	3					3							
Tritomaria exsecta	3	3		3	3		3				3	2					3					2											3	3					3	3				3	3	
Tritomaria exsectiformis	3	3		3	3		3				3	2					3								3		3			3									3	3				3		3

Taxon name	ML	Ord	Stat	Len	Per	LF1	LF2	Tub	Gem	Bul	Bra	Lvs	Sex	Fr	Sp1	Sp2	E	W	Sc	IR	NI	Cl	Elem	GBno	IRno	Cino	TJan	TJul	Prec	Alt	L	F	R	N	S	HM
Tritomaria polita	L	Jung	N	40	P	Ms	We		X				D	R	14	19			S				16	29			-0.1	11.2	2172	1070	6	8	4	2	0	0
Tritomaria quinquedentata	L	Jung	N	50	P	Ms	We		R				D	O	12	21			S				26	561	64		2.4	12.9	1613	1205	5	6	4	2	0	0
Ulota bruchii	M	Orth	N	20	P	Cu							M	A	20	26	E	W	S	IR	NI	Cl	73	1069	138	1	3.4	14.5	1197	450	5	5	5	4	0	0
Ulota calvescens	M	Orth	N	15	P	Cu							M	A	22	26	E	W	S	IR	NI		81	76	29		3.4	13.1	1887	430	6	5	5	3	0	0
Ulota coarctata	M	Orth	N	10	P	Cu							M	A	18	24	E	(W)	S	IR			42	20	1		2.2	13.0	1962	245	5	5	5	3	0	0
Ulota crispa	M	Orth	N	20	P	Cu							M	A	20	26	E	W	S	IR	NI	Cl	73	1130	225	4	3.5	14.4	1226	480	6	4	5	3	0	0
Ulota crispa s.l.	M	Orth	N	20	P	Cu							M	A	20	26	E	W	S	IR	NI	Cl	73	1506	273	4	3.4	14.5	1176	480	6	4	5	3	0	0
Ulota drummondii	M	Orth	N	10	P	Tuft							M	A	18	24	E	W	S	IR	NI	Cl	42	198	13	4	2.2	12.6	1656	620	5	5	4	3	0	0
Ulota hutchinsiae	M	Orth	N	20	P	Cu							M	A	16	18	E	W	S	IR	(NI)		42	157	46		3.1	12.7	1915	600	7	3	3	2	0	0
Ulota phyllantha	M	Orth	N	25	P	Cu		F					D	R			E	W	S	IR	NI	Cl	51	994	302	6	3.8	14.3	1232	420	6	5	5	4	3	0
Warnstorfia exannulata	M	Hypn	N	168	P	We	Mr						D	R	16	20	E	W	S	IR	NI		56	603	48		3.0	13.7	1407	1335	8	9	4	2	0	0
Warnstorfia fluitans	M	Hypn	N	128	P	Ms	Ac						M	O	16	24	E	W	S	IR	NI		56	602	26		3.1	14.2	1165	870	7	10	2	2	0	0
Weissia brachycarpa	M	Pott	N	10	PA	Tf							M	A	20	34	E	W	S	IR	NI	Cl	86	507	27	2	3.7	15.1	1010	580	4	4	6	3	0	0
Weissia brachycarpa var. brachycarpa	M	Pott	N	10	AP	Tf							M	A	24	34	E	W	S	IR	NI		86	70	1		4.0	15.6	901	170	7	5	5	4	0	0
Weissia brachycarpa var. obliqua	M	Pott	N	10	PA	Tf							M	A	20	28	E	W	S	IR	NI	Cl	86	204	5		4.2	15.5	991	580	8	3	7	2	0	0
Weissia condensa	M	Pott	N	15	P	Tf							M	F	14	24	E		(S)				92	19	1		4.2	16.1	854	75	8	2	9	2	0	0
Weissia controversa	M	Pott	N	10	P	Tf							M	A	16	20	E	W	S	IR	NI	Cl	66	1215	186	8	3.6	14.7	1117	580	7	4	6	3	0	3
Weissia controversa var. controversa	M	Pott	N	10	P	Tf							M	A			E	W	S	IR	NI	Cl	66	337	7		4.1	15.4	1059	550	7	4	6	3	0	3
Weissia controversa var. crispata	M	Pott	N	10	P	Tf							M	A			E	W	S				83	25			4.5	15.6	935	250	7	2	7	2	0	0
Weissia controversa var. densifolia	M	Pott	N	40	P	Tf	Tuft						M	A			E	W	(S)	IR	NI		83	70	6		4.5	14.8	1284	580	6	4	6	2	0	4
Weissia controversa var. wimmeriana	M	Pott	N	7	P	Tf							M	A	17	20	E	W	S				43	1			-1.3	10.7	1304	530	6	5	6	2	0	0
Weissia levieri	M	Pott	N	10	P	Tf							M	A	18	22	E	W					91	4			5.3	16.2	990	50	8	2	9	1	0	0
Weissia longifolia	M	Pott	N	10	PA	Tf	Ts						M	A	17	23	E	W	S	IR	(NI)		73	338	5	2	3.9	16.1	767	280	7	4	6	3	0	0
Weissia longifolia var. angustifolia	M	Pott	N	10	PA	Tf	Ts						M	A			E	W	S	IR	(NI)		73	177	3		3.9	16.0	774	280	7	3	7	2	0	0
Weissia longifolia var. longifolia	M	Pott	N	10	AP	Tf	Ts						M	A			E	W	S	IR	NI	(Cl)	73	140			3.8	16.1	717	580	7	5	5	4	0	0
Weissia mittenii	M	Pott	N	15	PA	Tf							M	A	18	20	(E)						71	130						130	7	6	5	4	0	0
Weissia multicapsularis	M	Pott	N	15	P	Tf							M	O	16	21	E	W					71	13	12	2	5.9	15.9	1032	110	7	6	6	3	0	0
Weissia perssonii	M	Pott	N	10	P	Tf							M	A	18	20	E	W	S	IR	NI		71	89	5		4.9	14.5	1320	300	8	2	8	2	0	0
Weissia rostellata	M	Pott	N	5	AP	Tf							M	A	22	27	E	W	S	IR	NI		73	31	5		3.7	15.1	998	245	6	4	6	5	0	0
Weissia rutilans	M	Pott	N	10	AP	Tf							M	A	22	28	E	W	S	IR	NI		73	128	4		4.2	15.2	1091	450	6	4	6	5	0	0
Weissia squarrosa	M	Pott	NA	10	PA	Tf							M	F	22	28	E	W	(S)				72	24			3.7	16.2	750	160	8	5	5	4	0	0
Weissia sterilis	M	Pott	N	15	P	Tf							M	A	18	20	E	W					71	36			3.7	16.2	761	180	8	2	8	2	0	0
Zygodon conoideus	M	Orth	N	5	P	Tuft	Tf	F					D	F	18	20	E	W	S	IR	NI	Cl	71	609	50	2	3.8	15.0	1175	350	6	4	6	5	0	0
Zygodon conoideus var. conoideus	M	Orth	N	5	P	Tuft	Tf	F					D	F	18	20	E	W	S	IR	NI		71	49			5.9	15.7	1155	350	6	4	6	5	0	0
Zygodon conoideus var. lingulatus	M	Orth	N	5	P	Tuft		F					Nil	Nil			E						71	1			3.5	16.1	855	90	6	4	6	5	0	0
Zygodon forsteri	M	Orth	N	5	P	Cu							M	A	10	10	E						82	4			3.9	16.7	684	50	5	5	5	4	0	0
Zygodon gracilis	M	Orth	N	70	P	Tf							D	R	12	14	E						73	3			1.3	13.0	1613	458	6	5	9	2	0	0
Zygodon rupestris	M	Orth	N	15	P	Tf		F					D	O			E	W	S	IR	NI		86	282	13		3.4	14.6	1324	500	6	4	6	4	0	0
Zygodon viridissimus	M	Orth	N	10	P	Tf	Tuft	F					D	O	14	16	E	W	S	IR	NI	Cl	73	1509	198	9	3.6	14.9	1051	560	6	4	6	5	0	0
Zygodon viridissimus var. stirtonii	M	Orth	N	10	P	Tuft	Tf	F					D	R			E	W	S	IR	NI	Cl	72	285	33	1	4.0	14.7	1095	560	6	4	6	5	0	0
Zygodon viridissimus var. viridissimus	M	Orth	N	10	P	Tf	Tuft	F					D	O	14	16	E	W	S	IR	NI	Cl	73	1319	169	9	3.7	15.0	1047	400	6	4	6	5	0	0

Taxon name	RH	RS	RW	SR	SO	PT	GS	DW	DV	DA	BR	EN	EW	AQ	A2	B1	B2	B3	C1	C2	C3	D1	D2	D4	E1	E2	E3	E4	E7	F3	F4	F9	FA	G1	G1R	G3	G3R	H2	H3	H5	I1	I2	J1	J2	J3	J4
Tritomaria polita		3																						3															3							
Tritomaria quinquedentata	3	3		3		3	1	2		2												2	3					3		3								3	3					3		
Ulota bruchii	1												2			1															3	3		2				1	1			1				1
Ulota calvescens													3																	3	1	3		3												
Ulota coarctata													3																	3				2												
Ulota crispa	1												3																	3		3		3		2		1	1							
Ulota crispa s.l.	1		1										3																	3	1	3		3		2		1	1				1			
Ulota drummondii													3																	3				3												
Ulota hutchinsiae	3												1																									3								
Ulota phyllantha	3		3										3					3			2	3		3			3			3		3		3		2			3	1	1			2		
Warnstorfia exannulata	1				3	3														3		3	3							3	3															1
Warnstorfia fluitans					3	3													3	1		3	3							3	3															
Weissia brachycarpa			3	3	3													3			2				3						1				2				3	2	3				2	
Weissia brachycarpa var. brachycarpa																					3														3				2	3	3				3	
Weissia brachycarpa var. obliqua			3	3														3							3						1				2				3	2	3				2	
Weissia condensa			3	3																					3													3	3							
Weissia controversa	2		2	3	3		2	1								2		3			2				3								3	2	3			3	3	3	1			3	3	
Weissia controversa var. controversa			1	3	3		2	1								2		3							3								3	2	3			3	3	3	1			3	3	
Weissia controversa var. crispata				3	3													3							3													3						3	3	
Weissia controversa var. densifolia	3		3	3	3		3	1													3				3														3					3	3	
Weissia controversa var. wimmeriana			3	3																					3													3								
Weissia levieri				3	3													3							3														3	3	3	3		3	3	
Weissia longifolia					3																				3														3	3	3			3	3	
Weissia longifolia var. angustifolia					3																				3														3	3				3	3	
Weissia longifolia var. longifolia					3																				3															3		3				
Weissia mittenii					3																												3							3	3					
Weissia multicapsularis			3	3														3															3	3					3					3	3	
Weissia perssonii	3		3	3														3																												
Weissia rostellata					3		3																			2								2						2						
Weissia rutilans					3		3																			3								2					3	3	3					1
Weissia squarrosa					3																													2					3	3	3					
Weissia sterilis					3																				3															2	2					
Zygodon conoideus			1	1									3					1									3	3		3	3		3	3		1						2				
Zygodon conoideus var. conoideus			1										3					1									3	3		3	3		3	3		1						2				
Zygodon conoideus var. lingulatus													3																				3	3												
Zygodon forsteri													3																				3													
Zygodon gracilis	3												3																									3	1					3	3	
Zygodon rupestris	2												3																										1							
Zygodon viridissimus	3		3										3					2									3	3		3		3		3					3	3					3	3	
Zygodon viridissimus var. stirtonii	3		2	1									1														1			1		3		3					3	3					2	2	
Zygodon viridissimus var. viridissimus	3		3	1				2					3					3									3	3		3		3		3					3	3					3	3	

85

Acknowledgements

We are grateful to several bryologists who helped to us to compile the data in this book. Jean Paton kindly gave us permission to extract data from *The Liverwort Flora of the British Isles*, which has been our main source for data on liverworts and which proved a joy to use because of the orderly and consistent way in which data are presented for each species. Other published works are acknowledged in the text but none has been used to the same extent as *The Liverwort Flora*. Jean Paton also commented on the draft altitude list for liverworts, and supplied a number of new maxima. David Holyoak very generously allowed us to use a copy of his unpublished, draft accounts of Cornish bryophytes, which will eventually provide the basis for a new bryophyte flora of that county. In compiling the altitude data we were fortunately able to draw upon Gordon Rothero's unrivalled knowledge of the Scottish mountains; we also incorporated information provided earlier for the *Atlas of Bryophytes* by Martin Corley and David Long. At Monks Wood, Marjorie King did much of the initial extraction of morphological data into spreadsheets. The Ellenberg values for bryophytes were developed under a project on Nitrogen Impacts on Biodiversity funded by Defra. For this, we relied on quadrat data in electronic form, and are grateful to Richard Alexander (Natural England), John Birks (Bergen), Dave Horsefield (Scottish Natural Heritage) and Ian Strachan (Joint Nature Conservation Committee). Dr Henk Siebel supplied Dutch indicator values for comparison. We thank Simon Smart for his encouragement for this part of the project and for supplying the Key Habitats dataset. We also thank Ron Porley for help in tracing sources of information on the bryophytes of sites rich in heavy metals.

Three of us work at the Biological Records Centre where the compilation of *BRYOATT* forms part of an agreed programme of work financed by the Centre for Ecology and Hydrology and the Joint Nature Conservation Committee; the Countryside Council for Wales also agreed to allow Sam Bosanquet to spend some of his working hours on this project. Finally, this compilation would have been impossible without the recording activities of members of the British Bryological Society, whose contributions to the recording schemes and publications run by the Society form the basis of much of the data summarized here.

Bibliography

Barrow, E.M., Hulme, M. & Jiang, T. (1993) *A 1961-90 baseline climatology and future climate change scenarios for Great Britain and Europe. Part I: 1961-90 Great Britain baseline climatology*. Climatic Research Unit, Norwich.

Bates, J.W. (1995) A bryophyte flora of Berkshire. *Journal of Bryology*, **18**, 503-620.

Bates, J.W. (1998) Is 'life-form' a useful concept in bryophyte ecology? *Oikos*, **82**, 223-227.

Blackstock, T.H., Rothero, G.P. & Hill, M.O. (2005) *Census catalogue of British and Irish bryophytes updated 2005*. BBS web publication http://www.britishbryologicalsociety.org.uk/

Blockeel, T.L. (1998) *Cinclidotus riparius* re-instated as a British and Irish moss. *Journal of Bryology*, **20**, 109-119.

Blockeel, T.L. & Long, D.G. (1998) *A check-list and census catalogue of British and Irish bryophytes*. British Bryological Society, Cardiff.

Bosanquet, S.D.S. (2006) *Tortella bambergeri* (Schimp.) Broth. in the British Isles. *Journal of Bryology*, **28**, 5-10.

Bosanquet, S.D.S., Graham, J.J. & Motley, G.S. (2005) *The mosses and liverworts of Carmarthenshire*. Privately published.

Braithwaite, M.E., Ellis, R.W. & Preston, C.D. (2006) *Change in the British flora 1987-2004*. Botanical Society of the British Isles, London.

Cortini Pedrotti, C. (2001) *Flora dei muschi d'Italia. Sphagnopsida - Andreaeopsida - Bryopsida (I parte)*. Antonio Delfino Editore, Roma.

Cortini Pedrotti, C. (2006 [2005]) *Flora dei muschi d'Italia. Bryopsida (II parte)*. Antonio Delfino Editore, Roma.

Crum, H.A. & Anderson, L.E. (1981). *Mosses of eastern North America.* 2 vols. Columbia University Press, New York.

Crundwell, A.C. (1976) *Ditrichum plumbicola*, a new species from lead-mine waste. *Journal of Bryology*, **9**, 167-169.

Crundwell, A.C. (1985) The introduced bryophytes of the British Isles [abstract of spoken paper]. *Bulletin of the British Bryological Society*, **45**, 8-9.

Damsholt, K. (2002) *Illustrated flora of Nordic liverworts and hornworts*. Nordic Bryological Society, Lund.

Davies, C.E., Moss, D. & Hill, M.O. (2004) *EUNIS habitat classification revised 2004. Report to European Environment Agency European Topic Centre on Nature Protection and Biodiversity*. EEA. http://eunis.eea.europa.eu/upload/ EUNIS_2004_report.pdf

Dierssen, K. (2001) *Distribution, ecological amplitude and phytosociological characterization of European bryophytes*. J. Cramer, Berlin & Stuttgart.

Düll, R. (1991). Zeigerwerte von Laub- und Lebermoosen. In *Zeigerwerte von Pflanzen in Mitteleuropa* (eds H. Ellenberg, H.E. Weber, R. Düll, V. Wirth, W. Werner & D. Paullißen), pp. 175-214. Erich Golze, Göttingen.

Ellenberg, H., Weber, H.E., Düll, R., Wirth, V., Werner, W. & Paulissen, D. (1991) Zeigerwerte von Pflanzen in Mitteleuropa. *Scripta Geobotanica*, **18**, 1-248.

Forrest, L.L., Davies, E.C., Long, D.G., Crandall-Stotler, B.J., Clark, A. & Hollingsworth, M.L. (2006) Unravelling the evolutionary history of the liverworts (Marchantiophyta): multiple taxa, genomes and analyses. *The Bryologist*, **109**, 303-334.

Frahm, J.-P. & Klaus, D. (2001) Bryophytes as indicators of recent climate fluctuations in Central Europe. *Lindbergia*, **26**, 97-104.

Goffinet, B. & Buck, W.R. (2004). Systematics of the bryophyta (mosses): from molecules to a revised classification. In *Molecular systematics of bryophytes* (eds B. Goffinet, V.C. Hollowell & R.E. Magill), pp. 205-239. Missouri Botanical Garden Press, St Louis.

Guerra, J., Cano, M.J. & Ros, R.M., eds. (2006) *Flora briofítica ibérica. Volumen 3. Pottiales: Pottiaceae, Encalyptales: Encalyptaceae*. Universidad de Murcia, Murcia.

Haines-Young, R.H., Barr, C.J., Black, H.I.J., Briggs, D.J., Bunce, R.G.H., Clarke, R.T., Cooper, A., Dawson, F.H., Firbank, L.G., Fuller, R.M., Furse, M.T., Gillespie, M.K., Hill, R., Hornung, M., Howard, D.C., McCann, T., Morecroft, M.D., Petit, S., Sier, A.R.J., Smart, S.M., Smith, G.M., Stott, A.P., Stuart, R.C. & Watkins, J.W. (2000) *Accounting for nature: assessing habitats in the UK countryside*. Department of the Environment, Transport and the Regions, London.

Hallingbäck, T., Lönell, N., Weibull, H., Hedenäs, L. & von Knorring, P. (2006) *Nationalnyckeln till Sveriges flora och fauna. Bladmossor: Sköldmossor - blåmossor. Bryophyta: Buxbaumia-Leucobryum*. ArtDatabanken, SLU, Uppsala.

Hill, M.O. (1988) A bryophyte flora of North Wales. *Journal of Bryology*, **15**, 377-491.

Hill, M.O., Mountford, J.O., Roy, D.B. & Bunce, R.G.H. (1999) *Ellenberg's indicator values for British plants. ECOFACT Volume 2 technical annex*. Institute of Terrestrial Ecology, Huntingdon.

Hill, M.O. & Preston, C.D. (1998) The geographical relationships of British and Irish bryophytes. *Journal of Bryology*, **20**, 127-226.

Hill, M.O., Preston, C.D. & Roy, D.B. (2004) *PLANTATT - attributes of British and Irish Plants: status, size, life history, geography and habitats*. Centre for Ecology and Hydrology, Huntingdon.

Hill, M.O., Preston, C.D. & Smith, A.J.E. (1991) *Atlas of the bryophytes of Britain and Ireland, Vol. 1. Liverworts (Hepaticae and Anthocerotae)*. Harley Books, Colchester.

Hill, M.O., Preston, C.D. & Smith, A.J.E. (1992) *Atlas of the bryophytes of Britain and Ireland, Vol. 2. Mosses (except Diplolepideae)*. Harley Books, Colchester.

Hill, M.O., Preston, C.D. & Smith, A.J.E. (1994) *Atlas of the bryophytes of Britain and Ireland, Vol. 3. Mosses (Diplolepideae)*. Harley Books, Colchester.

Hill, M.O., Roy, D.B., Mountford, J.O. & Bunce, R.G.H. (2000) Extending Ellenberg's indicator values to a new area: an algorithmic approach. *Journal of Applied Ecology*, **37**, 3-15.

Hill, M.O., Roy, D.B. & Preston, C.D. (2005). Appendix 11: Development of environmental indices (Ellenberg-style scores) for British bryophytes. In *Atmospheric nitrogen pollution impacts on biodiversity: Phase 1 - Model development and testing (CR0289). Final report to Department of the Environment, Food and Rural Affairs, Joint Nature Conservation Committee and English Nature* (eds S. Smart, C. Evans, E. Rowe, W. Wamelink, S. Wright, W.A. Scott, D. Roy, C. Preston, M. Hill, P. Rothery, J. Bullock, I. Moy, B. Emmett & L. Maskell). Defra, London.

Hulme, M. & Jenkins, G.J. (1998) *Climate change scenarios for the UK: scientific report*. Climatic Research Unit, Norwich.

Ignatov, M.S. & Ignatova, E.A. (2003) *Flora mkhov srednei chasti evropeiskoi Rossii. Tom. 1. Sphagnaceae - Hedwigiaceae (Moss flora of the Middle European Russia. Vol. 1. Sphagnaceae - Hedwigiaceae)*. KMK Scientific Press, Moscow.

Ignatov, M.S. & Ignatova, E.A. (2004) *Flora mkhov srednei chasti evropeiskoi Rossii. Tom. 2. Fontinalaceae - Amblystegiaceae (Moss flora of the Middle European Russia. Vol. 2. Fontinalaceae - Amblystegiaceae)*. KMK Scientific Press, Moscow.

Kürschner, H. (2002) Life strategies of Pannonian loess cliff bryophyte communities - Studies on the cryptogamic vegetation of loess cliffs, VIII. *Nova Hedwigia*, **75**, 307-318.

Kürschner, H. & Parolly, G. (1998) Lebensformen und Adaptionen zur Wasserleitung und Wasserspeicherung in epiphytischen Moosgesellschaften Nord-Prus (Amazonas-Tiefland, Cordillera Oriental, Cordillera Central). *Nova Hedwigia*, **67**, 349-379.

Kürschner, H., Tonguc, O. & Yayintas, A. (1998) Life strategies in epiphytic bryophyte communities of the southwest Anatolian *Liquidambar orientalis* forests. *Nova Hedwigia*, **66**, 435-450.

Long, D.G., Paton, J.A., Squirrell, J., Woodhead, M. & Hollingsworth, P.M. (2006) Morphological, ecological and genetic evidence for distinguishing *Anastrophyllum joergensenii* Schiffn. and *A. alpinum* Steph. (Jungermanniopsida: Lophoziaceae). *Journal of Bryology*, **28**, 108-117.

Mägdefrau, K. (1982). Life-forms of bryophytes. In *Bryophyte ecology* (ed A.J.E. Smith), pp. 45-58. Chapman & Hall, London.

Nyholm, E. (1986-1998) *Illustrated flora of Nordic mosses, 1-4*. Nordic Bryological Society, Lund.

Paton, J.A. (1969) A bryophyte flora of Cornwall. *Transactions of the British Bryological Society*, **5**, 669-756.

Paton, J.A. (1971) A bryophyte flora of the Isle of Man. *Proceedings of the Isle of Man Natural History and Antiquarian Society*, **7, suppl.**, 1-68.

Paton, J.A. (1999) *The liverwort flora of the British Isles*. Harley Books, Colchester.

Preston, C.D. (2004) An updated list of British and Irish bryophytes from which tubers have been reported. Field Bryology, **83**, 2-13.

Preston, C.D., Pearman, D.A. & Hall, A.R. (2004) Archaeophytes in Britain. *Botanical Journal of the Linnean Society*, **145**, 257-294.

Rodwell, J.S., ed. (2000) *British plant communities. Vol. 5. Maritime communities and vegetation of open habitats*. Cambridge University Press, Cambridge.

Rothero, G.P. (2002). Bryophytes. In *Flora of Assynt* (by P.A. Evans, I.M. Evans & G.P. Rothero), pp. 179-256. Privately published.

Schuster, R.M. (1966-1992) *The Hepaticae and Anthocerotae of North America east of the Hundredth Meridian*. Columbia University Press and Field Museum of Natural History, New York and Chicago.

Smith, A.J.E. (1978) *The moss flora of Britain and Ireland*. Cambridge University Press, Cambridge.

Smith, A.J.E. (2004) *The moss flora of Britain and Ireland*, ed. 2. Cambridge University Press, Cambridge.

Störmer, P. (1969) *Mosses with a western and southern distribution in Norway*. Universitetsforlaget, Oslo.

Szweykowski, J., Buczkowska, K. & Odrzykoski, I.J. (2005) *Conocephalum salebrosum* (Marchantiopsida, Conocephalaceae) - a new Holarctic liverwort species. *Plant Systematics and Evolution*, **253**, 133-158.

Touw, A. & Rubers, W.V. (1989) *De Nederlandse bladmossen: flora en verspreidingsatlas van de Nederlandse Musci (Sphagnum uitgesonderd)*. Stichting Uitgeverij Koninklijke Nederlandse Natuurhistorische Vereniging, Utrecht.

Walker, K.J. & Preston, C.D. (2006) Ecological predictors of extinction risk in the flora of lowland England, UK. *Biodiversity and Conservation*, **15**, 1913-1942.

Whitehouse, H.L.K. (1987) Protonema-gemmae in European mosses. *Symposia Biologica Hungarica*, **35**, 227-231.

Wigginton, M.J. (1995) *Mosses and liverworts of North Lancashire*. University of Lancaster, Lancaster.

Wilson, W. (1855) *Bryologia Britannica*. Longman, London.